"Happiness comes in largest measure
to those who live in closest harmony with nature."

O.C. SIMONDS

LOW-KEY GENIUS

THE LIFE AND WORK OF
LANDSCAPE-GARDENER

O.C.SIMONDS

BARBARA GEIGER

FERME ORNÉE PRESS / URBPUBLISHER

COPYRIGHT & CREDITS

FERME ORNÉE PRESS

URBPUBLISHER

LANDSCAPE-GARDENING

L andscape-gardening, as the term was used by O.C. Simonds and Bryan Lathrop, had its origins in the naturalistic, informal design style that was popular throughout the nineteenth-century into the first few decades of the twentieth. English landscape-gardener Humphry Repton (1752-1812) is credited with coining the title, and many practitioners in America adopted it, including Adolph Strauch, O.C. Simonds, and Frank Waugh.

A landscape-garden consisted of verdant lawns surrounded by and interspersed with irregular masses of shrubs and trees. The landscape-gardener kept man-made structures and objects to a minimum, blending them into the scene with dense vegetation when they were necessary. The showy plant displays and colorful carpet beds, so popular during the Victorian and Edwardian eras, were considered to be in poor taste and were strictly avoided. The color green in all its myriad hues predominated, with seasonal color provided by spring-blooming woody plants and autumnal leaf change. A landscape garden either did not contain geometrical shapes, straight lines, and symmetrical layouts, or concealed these kinds of formal spaces behind naturalistic plantings. For Simonds in particular the overall objective was to create a practical and easy environment for human beings that had the beauty of composition and harmony of a Barbizon school landscape painting.

The term is hyphenated throughout this book as that is how Simonds usually punctuated it; it is not hyphenated in quotations from other writers who did not.

CONTENTS

Ancestors in New England
The Move to Grand Rapids
Adventist Beliefs
Simonds's Youth
William LeBaron Jenney: Teacher and Employer
Early Chicago Cemeteries and Drainage Problems

In Good Taste
The Bryan and Lathrop Families' Influence at Graceland
Graceland's Neighborhood
Simonds at Graceland
Chicago
Lathrop Introduces Simonds to Landscape-Gardening
Partnership with Holabird
Superintendent Full-time
Fort Sheridan
Another Cemetery Designer Comes to Town
Sheridan Park

Rattlesnake Master

LIST OF BOTANICAL ILLUSTRATIONS

ALL BY ROBERTA SIMONDS

Each chapter in the book begins with an illustration of a plant that could have been found in a typical O.C. Simonds project, either naturally-occurring on site or added by the designer.

PREFACE AND ACKNOWLEDGEMENTS

My introduction to O.C. Simonds came through a blueprint. In the summer of 1995 my family and I took a tour of Rockcliffe Mansion in Hannibal, Missouri. While the guide was showing our group the butler's pantry, I noticed a blueprint in a battered old frame hanging on the kitchen wall and went to get a closer look. It turned out to be a plan of the grounds and was signed "O.C. Simonds and Company, Landscape-Gardeners, Chicago, Illinois, 1901." Odd, I thought, that the lumber baron who built this over-the-top mansion had sought out a garden designer from that far away. My curiosity was piqued so I jotted down the information from the blueprint to look into later. I began to make enquiries about Simonds but no one knew very much about him, other than that he was an important early designer of equal caliber with Jens Jensen, and that no one knew very much about him.

As I began my research in earnest, it became apparent just *why* no one had previously tackled a full-length biography of Simonds. The relatively few materials of his that still existed were scattered about widely, and it was difficult to even guess where holdings might be. The tiny collections were incomplete and random, and were geographically far apart. By the time I realized all of this, however, I had learned enough about my subject to know that he had lived in the same Ravenswood neighborhood of Chicago my grandmother had, that he had designed many of the places I frequented, and that he had been the long-term designer of Graceland Cemetery, part of my family's history too. During one research session at the Morton Arboretum special collections, I learned that Simonds's grandson Richard and his wife Roberta lived right around the corner, and librarian Michael Stieber very graciously put us in touch. Mrs. Simonds had salvaged what was left of O.C.'s (as the family called him and I soon began to also) correspondence and notes and sketches. From just being a name on a blueprint Simonds was becoming a real and tangible presence. There was no longer any question of not tracking down his story.

In fact, if I had chosen a research topic solely for the cooperative and gracious response of those possessing materials for it, I could not have picked a better one than O.C. Simonds. As I have greatly expanded and rewritten the original unpublished version of this biography, his family has continued to share information and insights. Throughout the years, Roberta L. Simonds has allowed me unrestricted access to the family collection, provided copies of letter and genealogies, and always found answers to my questions. Grandson Robert C. Simonds has also given me free access to the materials in his possession. Both branches of the Simonds family have more than once provided gracious hospitality when I came around to do my research at their Fennville, Michigan property. Much to my delight and to the book's visual appeal, Mrs. Simonds has allowed me to use several of her exquisite botanical illustrations for chapter headings, as well as reproducing photographs.

William M. Walker of Urbpublisher has been an invaluable colleague in the process of book creation. From his beautiful cover-to-cover design and his thoughtful and literate suggestions and corrections to the text he has provided a strong aesthetic and balance that complement the material beautifully.

A generous grant from The Graham Foundation for Advanced Studies in the Fine Arts made it possible to do both additional local and geographically far-flung research, which led to some of the richest discoveries.

Without Rommy Lopat's encouragement and enthusiasm the project might have continued to languish in-process.

And much appreciation to others who have been so helpful providing access to research materials along the way:

Michael Stieber, Nancy Faller, and the staff of the Sterling Morton Library at the Morton Arboretum for access to materials and for graciously allowing me to use photos from the collection;

Diane Dillon of the Newberry Library for granting me Scholar-in-Residence status, which allowed me the luxury of mining the Library's fabulous book collection, and special collections librarian Alison Hinderliter for assistance with primary sources in its special collections;

Janet Olson, archivist at Northwestern University and the Frances Willard/Women's Christian Temperance collection, for her help in locating items, for allowing me to use photos from the collection, and finding such remarkable documents as Anna Gordon's letters regarding Willard's death;

Ken Leone, Superintendent of Public Works for the City of Lake Forest, Illinois and Phil Alderks, Sexton, Lake Forest Cemetery, for their interest in Simonds and for access to historic materials and the use of photos;

Arthur Miller, special collections librarian at the Donnelly Library of Lake Forest College, for his interest and access to the collection;

Diane Oestereich for sharing her research on Simonds's work in Rock Island, Illinois and use of photos;

Deb Engmark, head gardener, for sharing information from the Brucemore Historic House archives and use of photos;

Deb Cooper, graduate student at Iowa State University, for information on Cedar Rapids cemeteries;

Sarah Camacho for research assistance and David Null of University of Wisconsin archives;

Jessica Henderson, my former Illinois Institute of Technology student, for her interest in the topic and her independent research;

Leone Falcone for her efforts to preserve Simonds's work at Forest Park in Lake Forest;

Library of Congress;

Cornell University Special Collections;

University of Maryland Archives.

And thank you to the School of the Art Institute for a supplemental research grant as part of a faculty enrichment program in 2009.

Other thoughtful researchers who shared findings with me over the years include Harold T. Wolff; Kathleen Cummings; Susan Cahill-Aylward, ASLA Director of Information; Thomas Brock of the University of Wisconsin and Shorewood Hills. Thank you also to Robert E. Grese for his generous interest and sharing of information early on; Hurley and Roberta Hagood, Hannibal historians; and Charles D. Kiefer, John Notz, Dean Sheaffer, and William Tishler for materials and conversation on the topic in 1997-99. And to many others along the way for their tidbits about and interest in Simonds, thank you.

Despite the amount of information gathered over the years, there are gaps in the Simonds story. As very few company records have come to light chances are they were destroyed when the company finally dissolved, apparently in the late 1950s. Extant materials are spotty, so when a relatively complete set of correspondence, invoices, etc. was available for a project (i.e. Morton Arboretum, Victor Lawson's Green Lake property, the University of Maryland) I have gone into more than usual detail, trying to take advantage of the opportunity to see a little more behind the scenes. There are many descriptions of Simonds's work throughout this book, but rather than belabor these with additional explanations about Simonds's perspective, I refer to the reader to his own book, *Landscape-Gardening*. Originally published in 1920, republished in the 1930s, and published again as a reprint edition in 2000, it is readily available in paperback as of this writing. The present biography tells Simonds's life story, the development of his career, his important connections and projects, and gives as much of a sense of his personality as possible. The information contained here will also provide a background and starting point for those undertaking further or project-specific research.

As you read this biography I hope that you will come to appreciate and enjoy Simonds's approach to landscape design as much as I have over the years of researching and writing it.

Barbara Geiger, May 2011

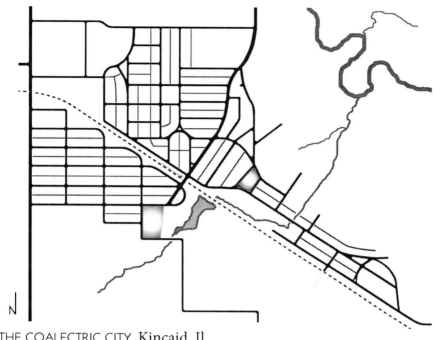

THE COALECTRIC CITY, Kincaid, Il.

TRACING O.C.

T he charge of graphically representing O.C. Simonds's designs for this biography is complicated by the paucity of original drawings for his built projects and the impermanence of the medium of landscape-gardening. Remaining are the hardscapes he shaped, historical imagery and maps, and that published by him or about him from which to work.

After Simonds's death his firm continued into the 1950's but most records were scattered, lost, or destroyed since. In her research, the author (with the help of others) has unearthed a valuable set of complete or near-complete plans for several of Simonds's projects. The most informative of these include the actual planting assignments as envisioned by Simonds. (See the Field plot in Graceland Cemetery in chapter two [2], the Martin home of Lake Forest, Il. plan [5], and the bermed boathouse plan for Chicago's Lincoln Park [6].)

In Simonds's book *Landscape-Gardening* his talents and those of his firm are showcased in exquisite detail with a series of prototypical example drawings illustrating the lessons and rules he championed. Designed to offer insight, they make the book a rich visual reference and requisite starting point.

It is the confluence of libraries, the internet, and freely accessible satellite imagery, though, that has enabled the construction of the handful of rudi-mentary project representations created for this biography. The subjects were primarily chosen for feasibility (simplicity being paramount) and availability of information (including maps, satellite imagery, and photographs). One of which, a cemetery in New York, is of an interesting split character. Another, the Coalectric City, sports a well-preserved array of details common to Simonds.

Noticing recurring details is the inevitable by-product of working with his projects. For example, the original subdivision plan for Berkeley Hills

BERKELEY HILLS PLAN, BELLE MEADE, TN

(top left) demonstrates a very literal example of a "garden room" and Simonds's willingness to delineate property lines with plentiful greenery. A quick internet map/satellite search reveals the neighborhood around Cornwall Avenue and Belle Meade Boulevard still remains a lush assortment of stately homes and well-matured trees.

Perhaps the most easily recognizable element strongly indicative of a Simonds design is the triangular split-road intersection (an example, middle left, is marked with a dark triangle in the map of Sheridan Park in Chicago). They were used by his contemporaries as well, but are common enough in Simonds's work that it is fair to consider them iconic elements of his street layouts.

MAP OF SHERIDAN PARK, CHICAGO, IL

Simonds's wonderfully illuminating quote regarding subtly running a road around a tree—as to not embarrass the tree with undue attention—provides an opportunity to understand the frequency with which he employed gentle curves in his projects. The Acacia Park Cemetery (bottom left) has since expanded beyond what is shown here, but this graphic illustrates well the curvilinear qualities that are often part of Simonds's layouts, though this project was handled by his office. The curves and split intersections are absent from the

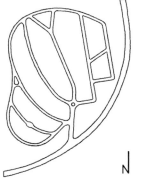
ACACIA PARK CEMETERY, BUFFALO, NY

right side (the eastern section; which satellites

reveal to have much younger trees). Acacia Park's alternating layout reflects a handsomely integrated change in style.

Other contrasts, though, are often much more abrupt and can be interpreted as potential edge markers of Simonds's involvement. For example, in preparing the map for the Coalectric City in chapter eight the challenge involved removing streets that expressed "newness" through building style (a herringbone mobile home park would be an unlikely component to most 1913 Simonds designs), missing elements (sidewalks and alleys were included in a town intended to be much bigger than it ever became), and some modern anachronisms (the new highway). There are also abandoned sidewalks that may imply the city's original eastern entrance was a split-intersection.

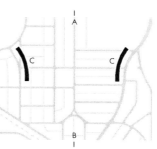

SUBTLE SYMMETRY IN KINCAID, IL

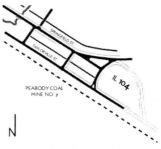

KINCAID'S ABANDONED SIDEWALKS

Localized energy as an idea is as relevant now as it was when Kincaid was new. In 1913 that idea was a town built around an electricity generating station powered by its own coal mine. Located on a rail and early auto route and shaped by a river watershed, Simonds's approach was to have his design respond in concert with these local conditions. Lowlands were reserved for gardens, the town's civic and commercial center was positioned on a small hill just north of the rail depot, and streets and lots purposefully skirted the topography.

The street layout has remarkable balance for its irregular shape. Kincaid is evidence of Simonds's controlled use of symmetry, here establishing a formal north-south axis (A-B), which centers a small grid. That grid then flows across flat prairie until encountering changes in elevation or existing roads. These edge conditions are then shaped in response to the axis (note the mirrored curves [C] of certain streets), elevation, or connections to the rest of the town.

These few qualities are by no means exhaustive, nor certainties themselves; they are humbly offered as evidence of the effort invested to restore what time has withdrawn from all of us interested in O.C. Simonds's work.

It was a particular joy to work with Roberta Simonds's illustrations.

William M. Walker, May 2011

LOW-KEY GENIUS

THE LIFE AND WORK OF
LANDSCAPE-GARDENER

O.C.SIMONDS

INTRODUCTION

Ossian Cole Simonds (1855-1931) helped shape the look of American landscapes for fifty-three years, from 1878 until 1931. In this time he tackled a range of projects from small urban backyards to 4,000-plus acre gentleman's estates. Simonds learned the art and profession of landscape-gardening (as he always called it) at Graceland Cemetery, with which he was affiliated for his entire career, under the tutelage of Bryan Lathrop, a powerful Chicago real estate developer and the treasurer and later president of Graceland. The simple but powerful guiding principles that Simonds developed in the early years of his career formed the bedrock of his approach to design for five decades. Essential to his work was respect for and enhancement of the spirit of the place—the genius loci—anywhere and everywhere he made a design. He observed and worked with the natural qualities of a site: its topography, water, vegetation, and its views; the kind of light and the sky. Thus Simonds avoided formal and geometric shapes because they typically masked rather than enhanced the uniqueness of a site. Another hallmark of his work was the predominant use of indigenous plants beginning in the 1870s when they were still "weeds" to most people. To pull these various elements together Simonds used contemporary theories of composition for landscape painting, creating with the actual stuff of nature instead of canvases and paint. These scenes provided more than beauty and inspiration, though. Simonds's underlying concern was that they function as very practical and safe human environments.

Although Simonds developed and refined this naturalistic style of design, he did not see himself as breaking new ground. Throughout his long and productive practice he continued to acknowledge those he had learned from, in particular his mentor Bryan Lathrop. He also recognized his debt to Adolph Strauch, the Prussian landscape-gardener* responsible for shaping the landscape of Spring Grove Cemetery in Cincinnati. Simonds became well-versed in the writings of such early nineteenth-century English designers as Humphry Repton and John Claudius Loudon, and of course he was heavily

---

* Simonds usually hyphenated the term "landscape-gardener," so that is the format used throughout this book, unless the term is used in a quote where it was not hyphenated.

influenced by the great Frederick Law Olmsted, whose work in Jackson and Washington Parks and in the town of Riverside set the direction for Chicago landscapes that followed. Rather than expressing any great new theories or personal diatribes in his published writings or his correspondence, Simonds maintained a low personal profile, focusing on the project at hand, the clients' needs, or the subject he was teaching. Obviously he was modest and he seems to have also been good-natured, judging from the tone and content of his more personal letters. He cared about young people coming up in the profession, hiring many throughout the years and giving them a professional start. He was especially lucky to find a young man named J. Roy West—West stayed in the Simonds firm from his first job in 1896 until his own death in 1942. Simonds made it clear, in the records that still exist, that he thoroughly enjoyed his activities as a landscape-gardener, believing it to be the best of all possible professions.

SIMONDS'S* SIGNIFICANCE

As a major contributor to the establishment of an informal, naturalistic style of landscape design in the Midwest and to the development of landscape architecture as a profession in the United States around the turn of the twentieth-century, Simonds is a key figure in the history of American landscape architecture for a number of reasons. First, Simonds's plans and actions have had an enduring effect because more often than not he worked with "raw" space—areas that were shaped and molded from the wild or from farm fields. Parks, cemeteries, school grounds, golf courses, and arboretums are seldom completely redesigned once built, although plantings and some design features may deteriorate or be altered without regard to the context of the overall plan. Thus many of these sites still bear the overall configuration that Simonds had created. Judging from available records and from allusions to projects for which no records exist, Simonds was a prolific designer, his firm producing about 1,000 jobs over the years. Less skilled imitators produced rather generic work for parks and private grounds, adding another layer of continuing influence for naturalistic designs.

---

* A note on style: traditionally, last names ending with an "s" have been made possessive by adding just an apostrophe. Grammatically, though, that makes no sense, and as current usage also favors adding the additional "s" to make such a name truly possessive, "Simonds's" is the form that is used throughout the pages to follow.

Second, Simonds's powerful, prominent clients promoted his naturalistic approach for the public and private projects with which they were involved. This helped to further the widespread acceptance and use of indigenous plants as the primary kind of vegetation, creating distinctively local scenery. Although Simonds's designs were not unlike those produced by the Olmsted and his firm, Olmsted preferred a "tropical" look reminiscent of southern bayous and lagoons for what he saw as more inherently soothing qualities.

Third, Simonds's connections with other late-nineteenth-century practitioners such as William LeBaron Jenney, Horace W. S. Cleveland, Frederick Law Olmsted, and Jens Jensen are helpful in creating a more complete picture of the beginnings of their profession. In this context, his story adds to our knowledge of the design and development of public and private sites at a time in history that has had lasting influence.

Fourth, Simonds was concerned for and worked to save our natural resources. Never an activist, he presented his ideas gently, as part of a design approach. In this way he encouraged towns to stop dumping filth into their rivers, to replace factories on the water with public parks, and to preserve or reestablish native forests.

And fifth, Simonds had a lasting impact through the many professional organizations of which he was a founder or early member. He was a founding member of the American Society of Landscape Architects (ASLA), the American Association of Cemetery Superintendents (AACS), the American Park and Outdoor Art Association, (APOAA), and was active in many of Chicago's prestigious social and professional clubs, including the influential Cliff Dwellers. Simonds designed hundreds of public and private grounds—many for fellow club members—and had an international reputation in his heyday.

Yet, outside the realm of landscape architectural history, he remains relatively unknown today. Timing played a part in his being lost to history. As described in the chapters that follow, his declining health and less direct involvement in his company occurred just at the time of the stock market crash, and he died in the early years of the Great Depression, when work was scarce even for the most successful firms. Although he mentored a number of young designers, he had no following *per se,* and most of his interns adopted the new formal approach that was in demand in the 1920s. Simonds's own modest demeanor and focus on topics other than himself contributed to his loss of visibility. In hindsight, it is obvious that Simonds warrants greater recognition—both within and without the landscape design professions— because of the magnitude and quality of his work and its continuing influence on our use and appreciation of native plants.

RESTORING AN O.C. SIMONDS DESIGN

Many of the properties planted by Simonds have passed the one-hundred year mark and, because of the relative dearth of existing plans (due to subsequent loss or never having been drawn at all), restoring or reconstructing these sites appropriately can be difficult. If a plan and/or historic photograph is available, that is the natural place to start. But a word of caution: even with a plan specific to a site, it is quite easy to still miss the mark. Much of what Simonds put in to a design is not so readily observable in plan view. The landscape historian or landscape architect working on such a project needs to develop a broader understanding of Simonds's philosophy and become familiar with his techniques in order to restore a site to its original form and spirit. In fact, by understanding his approach to vistas, to grading, to road layout, to plant massing, and his preferred plants (see Appendix B for a sample list), one can approach a restoration more genuinely in the spirit of Simonds than by just following an original plan. Learning "how to think like Simonds" will reward a designer with delightful new ways to see the landscape.

Over the years writers have often referred to Simonds as a "Prairie style" designer, taking their cue from Wilhelm Miller's 1915 publication, *The Prairie Spirit in Landscape Gardening*. While this title has a certain cachet, it sends the writer or researcher off on the wrong track now. Simonds seldom, if ever, planted grasses and sedges, yet those are the plants most affiliated with the very literal approach to natural and prairie landscape design today. As you will read in Chapter 8, Simonds rejected the "Prairie style" name and motive, finding more inspiration in ravines, forests, and the vegetation found around rivers, streams, and ponds. In studying to restore a Simonds work it is best to leave the Prairie idea out of the process, allowing yourself to encounter the design's reality without preconceptions.

Appendix A lists known Simonds and Company and Simonds and West projects. At least ten Illinois properties that are listed in the National Register of Historic Places were affiliated with Simonds; Rockcliffe Mansion in Missouri is an eleventh (listed only for the building). Other significant properties include the Cummer estate in Florida and the Barber farm in Ohio. No doubt more Simonds landscapes will come to light as ongoing research at historic homes uncovers more information. I hope this biography will be useful to those continuing research on this prolific but low-key genius.

chapter 1

FAMILY BACKGROUND AND EARLY YEARS

1630-1878

Bearberry

THOMAS COLE'S Italian Sunset 1845.

AN IMAGE from George Putnam's *The Home Book of the Picturesque.*

AMERICAN LANDSCAPES

A mericans were proud of their continent in the nineteenth-century. Quintessential Hudson River Valley painter Thomas Cole (1801-1848; an Englishman, actually) created dozens of images during the 1830s of the "wild" nature of the east coast, showing its sublime beauty, its Rousseau-esque innocent savages, and its implicit superiority to the worn-out landscapes of Europe. At the same time, Ralph Waldo Emerson (1803-1882), Henry David Thoreau (1817-1862), Margaret Fuller, Countess Ossoli (1810-1850), and their Transcendental colleagues explored the same world of nature from theological and philosophical perspectives, finding that all of nature was imbued with holiness and spirit—a distinct departure from the belief system that supported Jonathan Edward's sermon "Sinners in the Hands of An Angry God" less than a century before. James Fennimore Cooper, writing in George Putnam's 1852 *The Home Book of the Picturesque,* explored the aesthetic contrasts between the European and the more rugged American landscapes.

It was in this environment that Frederick Law Olmsted (1822-1903), the originator of American landscape architecture, was born and grew up in Hartford, Connecticut. Olmsted's direct inspiration came from American horticulturalist Andrew Jackson Downing (1815-1852) and from the verdant, expansive English landscape gardens of the previous century. He believed that such scenery and contact with nature supported human health and happiness, a theme that underpinned all of his landscape work throughout his long and productive career. He was also a neighbor of Putman's in 1850 and was intimately acquainted with serious discussions about landscape preferences. Olmsted's philosophy both supported and was supported by the continuing influence of Transcendentalism, so that by the time he and partner Calvert Vaux (1824-1895) won the design competition for New York's Central Park in 1857, few citizens—other than real estate speculators—doubted the need for green space in cities.

Just three years before work began on Central Park, future landscape-gardener Ossian Cole (O.C.) Simonds was born near Grand Rapids, Michigan. From the beginning of his practice in 1878, Simonds was aware of Olmsted,

Emerson, and other east coast designers and philosophers, reading their writings and acknowledging their influence on the projects he designed. By the time he published his book *Landscape-Gardening* after World War I in 1920, he was also sensitive to the nationalism that resulted from the war and began chapter 1 explaining that "The purpose of this book is to help make our country more beautiful. 'Our country' refers especially to the United States." Yet his next sentence acknowledged Canada and indeed he quoted Thomas Paine's comment that "The world is my country." This was characteristic of Simonds's gentle, curious spirit, and yet paradoxically, he would make his name designing regionally specific landscapes. One of the first to regularly use and recommend native plants, he appreciated *every* region he worked in and applied his design principles to make the most of each locale. And unlike the sublime drama of Cole's paintings or Coopers essays, Simonds's genius with landscape showed best with quiet, subtle, low-key environments in a variety of climates and topographies. It was in making everyday landscapes beautiful that his talent shone.

ANCESTORS IN NEW ENGLAND

More of a Michigander and Midwesterner than a New Englander, Ossian Cole Simonds was born in a log cabin on a farm near Grand Rapids, Michigan, on November 11, 1855; his family had already been on this continent for more than two centuries. Ancestor William Simonds had emigrated from England to Woburn, Massachusetts with his wife Judith Hayward in 1639.[1] Their descendent John Simonds was born in Massachusetts in 1760 and his wife-to-be Sabra Cole was born in New York in 1793.[2] Sabra and John, O.C.'s grandparents, moved to Vermont after they married, where they raised a large family. Their son Joel was born in 1813, and several years later, the family moved to Genesee in Alexander County, New York. Here Joel met Emily Toby, also from Vermont, and they were married in Genesee on April 12, 1838.[3] Through additional land purchases, the Simonds family farm expanded from sixty-eight to 225 acres, including 125 acres that Joel bought in 1842.[4] His older brother Ossian* moved away from the family, leaving responsibility for the farm to Joel who taught

---

* Ossian is a mythic ancient Scots poet whose works first appeared in 1760, purportedly 'discovered' by James MacPherson in his studies of Gaelic poetry. No family records explain the how the name began to be used by the Simonds.

school for ten winters to earn extra income.[5]

Joel and Emily's second child, Omar, was born in the spring of 1844; their first had died at birth.[6] Two more children came along, Emma in 1847 and Charlie in 1848.[7] By 1849, Joel's traditional Baptist beliefs had altered so that he now understood immortality to be conditional, and soon thereafter he joined "the Adventist cause," and began preaching its doctrines.[8]* Emily Simonds died of dysentery on September 25, 1851, and Joel picked up his life as a widower with three young children.[9]

THE MOVE TO GRAND RAPIDS

Joel sold part of his farm during the spring of 1853 and the following year married Harriet Newell Garfield. With the children from his first marriage, they left western New York state to move to Michigan.[10] They settled in Grand Rapids, and although he had not enjoyed farming back east, Simonds bought eighty acres of farmland from a Mr. Burton. He defended selling some of his property back east and buying more out west in a letter to his brother Ossian in August 1855. Joel explained the value of subdivision, asking, "Is not the dividing up the farms, one of the leading influences which cause the rise of property [sic]."[11] Perhaps he discussed this philosophy at home over the ensuing years; his not-yet-born son Ossian would be involved in exactly this process many times throughout his career.

The Simondses were now "rather a contented family" in the their new surroundings. As Harriet wrote to relatives in New York, ". . . we have none of us been homesick. The children have been much better pleased and satisfied with our home here than I thought they would be."[12] Relatives from New York came for extended visits, easing the transition. Omar and Charlie, the two boys from Joel's first marriage, helped with harvesting and other jobs, and the whole family enjoyed the abundant strawberries and blackberries that year. The family was "vegetarian strictly" and believed in "No Drugs;" the adults, at least, found it healthful and "delicious living."[13]

Joel and Harriet may have chosen Grand Rapids, Michigan, for their move

---

* Joel may have actually joined the Millerites, a large sect that preceded the Seventh-Day Adventists and also preached that Christ's return (the Advent) was imminent. Named for their leader William Miller, the religion was popular in New England in the 1840s. See David Armstrong and Elizabeth Metzger Armstrong, *The Great American Medicine Show* (New York: Prentice Hall, 1991), 99-106 for a readable account.

because like-minded people had already settled in the area. Anne B. Henderson, a farm girl from Allegan County, married the Reverend Henry Stephen Chubb, the leader of a vegetarian sect called the Bible Christians. They had settled in Grand Haven, about twenty-five miles west of Grand Rapids, in the early 1850s and it is likely that some of Chubb's followers settled there as well.[14]

By 1855 Grand Rapids was a thriving new community with "flouring mills, Saw Mills, Machine shops [for manufacturing steam engines], Planing Mills, Sash and door factories, Axe factory, Wagon hub factory, [and] Furnaces and Boat Making."[15] Simonds wrote to his brother back east that there were several hundred teams on the plank road each day going to Kalamazoo. By August 1855 the farm had grown to 150 acres and Simonds drew up plans to build a new house for his family and for fencing his land. His wife was expecting a baby that November and, with three children already and frequent visits from many relatives, they needed more room.

Two railroad companies were laying track through the town and even though the line would go through their property, the Simonds family found the progress exciting. Joel was pleased with the "very rich soil, dark sand, with some gravel" on his farm on Plaster Creek. The family grew corn, potatoes, and apples, as well as vegetables and berries.[16]

Harriet's baby was born on November 11 and they named him Ossian Cole after Joel's brother and mother. His younger sister Julia was born to the family three years later. In 1860, the Michigan census listed the Simonds family's real estate holdings at $8,000, with an additional $2,000 in personal property; they were well off by contemporary standards. By then the household included Joel, forty-seven, a farmer; Harriet, his thirty-four year old wife; children Omar H., sixteen, a farm laborer, Charlie O., twelve, Emma, thirteen, Ossian C., four, and Julia L., one year. Grandparents John and Sabra Simonds, a gardener aged eighty and his sixty-seven year old wife, also lived there.[17]

ADVENTISTS BELIEFS

Like the Simondses, most of their neighbors had come from New York state. Harriet Simonds's brother Samuel W. Garfield and his wife Harriet bought the adjoining farm; they were the parents of Charles W. (1848-1938, the Simonds children's first cousin), who would be O.C.'s life-long close friend.

Other New Englanders settled in the small community of Otsego, less than thirty miles south of the farm, and, in 1860, the group began calling themselves Seventh-Day Adventists. Among this group were James and Ellen G. White. After experiencing a life-changing vision in June 1863, Mrs. White became the new religion's prophet and leader.

Many of the precepts that Mrs. White recorded in a sixteen-page manuscript the day after this event were similar to those the Simonds family already followed. They forbade the consumption of meat, alcohol, tobacco, or drugs. Eating fruit, grains, and nuts instead was advocated along with cleanliness, fresh air, clear water, and sunshine.[18] Already believers, Joel and Harriet officially became Seventh-Day Adventists. For the next several decades Mrs. White continued writing the rules she believed God was giving her. Chief among these were injunctions to "Get out of the cities into rural districts . . ."[19] She pursued this idea for many years in such pieces as "Manifold Benefits of Active Out-of-Door Life" (1876), "With a Piece of Land and a Comfortable Home" (1894), and "The Refuge of Country Places (1908).[20] The life of the Simonds family on their farm quite naturally fulfilled these suggestions and inculcated in O.C. and Julia a lifelong belief in the importance of nature.

SIMONDS'S YOUTH

While growing up, young O.C. explored the woods and fields around his family's farm and he developed a knowledge of local plants, soil, and waterways. He attended high school in Grand Rapids, graduating in 1874. A pioneering naturalist named Emma Cole (1845-1910) taught there for twenty-six years. Cole had studied botany at Cornell University, traveled extensively in Europe visiting gardens and arboreta, and later worked for the Arnold Arboretum at Harvard University. She devoted many years to studying Western Michigan's native plants, publishing *Grand Rapids Flora* in 1910, and later donated her herbarium collection to the University of Michigan.[21] Despite the coincidences—O.C.'s half-sister Emma was born in 1847, and Cole is of course his middle name—no records indicate any relationship, or that O.C. studied with her. Whether or not there is a direct connection, Miss Cole's presence here for a quarter-century gives an indication of the interests and values of the faculty that Simonds knew.

By the time O.C. was in high school, Grand Rapids had grown out to the boundaries of the Simonds farm and Joel sold the land, moving the family into town. Instead of farming, he began marketing a patented collapsible fencing system for a few years, then moved on to other businesses.[22] They were affluent enough for O.C. to enroll in the civil engineering program at the University of Michigan in Ann Arbor. To earn money during his college years, Simonds used his drafting skills to make patent drawings for a half-uncle who was in partnership with an attorney.[23]

For three summers during college, Simonds also worked as a recorder for the United States Lakes Survey.[24] John Butler Johnson, a fellow engineering student, was employed by the survey as a full-time assistant. The two of them worked along the Michigan coast near Saugatuck and fell in love with the land just to the south around Pier Cove, a tiny town built among the sand dunes in Allegan County.[25] They decided they would purchase property there as soon as the opportunity arose and their finances permitted. Johnson continued surveying in other areas of Michigan and in Illinois while Simonds returned to school in the fall.

WILLIAM LE BARON JENNEY

Stationed at the U.S. Lake Survey Camp at Summit, in near southwest Cook County, Illinois in July 1877, Johnson wrote to Simonds back in Michigan, reporting on his Chicago area adventures. Of particular interest were the activities of Major William Le Baron Jenney (1832-1909), with whom Simonds studied architecture in a new program at the University of Michigan's School of Engineering.[26] Johnson called on Jenney at his Chicago office one Saturday in mid-July, to find him alone, ". . . apparently there was nothing going on at all." Jenney explained that his "workmen are out," but Johnson "suspected he hadn't any at all."[27]

The following week, Johnson and two other men from his survey team took the Chicago, Burlington, and Quincy Railroad out to Riverside, the new suburban town designed by Frederick Law Olmsted and Calvert Vaux. Jenney had assumed town planning duties in 1871 after Olmsted and Vaux left and had designed a hotel and several houses there, including one for himself. Johnson thought it "a very pretty place indeed," a "residence park," with some fairly

O.C. SIMONDS as a young man.
SIMONDS FAMILY COLLECTION

nice frame houses.+ The group passed Jenney's home, but did not stop because he had guests with him on the portico. Overall, Johnson was not impressed with the town, telling Simonds "the enterprise is busted and the place on the decline."[28]* Despite Johnson's unenthusiastic reports about Jenney, Simonds continued to study architecture with him, and, when he graduated with his C.E. in 1878, Simonds accepted Jenney's invitation to work as an assistant in his Chicago office and moved that summer.[29]

Jenney was a landscape designer, as well as an architect and engineer. He had studied civil engineering at the Ecole Centrale des Arts et Manufactures in Paris from 1853 to 1856, where "landscape engineering" was part of the program. He would have seen Napoleon III's massive modernization of the city under the direction of Georges-Eugene Haussmann, which was fully underway during these years. After returning to America, Jenney served as a Union major during the Civil War and had the opportunity to meet Frederick Law Olmsted

+ Jenney commuted via train to teach at Ann Arbor, a 450+ mile round-trip each week, maintaining his professional practice back in Chicago during this time.
* Johnson did not explain in this correspondence why he was so under-impressed with Jenney. It did not seem to faze his friend Simonds.

at the Siege of Vicksburg. He greatly admired Olmsted's work on New York's Central Park and, after the war, they began a correspondence that continued for the rest of their lives.[30]

Jenney moved to Chicago just at the time the West Parks Commission was seeking someone to design a series of parks and boulevards (and just at the time that Olmsted and Vaux were resigning their Riverside commission to create a vast landscape for the South Parks Commission).* He and a partner procured the job and in 1870 Jenney wrote his first report for the Board. In addition to creating a park and street plan, he devised a drainage system to augment the sewers by digging small lakes that would function as reservoirs. The excavated soil was used to create some variation in the otherwise flat terrain, and Jenney fashioned a landscape plan around these water features and berms.[31] Jenney's topographical skills won him a contract to plan an expansion of Graceland Cemetery in 1878.

EARLY CHICAGO CEMETERIES AND DRAINAGE PROBLEMS

Knowing how to create a beautiful park by draining swampy land was a valuable skill in Chicago in the 1870s. Converting the low lying areas surrounding the rapidly growing city into usable, salable real estate enabled developers to build new residential and industrial sections; it also solved the problem of soggy burials. The third and last of Chicago's city cemeteries was located on the grounds of what is now the Chicago History Museum's site at the south end of Lincoln Park at Clark and North Avenue. Because of the cemetery's sandy soil and high water table, coffins and corpses occasionally rose to the surface, propelled by the alternating freezing and thawing during Chicago winters. This was a miserable situation. Citizens like William Barry and Charles Dyer and physician John Rauch, who was active in the new sanitation movement, urged the city to close the cemetery altogether and to re-inter bodies elsewhere. The city closed the cemetery to new burials in 1860 and subsequently ordered the removal of remains with a view to turning the grounds into a city park (later named for Abraham Lincoln).[32]

Real estate developers saw a fine opportunity and private companies

---

* The Illinois State Legislature had written legislation in 1869 creating and authorizing three separate park commissions in the City of Chicago, Lincoln Park being the third.

formed to purchase land far from the city center on which to build dry and sanitary rural cemeteries. Over the next several years most of the remains were removed to three new, private, non-sectarian burial grounds—Oak Woods, Rosehill, and Graceland.

Oak Woods, on Chicago's south side at Cottage Grove and 67th Street, was, in 1854, the first of the major landscape cemeteries to be chartered by the State, although it did not receive its first official burial until 1860. Oak Woods was also distinctive in being the only Chicago cemetery with a Confederate burial section, holding the remains of more than 4,000 southern soldiers who died at the infamous Camp Douglas, a Union prison just a few miles north of the cemetery. Some of the Confederates had been buried originally in the city cemetery, then moved to Oak Woods at Army expense when it was closed. (Others who died of cholera and other infectious diseases were buried in a small graveyard at the camp, near Cottage Grove and 31st Street, and later removed as well.) Needless to say, the removal effort was not given kindly or careful attention, and remains still come to the surface as of 2011 when any digging is required at the south end of Lincoln Park.

The new cemetery's president and founder was Jonathan Young Scammon, an important early Chicagoan who had settled here in 1836 and was buried here upon his death in 1890. Scammon was instrumental in establishing the public school system and other early improvements, and was a Swedenborgian like Daniel Burnham and his family. He and his fellow board members were proud to have employed the famous landscape-gardener Adolph Strauch to design the original naturalistic, open lawn arrangement for Oak Woods.

The cemetery's initial advertising was addressed "To those about [to] exchang[e] their lots in that portion of the City Cemetery now being vacated, and all others who contemplate buying a Cemetery lot—particularly those living in the South Division, and that portion of the West Division south of Lake Street—we would present the claims of OAK WOODS CEMETERY." A description of the improvements that were underway was followed by an announcement that "In drawing the plan of the grounds, the Company were fortunate in securing the services of Adolph Strauch, Esq., Superintendent of Spring Grove Cemetery, Cincinnati, who, probably, has no *superior* as a landscape gardener and manager of cemeteries."[33] The motives were the same: "to make [the cemetery] in fact a rural cemetery, ornamented and kept like a highly cultivated park, at the same time investing it with all the sacredness pertaining to a burial place of the dead."[34]

On the north side, Rosehill ("Roe's Hill" initially) was located about seven miles north of downtown Chicago at Ravenswood and what is now called Peterson Avenue and was incorporated in 1859. Eminent landscape-gardener William Saunders (1822-1900) of Philadelphia created the initial layout. The impressive entry gate on the east side of Rosehill was designed by architect William Boyington of limestone in a neo-gothic style, the same as his water tower at Chicago Avenue and Pine Street (now Michigan Avenue). Native oaks and other mature trees graced the site, which would become the largest of these three key cemeteries.

A year later, Graceland received its charter from the state; its entry was at the corner of Green Bay Road and Graceland Avenue (now Clark and Irving Park), two miles closer to the city than Rosehill, but still far out in the country. Both cemeteries, as well as Wunder's Lutheran Cemetery to the south of Graceland, St. Boniface Catholic Cemetery to the north, and Calvary Catholic Cemetery a few miles north at the southern end of Evanston, were all situated along geologic features known as the Graceland and Rose Hill Spits. Formed by an ancient version of Lake Michigan as it ebbed and flowed, the spits are high, dry ridges formed of sand—perfect for burial grounds. A train line ran from downtown north along the eastern edges of Graceland and Rosehill and the western side of Calvary, making funeral trains an easy and efficient way to transport bodies and families to these locations.

Although established for nearly twenty years when Simonds began working with Jenney on the Graceland project, Chicago's new rural cemeteries were just beginning to fulfill their development potential in 1878. Simonds could look forward to a long and fruitful career.

CHAPTER ONE ENDNOTES

[1] *The National Cyclopedia of American Biography*, Vol. XXII (New York: James T. White and Company, 1932), 91.

[2] 1860 Michigan census, Paris Township, Kent County. Information in the Simonds Family Collection of Richard and Roberta Simonds (hereafter noted as "SFC").

[3] *National Cyclopedia.*

[4] Benjamin Cole Simonds, *Family Record of John Simonds* (Batavia, New York: J.F. Hall Printers, 1891), 11; SFC.

[5] Ibid.

[6] Ibid.

[7] Census, 1860.

[8] Benjamin Cole Simonds.

[9] Ibid.

[10] Ibid.

[11] Joel A. Simonds to Ossian H. Simonds, August 18, 1855, The Joseph Downs Collection of Manuscripts and Printed Ephemera, Winterthur Museum, Garden and Library, Winterthur, Delaware.

[12] Harriet Garfield Simonds to "Br. Ossian and Family," August 22, 1855, Winterthur.

[13] Joel A. Simonds to "Br. Ossian and Family," August 19, 1855, Winterthur.

[14] Gerald Carson, *The Cornflake Crusade: From the Pulpit to the Breakfast Table* (New York: Rhinehart and Company, Inc., 1957), 20-22.

[15] Ibid.

[16] Joel A. Simonds to Ossian H. Simonds, August 22, 1855, Winterthur.

[17] Michigan census.

[18] Armstrong.

[19] Ellen G. White, Letter 5, 1904 in "Country Living: An Aid to Moral and Social Security" (Hagerstown, MD: Review and Herald Publishing Association, compiled and reprinted 1946), 10.

[20] Ibid., 13, 16, 18.

[21] "Making a Difference: Outstanding Women of Grand Rapids: (exhibit at the Grand Rapids Public library, July 1997).

[22] Miscellaneous receipts, letters, and copyright applications, SFC.

[23] Edward A. Renwick, "Recollections" (unpublished and undated paper), SFC.

[24] Lieutenant-Colonel C.B. Comstock, Corps of Engineers, "Report upon the Primary Triangulation of the United States Lake Survey" (Washington, D.C.: Government Printing Office, 1882). Many thanks to Rob Nurre for the information pertaining to the Lakes Survey.

[25] Pier Cove Ravine Trust Association brochure, undated, privately printed, SFC.

[26] National Cyclopedia; and Theodore Turak, William Le Baron Jenney: A Pioneer of Modern Architecture (Ann Arbor, MI: UMI Research Press, 1986), 143.

[27] John Butler Johnson to O.C. Simonds, July 15, 1877, SFC.

[28] Ibid.

[29] National Cyclopedia.

[30] Theodore Turak, "William Le Baron Jenney: Pioneer of Chicago's West Parks," Inland Architect (March 1981), 39-45.

[31] Ibid.

[32] http://hiddentruths.northwestern.edu/city_cem_main.html

[33] Undated brochure introducing Oak Woods Cemetery; courtesy of Eunice Nowak, General Manger, Oak Woods.

[34] Ibid.

chapter 2

GRACELAND:
THE BEGINNING OF A MASTERPIECE

1878-1885

Goldenrod

MILLS MAUSOLEUM with restored brambles as specified in original Simonds plan, Graceland Cemetery, Chicago.

IN GOOD TASTE

G raceland Cemetery's founders were the cream of Chicago society. William B. Ogden (a future mayor of Chicago), E. H. Sheldon, Dr. S. Sawyer, and presidential portrait painter George P. A. Healy started the Graceland Cemetery Company early in 1860 and served as its directors. Thomas Barbour Bryan, a lawyer and real estate magnate, filled the office of president of the board from the beginning; his infant son Daniel was Graceland's first burial when his body was moved there from the old city cemetery. The "Charter of the Graceland Cemetery, approved Feb. 22, 1861," in the collections of the Chicago History Museum, listed the cemetery offices as being conveniently located in "Bryan Hall, Chicago, Ill." Bryan's intention was to make Graceland "the Mount Auburn of the West,"[1] and to that end, he hired the best designers of the day. He was in agreement with Mayor James H. Woodworth who had told the *Weekly Chicago Democrat* in March 1848 that beautifully planted cemeteries were a reflection of a "high state of morality," addressing sanitary issues and thereby showing respect for the dead.

The "Origin of Graceland Cemetery" explained that Thomas B. Bryan sent for "William Saunders, the eminent landscape gardener of Philadelphia," to consult "as to the adaptation of the land to the purposes desired." The *Chicago Daily Tribune* reported that he came with the recommendation of Laurel Hill's president. Saunders "expressed surprise that so beautiful a tract, at such a convenient distance from the city, and so admirable adapted to Cemetery purposes, had not been previously so appropriated." He went further to assure Bryan that ". . . without qualification [it] . . . possessed . . . every requisite for a beautiful rural Cemetery."

Saunders had emigrated from Scotland in 1848 and set up a landscape gardening company in Philadelphia from 1854-1862, during which time he and a partner expanded the previous design for Laurel Hill, an early rural cemetery near that city. Saunders then accepted the position of superintendent of experimental gardens at the United States Department of Agriculture, where he remained until his death in 1900.[2] While employed at Laurel Hill he worked on the initial layout for Rosehill's 300 acres. Later, the Graceland trustees hired him as a consultant, where he worked with local landscape-gardener Swain Nelson (1829-ca.1912) on that cemetery's 119 original acres.[3] He would also be responsible for the design of the new military cemetery at Gettysburg for President Lincoln in 1863.

Nelson, who had emigrated from Sweden in 1854, started a practice in Chicago in 1856. In 1862, he worked with Saunders designing the west side of Graceland, and, over the next few years, Nelson worked on plans for Union Park and the new Lincoln Park. He subsequently opened a nursery for which he is better remembered today than for his design work.

Horace William Shaler Cleveland (1814-1900) was the next eminent landscape architect to work at Graceland. He opened an office in Chicago in 1869, having previously worked with Olmsted and Vaux on Prospect Park in Brooklyn and other projects. He attended to Graceland's design and planting needs for a few years beginning in 1870. Shortly after arriving here, Cleveland wrote an essay on "The Public Grounds of Chicago: how to give them Character and Expression." He expanded these ideas two years later in "A Few Hints on Landscape Gardening in the West," which included "The Relationship of Engineering to Landscape Gardening," by his new partner, civil engineer William M. R. French (1843-1914). While Cleveland and French each contributed his own area of expertise to the projects they shared, Cleveland as the designer and French as the engineer, French's essay described the benefits that could be expected if one man was qualified in both fields.[4] Within a decade, Simonds would be the person to fulfill that role.

In 1872, the South Parks Commissioners appointed Cleveland as landscape architect to succeed Olmsted and Vaux and to supervise park construction. He published another essay that year, entitled "Parks and Boulevards in Cities." While in Chicago, he also designed many private estates in the area and continued his work with cemetery design, writing "A Few Words on the Arrangement of Rural Cemeteries" in 1881. "The Culture and Management of our Native Forests for Development as Timber or Ornamental Wood," printed the following year, expressed his concern with the wasteful forest practices in the United States.[5][*]

---

[*] When Cleveland later relocated to Minneapolis, French (brother of sculptor Daniel Chester French) remained in Chicago, where he became the director of the new Art Institute, a position he held until his death. Like Simonds, French found no contradiction between his engineering background and his role as arbiter of aesthetic taste.

Cleveland stressed the importance of designing with the natural terrain and taking advantage of natural views. He believed that "the test of the architectural skill of a designer can only be attained by a careful examination of [the plan's] adaptation to the ground."[6] He had been hired at Graceland especially for his expertise in working with natural landscape features. However, a number of serious misfortunes soured Cleveland on Chicago, including the loss of all his files in the Chicago fire, the increasingly difficult illnesses of his wife, and the death of a son. He accepted a position with the city of Minneapolis and left Chicago permanently by 1886.[7]

BRYAN AND LATHROP FAMILIES' INFLUENCE AT GRACELAND

If Graceland Cemetery was a virtual hotbed of landscape design talent, it was a result of the vision and influence of the Bryan and Lathrop families. In 1856, just a few years before the inception of Graceland Cemetery, Thomas Barbour Bryan began purchasing what would accumulate to 1,000 acres of land for his personal estate directly west of the city in an area called Cottage Hill (today's Elmhurst). Here, he tried his hand at landscape-gardening by having mature elm trees transplanted from the banks of the nearby Des Plaines River— some with trunk diameters as large as eighteen inches.[*] The Prairie Farmer reported that his twenty-one room mansion called "Byrd's Nest" after his wife's family name, was "surrounded by thousands of newly planted trees."[8] Bryan's sister and her husband Jedediah Lathrop, from Alexandria, Virginia, came for a visit with their children in 1864, and decided to stay, purchasing twenty-six acres from him. Later, when Bryan's brother-in-law Lathrop had elm trees left over from a development project in nearby Noyesville (now River Forest), the two men planted them along Cottage Hill Avenue, establishing a precedent for Elmhurst streets and a rationale for the new name of the town.[9]

Lathrop's eldest son, born August 6, 1844, was named Bryan, after his uncle. During the Civil War young Bryan traveled and studied in Europe, becoming a connoisseur of fine art, music, architecture, and landscape design. When he

---

[*] They were ahead of the times in this kind of endeavor. Simonds would take it to new limits in moving trees for the cemetery, and in the twentieth century nurserymen would still brag about the size of trees that they had successfully transplanted. Nelson's men, for example, talked about the twenty-four inch diameter elms with twenty-two foot root balls they had moved. ("Notes from the Past: Swain Nelson Nursery," Roger E. Stevens, *The Landscape Contractor*, January 1994, 39.)

returned to Chicago, he joined his uncle's real estate business and worked with him in the offices of the Graceland Cemetery Company.[10] Compared to the rich cultural heritage in European cities, he found Chicago lacking in beauty and refinement—especially in its designed landscapes.* This, combined with the influence of his father's and uncle's interest in tree planting, led Bryan Lathrop to develop a fervent interest in landscape-gardening, a concern he brought to his work at Graceland.[11] [Because of the significance of the Bryans and Lathrops at Graceland and in the field of horticulture, a chapter on this significant extended family is devoted to them at the end of this publication.]

GRACELAND'S NEIGHBORHOOD

By 1867 the Graceland property in Lake View Township comprised 275 acres and many of the town residents objected to the cemetery company holding so much land. They contended that a large cemetery was not an asset to those living around it and wanted Graceland limited to its original chartered acreage. The Graceland Cemetery Company published a defense of its position in 1872, arguing that, if they did not own this "low and unsightly" land, it would never have become "anything more picturesque than a cabbage garden."[12] The issue was brought to court and, eventually, in 1879, a compromise was agreed upon whereby Graceland Cemetery was restricted to 125 acres.[13] The other 150 acres surrounding the cemetery (except to the south, already developed as small sectarian burial grounds) would eventually be platted and developed as residential subdivisions, under the direction of Graceland's new landscape-gardener.[14]

Even so, the cemetery's allotted development was beginning to spread into the soggy soil of the former celery fields on its property east of the Graceland Spit. When the trustees hired Jenney as their landscape designer in 1878, they asked him to devise a drainage plan to make the low-lying land usable as a burial ground. Jenney developed a lake drainage reservoir similar to the one he had used at the West Parks and he sent Simonds, his new assistant with an engineering education, to supervise the job.[15]

---

* Bringing Chicago up to European aesthetic standards was an acceptable common goal for Chicago's well-traveled sophisticates by the turn of the century. Henry B. Fuller expressed similar sentiments through Truesdale, the main character in *With the Procession*, his historical novel about the Gilded Age in Chicago. (New York: Harper Brothers, 1895; Chicago: University of Chicago Press, 1966), 73.

LAKE WILLOWMERE, Graceland Cemetery, Chicago.   AUTHOR PHOTO

SIMONDS AT GRACELAND

Simonds's first assignment at Graceland was to run a line of levels from the cemetery to Lake Michigan to determine if Jenney's plan to develop a reservoir and drainage system would work. Calculations proved that it would, and in May the Board of Managers unanimously resolved

> That the plans made by W.L.B. Jenney for the improvement of the lowlands and of the west portion of the grounds embraced in the new lines of Graceland . . . are hereby accepted.[16]

Simonds supervised the installation of vitrified pipe running from the lagoon at Graceland east to Broadway Avenue, and the construction of a thirty-inch brick sewer from there to Lake Michigan. This was completed by spring of 1879 (the same year the dispute with the town of Lake View was settled) and, after draining the lagoon through their pipe system, Jenney and Simonds discovered they could easily excavate the sand and gravel under the marl of

RESTORED SIMONDS plantings at Graceland Cemetery.   AUTHOR PHOTO

the lagoon bed to create a small lake. The managers authorized the president and treasurer "to accept the lowest responsible bid and make contracts for the excavation of soil according to the plans and specifications of Mr. Jenney." Removing enough of the sand and gravel to form the lake, Simonds used this material to raise and grade the surrounding areas, much as Jenney had done in the West Parks.[17]

Despite the success of his first project, however, Simonds's new career had a potential drawback—cemeteries could have ghosts. Writing to fraternity brother Asa Whipple at the University of Michigan in November 1879, Simonds admitted that "although not very superstitious, I have spent most of the time for the last year in trying to find out whether there really is such a thing as a ghost." He searched for them himself and asked night watchmen about their experiences with the supernatural, but in vain. Simonds finally relaxed his vigilance, although he told Whipple he intended to keep "searching for a returned specimen from the next world and when I am successful expect to take the individual on a lecturing tour."[18]

CHICAGO

For Simonds, adapting to life in Chicago had challenges more material than haunted graveyards. Ellen White's 1864 tract, "An Appeal to Mothers," reminded Adventists that there was to be no drinking of alcoholic beverages in Adventist homes, no drugs, no meat, no spicy foods, nothing of a sexual nature, and that there were to be just two meals a day, one at 7 am and the other at 1 pm; 'gluttony' was not part of a healthy life-style. An Adventist retreat not far from Grand Rapids at the Western Health Reform Institute on eight acres in Battle Creek in 1866 foreshadowed greater things. While there a twelve-year old John Harvey Kellogg had set the type for White's booklet called *Health, or, How to Live*; by 1876 Kellogg was the superintendent of the Institute. In 1902 he changed its name to the Battle Creek Sanitarium and developed it into a world-famous spa and health center.[19]

Whether or not Harriet Simonds had followed White's edicts closely or not, the change in lifestyle for O.C. when he went to college in Ann Arbor must have been an eye-opener, and his later move to Chicago must have been even more jolting. At a typical club dinner there would have been more meat served in one night than he had ever eaten in his life. [See the menu for the Architectural Sketch Club's feast in the winter of 1888 in the sidebar].[20] Although Simonds continually and agreeably associated with men at the top of the business world throughout his long career, he remained modest, conservative, and enjoyed the simpler things of life, apparently unaffected by such displays of opulence. From early on he believed that natural resources were to be used wisely and were not something to squander.

LATHROP INTRODUCES SIMONDS TO LANDSCAPE-GARDENING

Simonds had worked for Jenney at Graceland for more than a year before he laid to rest his concerns about phantoms. Bryan Lathrop had shared his enthusiasm for landscape-gardening with him during that time, and the two had gone to Mount Auburn Cemetery near Boston, Spring Grove in Cincinnati, and other cemeteries in Cleveland, Buffalo, New York, and Philadelphia—with Simonds on the watch for ghosts. At Spring Grove, they met its renowned

─────── ARCHITECTURAL SKETCH CLUB 1888 FEAST MENU ───────

The Architectural Sketch Club's feast in the winter of 1888 began with blue point oysters, two soups, green turtle and game broth, followed by the fish course with boiled trout with lobster sauce and baked black bass. Then on to the first "boiled course" with leg of mountain sheep and deer tongue, before moving on to the meat of the meal, so to speak.

The "roast" course included choices of black tail deer, mountain sheep, saddle of antelope, loin of venison, loin of elk, opossum, coon, black bear, wild goose, sand hill crane, ruffled grouse, mallard duck, Virginia partridge, red head duck, sage hen, brant, wood duck, jack rabbit, squirrel, butter ball duck, prairie chicken, blue winged teal, wild turkey, widgeon, pheasant, plover, snipe, and quail. This was accompanied by "Ornaments" of "the bear back rider" and "the hunter's mishap."

Then the "broiled" course: venison steak, fox squirrel, prairie chicken, butterball ducks, partridge, blue wing tea, pheasant, plover, black birds, snipe, reed birds, red wing starling, quail, and marsh birds.

The main course offerings under "entrees" included English hare braise a la financier, breast of duck, and squirrel pie hunter style. A few vegetables lightened the load: boiled and mashed potatoes, stewed tomatoes, turnips, green peas, sweet corn, sweet potatoes, and celery.

After refreshing the digestion with these, on to "ornamental dishes" of pyramid of game en Bellevue, aspic of birds a la royal, pattie of liver *sur socle*, bone quail in plumage, and red wing starling *au naturel*; then boned wild turkey, quail, snipe, ducks, prairie chicken, and partridge to choose among. Prairie chicken salad with dressed celery finished the main offerings.

Such a dinner required a suitable selection of desserts. So macaroons, cream almond cake, confectionery, ladyfingers, "assorted fancy pyramid," "Siberian sorbet," and vanilla ice cream followed. Finally offerings of oranges, figs, grapes, nuts, raisins, coffee, crackers, and cheese, and not on the menu but one presumes, cigars and perhaps brandy.

superintendent Adolph Strauch, who was in a trench showing the workmen how to properly lay drainpipe when they arrived.[21] Strauch was a Prussian landscape-gardener who had worked at the Royal Botanical Gardens in London, immigrating to America shortly after the Crystal Palace Exposition of 1851.[22] During his tenure at Spring Grove, Strauch refined the rural cemetery concept, minimizing curbing and fencing, and discouraging the use of monuments. He had created an open lawn cemetery reminiscent of the open expanses of turf punctuated by groups of trees and shrubs found in English parks (and in New York's Central Park). Strauch's techniques made a lasting impression on Simonds, as did his use of the term "landscape-gardener."[23]

Lathrop introduced his protégé to the concept of landscape-gardening as the fine art of creating a landscape *in situ* instead of on canvas. As early as 1851 James Fennimore Cooper had written that ". . . a union of art and nature can alone render scenery perfect." * Soon Simonds was reading books on landscape painting by English art critic Philip Gilbert Hamerton. In the 1860s, Hamerton had become fascinated with the use of imaging devices similar to the Claude glasses popular in eighteenth-century England. Hamerton, however, preferred a much larger-scale, using plate-glass windows to frame the landscape views instead. He had strong beliefs regarding the positive emotional value of landscape painting, especially when contrasted with "accurate draughtsmanship" which "if it is applied to landscape, must lead to topography as inevitably as accuracy in writing leads to prose."[24]

In *Landscape*, published in 1885, Hamerton expressed what was to become a fundamental principle in landscape-gardening, that

The curious truth that very much of the impressiveness of natural scenery depends upon the degree in which *mass* appears to predominate over *detail*. An extremely detailed view of anything is rarely, if ever, impressive.[25]

A decade later, Hamerton wrote *Imagination in Landscape Painting*, in which

---

* Cooper, W.C. Irving, and other popular American authors contributed to a collection called *Home Book of the Picturesque*, published by G.B. Putman in 1851, in which they defended the majesty of natural American scenery against the highly designed gardens of Europe. They expressed opinions on landscape aesthetics in general, Cooper going so far as to say that, "It is only in very particular places and under very dull lights, that the contrast between white and green is agreeable," more than fifty years before Frank Lloyd Wright would express a similar judgement.

OAK WOODS Cemetery, Chicago.   AUTHOR PHOTO

he defended the virtue of "perfectly passive enjoyment natural scenery" as a
desirable way of allowing "the repose of the intellect," a sentiment Olmsted
shared with him.[26] Simonds, too, adopted these as his guiding principles.

Lathrop further suggested that Simonds read J.C. Loudon and Humphry
Repton, influential English horticulturists and designers. Simonds took both
the contents and the title of Repton's 1803 book *Landscape Gardening* seriously.
Loudon's 1843 book *On the Laying Out, Planting, and Managing of Cemeteries*
may well have been the first published discussion linking horticulture,
landscape gardening, and burial grounds, and Simonds and Lathrop could have
found explicit guidance there.[27] Simonds also eagerly read William Robinson's
important contribution to public parks, *Parks and Gardens of Paris*, and A.J.
Downing's articles in *The Horticulturist* and his *Rural Essays*.[28]

With this kind of tutelage, the young civil engineer stepped into a profession
with an international lineage and local roots. He began to understand that with
these skills he could transform a barren site into a place of beauty and solace;
graveyards did not have to be the spooky places he had known back in rural

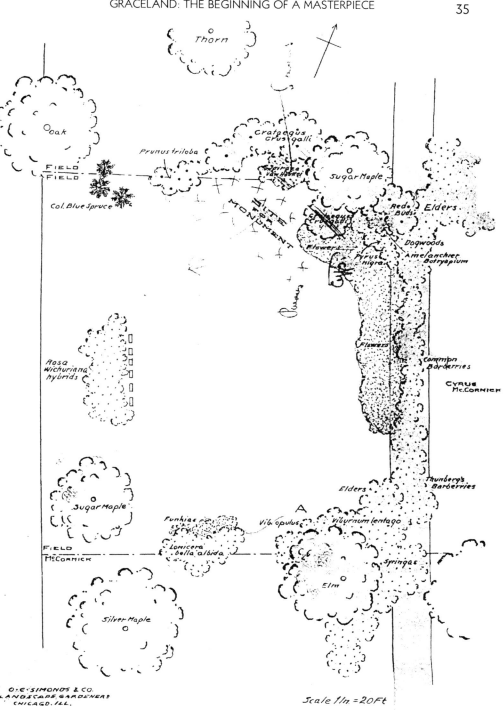

GRAVE SITE PLANTING PLAN establishes a "room" in the outdoors.

Grand Rapids. And in the words of the Oak Woods brochure again, "Good taste would seem to suggest that a rural Cemetery should partake more of the character of a cheerful park or garden than a common grave yard, where everything has a gloomy and dismal appearance, and every inch of ground is used for graves." A few miles north at Graceland Lathrop concurred, and Simonds felt the same as he got to know Strauch. Later in his career, Simonds was honored to design additional ground at Oak Woods, working directly with Strauch's original planning.

Simonds began putting these all ideas into practice at Graceland, combining them with his pragmatic engineering skills. Perhaps it was his openness to the idea of creating landscape pictures with natural-looking scenery that solidified his relationship with Lathrop. Jenney believed, as did Lathrop, that one found "in Paris above America . . . not language and manners . . . but appreciation of beauty and excellence more especially in the fine arts."[29] Jenney, though, leaned more towards the ideas of French architect and engineer Eugene Viollet-le-Duc, requesting his book, *Discourses on Architecture*, as a text for his class at the University of Michigan in 1876. Viollet-le-Duc's approach to design was that of an engineer: rational, intellectual, geometric, and precise. The approach preferred at Graceland, while also rational and intellectual, was closer to the craftsman-like approach of John Ruskin, employing local materials in an informal manner.[30] * In any case, Simonds left Jenney's firm to start a partnership with William Holabird in 1880, taking the Graceland account with him.

That Simonds was able to keep the Graceland account when he left Jenney's employ suggests that Jenney's initial drainage and expansion contract had been fulfilled and the work now consisted mainly of maintenance and small projects. It may also say something about the generosity of Jenney as an employer and teacher. Irving K. Pond was a fellow Michigan architecture student with Simonds and later recalled "Jenney's office very warmly as a 'springboard' from which he explored various professional options, always with the advice and support of the boss."[31] Jenney was also a tough businessman, though, going after the Lincoln Park contract that had already been awarded to Swain Nelson (as did H.W.S. Cleveland). The Bryans and Lathrops continued to socialize with Jenney, inviting him to a party in 1892 at "Byrd's Nest," the Bryan estate in Elmhurst.

---

* One of Ruskin's maxims was "Taste is not only a part and index of morality, it is the only morality. The first, and last, and closest trial question to any living creature is "What do you like?" Tell me what you like, I'll tell you what you are." Lathrop and Simonds thought along similar lines and promoted what they considered to be "good taste."

PARTNERSHIP WITH HOLABIRD

William Holabird was another fledgling architect who had worked at Jenney's office with Simonds. When the two left to set up their own practice in the Major Block in downtown Chicago, Graceland was their only client. Kindly Bryan Lathrop commissioned the struggling firm to design furniture for his office in 1882, and from 1881-83, alterations and buildings at Graceland that included a train station and cemetery office on the east side of the property.[32] In the spring of 1882 Martin Roche joined the partnership and their architectural commissions slowly began to increase.[33] Lathrop's wife Helen Aldis was the sister of Owen and Arthur Aldis, real estate investment managers in Chicago for the Brooks Brothers, New England financiers. The Aldis brothers commissioned many of Chicago's early high-rise office buildings on their behalf, much of the work going first to Burnham and Root and later to Holabird and Roche.

Joel and Harriet Simonds moved to Chicago in 1880 to live with their son, and he continued to maintain close ties with friends and relations in Grand Rapids. O.C. especially kept in touch with a young lady named Martha Elnora Rumsey (1857-1938), and by January of 1881 they were engaged; they married on May 12 that year in Grand Rapids.

Simonds had continued to make patent drawings for his half-uncle, but he now turned that work over to Edward Renwick (1860-1941), five years his junior and the son of old family friends. While visiting his hometown in the spring of 1882, Simonds suggested to Renwick that he come to Chicago and work for him at Graceland that summer. He thought his friend did not look well and that being "out of doors all the time . . . will be good for you." Grand Rapids was short on opportunity at the time so Renwick accepted the offer.

By this time, Simonds had purchased four acres of land just three blocks northeast of the cemetery's east entrance, and had built a house that included separate quarters for his parents.* It was the only residence for "miles around," as a history of the neighborhood describes it, and one of his few neighbors was the poet Eugene Field. At the time his address was 1431 Sulzer Street; the street became Montrose, and with the renumbering of addresses in 1908 and 1909, the Simonds house became 929 Montrose. Renwick boarded with Harriet and

---

* O.C. and Mattie lived in this large but unpretentious home for the next forty-three years.

Joel his first summer in Chicago because they lived close to Graceland, where he was working. Because O.C.'s father was, as Renwick put it, 'an odd Josy' differences of opinion caused friction. The elder Simonds still adhered strictly to a vegetarian diet, which did not suit Renwick's taste at all. Then, when O.C. asked his friend to take "some rather special photographs" of his new house and grounds, Edward discovered, upon pulling his head out from under the camera's focusing cloth, that Joel had taken out each of the eight "precious twelve by fourteen" exposed plates to look—ruining them all. He also found Joel's lectures on religion irritating. Renwick remembered these incidents more than forty years after they occurred; one can only speculate as to their effect on the relationship between Joel and his own son.

Simonds worked exclusively for Graceland, despite his partnership with Holabird. But this job did not bring money into the office, so he contributed to the partnership's expenses out of his own pocket. When Renwick completed his surveying work at Graceland that fall, Simonds suggested that Renwick fill in for him "at the munificent salary of $6.00 a week, a proposition to which Mr. Holabird agreed, in lieu of Simonds paying rent." So Renwick began working at Holabird, Simonds, and Roche that October, but he soon discovered that he did not know enough about architectural rendering for the job. Surprisingly, it was Joel Simonds, with whom he was still boarding, who taught him the basic drawing principles he needed for the job.[34]

With winter coming, Renwick began to dread the mile and a quarter walk from the Simonds's house to the public transportation he took downtown to his new job, and he sought closer quarters. One night he struck up a conversation on the train with A.P. Brink of Brink's Express, and within a few days, he rented a room at the Brinks' home in Ravenswood, where he would live for the next few years. Renwick remained at Holabird and Roche (later Holabird and Root) for his entire career, establishing himself as a respected Chicago architect.

SUPERINTENDENT, FULL-TIME

Simonds became so involved with the landscape work at Graceland that all questions about the grounds were now directed to him. Thus, it was natural that in 1883 he accepted the full-time position as superintendent of Graceland, and resigned from his architectural partnership. The firm changed its name

O.C. AND MARTHA Simonds's home at 1431 (later 929) Montrose Avenue. STERLING MORTON LIBRARY

to Holabird and Roche and, by the 1890s, would become one of the premier architectural offices in Chicago. Simonds set up his office in Graceland Station, the just-completed frame building designed by his former partners on the east side of the cemetery—and just a three-block walk from his new home. The Simonds's first child, Gertrude Elnora, was born that February.

The lake he helped design for the cemetery was named "Willowmere," and shortly after its completion, Simonds began planting its banks to create an idealized naturalistic shoreline. Another pond called Hazelmere was developed later on the east side of the cemetery near the station building, but later drained and filled with soil. By January of 1885, his titles—and duties—at Graceland included superintendent, landscape-gardener, engineer and surveyor. His five-year contract stipulated that he receive a $3,000 per-year salary, on the condition that "Mr. Simonds . . . devote his entire time, during said period of five (5) years, to the interests of the Graceland Cemetery Company." He had already drawn and submitted a plat for the company's proposed subdivision for 106 of its divested acres. The managers authorized him to use the "plat as a basis for the grading of streets, [and] the planting of trees . . ." before its designation as the official plat.[35]

FORT SHERIDAN

While all these responsibilities were more than a full-time job, what the board of managers intended by their direction that Simonds "devote his entire time . . . to the interests of . . . Graceland" is intriguing. For, by 1887, he was designing the landscape and drainage/sewer system for Fort Sheridan on a high and wooded bluff that overlooked Lake Michigan in Highwood, Illinois, about twenty-five miles north of Chicago.[36] Brigadier General Samuel B. Holabird, William Holabird's father, was U.S. Army quartermaster general at the time, and it was Holabird and Roche who received the commission for designing the new fort's buildings; Simonds was brought on to design the landscape—the parade grounds, the roads, and the parklands surrounding the officers' houses.

Increasing labor unrest in Chicago had culminated in the "Haymarket Riot" in May 1886, and Chicago's leading businessmen—members of the influential Commercial Club—responded by looking for a way to have an army presence here with troops at the ready. They created a subscription drive to raise the money to buy 600 acres of land north of Chicago to give to the United States government as a military base, with the stipulation that troops be stationed there. Club members Adolphus Clay Bartlett, Marshall Field, John Glessner, Charles Hutchinson, and Cyrus McCormick gave generously. Daniel A. Jones, owner of about twenty-five acres of the Highwood property chosen for the fort, asked only $250 an acre, taking a loss in lieu of a direct contribution. The mystery of what the Graceland Board of Managers meant about Simonds's full-time devotion to its business while he was also working on this very high-profile project is solved when the names of these Commercial Club members are compared to the major lot-holders at the cemetery: it is the same group.

Simonds was already familiar with the bluffs and ravines of Chicago's North Shore when he took the Fort Sheridan job. A few years earlier he had visited "Mr. Millard" (as Simonds referred to him), another Michigan transplant, at his new home in Highland Park, just south of Highwood. Millard purchased a sizable tract of land with several ravines, on a steep cliff next to the lake. Simonds was so impressed with this natural terrain

THE CAMPANILE at Ft. Sheridan, by Holabird and Roche ca. 1888.

that he would recall this visit fifty years later.[37] Although the extent and duration of his involvement with the fort can only be surmised now, as the records detailing his work have not been found, he seems to have been responsible for preserving the ravines in their natural condition (it was common practice at the time to fill them in or use them as refuse dumps) and for providing scenic drives with lake vistas. The *Chicago Daily Tribune* reported on the progress on page one of its January 23, 1889 edition, in a piece entitled "Our New Military Post: Fort Sheridan will be the Finest in the Country." A plan view showed the layout with the large parade ground in the center, Simonds's winding roads, and two cul-de-sacs with dramatic lake views for the officers' homes produced by Holabird and Roche. The article stated explicitly that "The plans of the post were prepared under the direction of Gen. J.D. Bingham and O.C. Simonds, civil engineer and landscape gardener, parking the plat," confirming in a contemporary primary source his role at the fort.

New Yorkers felt warmly about the new fort as well, but not with the pleasure and pride of the Chicagoans. Two years before the glowing *Tribune* article, the *New York Herald* published several pieces in January 1887 expressing its feelings about the Fort. A four-column, page two commentary on January 17 summed up the New Yorkers' point of view:

> "Chicago's Alarm; Her Citizens Thoroughly Scared by the Rising
> Spectre of Anarchism; To Become a Garrison City; Nearly a Square
> Mile of Land Offered to the Government for Barracks; Chicago Wants
> Twelve "Companies" of a Thousand Men Each; SCHEME OF THE
> COMMERCIAL CLUB; etc."

The *Tribune* did not take these attacks lying down. It responded with its own piece, saying,

> "The *New York Herald* has gone into four and a half columns of
> hysterics because there is a probability that a military post will be
> located at Highwood, one of our northern suburbs, and charges the
> scheme to the fears of the businessmen of Chicago . . ."

FORT SHERIDAN aerial panoramic 1908. G. R. LAWRENCE CO. LIBRARY OF CONGRESS LOT 5785 NO. 38

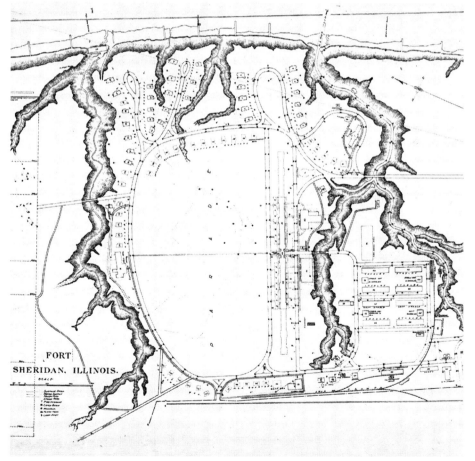

FORT SHERIDAN grounds map in 1904. LIBRARY OF CONGRESS HABS ILL,49-FTSH,1-

to which, of course, the *Herald* responded vigorously with a new piece entitled:

"Shaking in their shoes; Fright that Shook Shekels out of Chicago Cash Boxes; Anxiety to have an Armed Camp; What Members of the Commercial Club Say and Won't Say; The Truth Evident All the Same; And the Club Wants to Save the City from the Commune"

and from the *Cincinnati Enquirer*:

"Garrison Chicago; With Government Troops, Well Armed, For the Nabobs of that City are Terribly Alarmed."[38]

And so it went. Trial by fire for Simonds as he stepped into his first landscape design project away from Graceland in a blaze of publicity in New York and Chicago. And to clinch matters, when word got out that General Holabird's son had won the design contract for the fort, the reaction was so negative that the army created legislation in 1896 "that expressly prohibited the employment of a private architectural firm to design military installations expect by special act of Congress."[39]

ANOTHER CEMETERY DESIGNER COMES TO TOWN

Other real estate developers saw the opportunity that the new rural cemeteries presented and began to establish smaller outlying sites. A group formed to start Mount Hope, on the far southwest side of the city, and like the three major cemeteries, hired well-known landscape designers. Initially they asked Cleveland to consult, but as he declined to stay on to function as the superintendent as well, they instead hired Jacob Weidenmann, who agreed to do so. Weidenmann was well known, and was well-liked by Frederick Law Olmsted, whom he knew from projects in Hartford, Connecticut in 1862. Olmsted advised him not to take the Chicago position, but needing the work, Weidenmann accepted it anyway. He moved his family and business across the country in 1886, working on the cemetery plans throughout the winter so they would be ready to implement in the spring. He also took on the development of a plan for the grounds of Northwestern University and adjoining Garrett

"SIMONDS WAY" street sign in the Town of Ft. Sheridan.   AUTHOR PHOTO

Biblical Institute up in Evanston, in October 1887.[40] So at first it looked like things would go very well for him here, after all.

But one of the Mount Hope board members, a dry goods merchant named Rollins, believed that he knew better how to go about this work and simply over-rode Weidenmann's directions. When the board evaded meeting with him and canceled his contract, seasoned Chicago architect John Van Osdel (interred at Rosehill Cemetery), with whom Weidenmann had become friends, recommended that he sue Mount Hope. When the case finally came to court nearly two years later, it was Thomas Barbour Bryan who represented him. The court ruled in Weidenmann's favor and awarded him the entirety of payment for his five-year contract. He had already moved back east by then.[41]

Thus in his first decade as a landscape-gardener, Simonds was exposed to Strauch, Cleveland, Weidenmann, and Olmsted—strong, experienced designers—and to the difficulties even they faced in their professional pursuits. He also found himself in what must have been an encouraging environment for someone in his new line of work—endorsement from Thomas Bryan, Bryan Lathrop, and Adolph Strauch. Rural cemetery design and management was, in the 1880s, an up and coming profession whose practitioners could easily move into landscape design in general and into the nascent urban planning field.

THE TRIANGULAR MEDIAN areas eased turns into and out of Sheridan Park by mitigating the slight angle of its side streets, as well as providing character defining elements to this neighborhood. The north wall of Graceland Cemetery can be seen across Montrose Avenue. This point marked by a triangle on the map.   W. M. WALKER

SHERIDAN PARK

After the Fort Sheridan work, Simonds's next project off the cemetery grounds was the designing of landscape "improvements" for Sam Brown's Sheridan Drive Subdivision, better known by the name of Sheridan Park. North of Montrose Avenue, on property formerly owned by the cemetery company, it had been subdivided In 1891. When a new train station called Sheridan Park was built the name soon applied to the entire neighborhood. It encompassed the ninety acres of land west of Sheridan Drive, on high, well-drained land, with Graceland to its south and St. Boniface Cemetery north across Lawrence Avenue. (Simonds's own four-acre estate was located on the southeast corner of Montrose and Sheridan.) Brown included Simonds's name and a description of his work on Sheridan Drive in his advertisements promoting the charms of Sheridan Park. The streets were to be beautified, according to an article entitled "A Novel Feature," by plantings of red dogwood, barberries, syringes, snowberries, Indian currants, Japan quinces, snowballs, high bush cranberries,

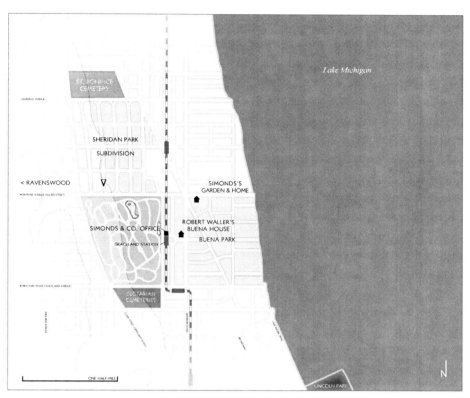

THE NEIGHBORHOOD around Graceland Cemetery ca. 1890s. The roadways in the eastern half of Graceland were designed by Jenney and Simonds. The streets in the Sheridan Park subdivision were Simonds's work; notice the subtle curve of several of the north-south streets, echoing the angle of Clark Street (Green Bay Road) to the west.

sumachs [sic], hydrangeas, elderberries, hazels, spireas, and honeysuckles, a veritable who's who of Simonds's favorite plants.[42]

In 1890, after Chicago won the right to host the World's Fair, Burnham and Olmsted led a team to determine the location for this monumental event. Amongst the locations they considered was a site in Lake View Township not far from Graceland; one account reports that Sam Brown, Jr. claimed that the spot was the same one he developed the following year as Sheridan Park.[43] Mr. Brown apparently knew what he was doing. In one month he sold over $200,00 worth of lots, and more than half of that within the first week. The roster of architects who designed both the private residences and the new-style apartment buildings included some important names—E.E. Roberts, James Gamble Rogers (who may have designed a building for Bryan Lathrop at 4741 North Dover), and William LeBaron Jenney, who built himself a new home a few blocks east on Bittersweet.[44]

Just a few years before Brown began his new residential district with the cemetery's divested holdings, Robert Waller had begun subdividing his family's land in 1887, creating the beginnings of "Buena Park" to the southeast of the Sheridan Park location. The Waller family had settled there in the 1850s and was Simonds's neighbor in their "Buena House" at the corner of streets now called Sheridan Road and Buena Avenue. Over the years their property had grown to include the land between Irving Park Road (Graceland Avenue at the time) on the south; the Chicago, Milwaukee, and St. Paul Railroad on the west (just outside the east wall of the cemetery); Sulzer Street (now Montrose) on the north, and the lake on the east. Robert hired architect James Gamble Rogers in 1892 to create attractive brick and stone houses to line the new streets of Buena Park. Aware of the needs of the population moving into these areas, Waller served as the president of the Lincoln Park Commissioners in 1893-94 with the express purpose of getting Lake Shore Drive extended north from Fullerton through the park. This was accomplished, but in the meantime, Governor John Peter Altgeld (buried at Graceland) had Waller removed from the position for "refusing to pad the payroll with party appointments." As Lake View Township real estate magnates, Waller and the Graceland board must have known each other well. Along with Lathrop and Bryan, Waller had served as one of the original directors of the World's Columbian Exposition, and his wife Lina was an active member of the Friday Club, a woman's literary group in which playwright Mary Reynolds Aldis, Arthur Aldis's wife, played a leading role. After the Lincoln Park fiasco, Mayor Carter Harrison II asked Waller to serve as city comptroller, at which he succeeded famously. He died of pneumonia in 1899 before being able to serve a second appointment and was buried at Graceland.[45]

Within just ten years after Simonds's arrival in this rural district of truck farms and celery fields these two new neighborhoods had developed around him, providing an opportunity for Simonds to practice his growing capabilities as a planner and landscape-designer.

CHAPTER TWO ENDNOTES

[1] A.T. Andreas, *The History of Cook County* (Chicago: A. T. Andreas, 1884), 720. Mount Auburn Cemetery in Cambridge, Massachusetts is considered America's first rural cemetery (in the sense of this new movement), established in 1831.

[2] *Who's Who in America: Historical Volume 1607-1896*, USDA National Agricultural Library, Beltsville, MD. Oddly, another William Saunders simultaneously served as the first secretary of the Canadian Department of Agriculture.

[3] Helen A. Sclair, "The Story of Graceland: A Prairie Landscape," (privately printed history, Trustees of Graceland Cemetery and Crematorium, 1995), 5.

[4] H.W. S. Cleveland, *A Few Hints on Landscape Gardening in the West*, with *The Relation of Engineering to Landscape Gardening*, by W. M. R. French (Chicago: Hazlitt & Reed, Printers, 1871). French, the brother of sculptor Daniel Chester French whose work would adorn the World's Columbian Exposition, the Marshall Field family plot at Graceland, and eventually the Lincoln Memorial in Washington, D.C., became the first Director of the Art Institute of Chicago.

[5] Theodora Kimball Hubbard, "H.W.S. Cleveland: An American Pioneer in Landscape Architecture and City Planning," *Landscape Architecture*, Vol. 20, No. 2, (1930), 92-111.

[6] Cleveland, "A Few Hints," 17, 34.

[7] Hubbard, Ibid.

[8] Don Russell, *Elmhurst: Trails from Yesterday* (Elmhurst, Illinois: Elmhurst Sesquicentennial Planning and Steering Committee, 1977).

[9] *Elmhurst! 150 Colorful Years* (Elmhurst, Illinois: Elmhurst Sesquicentennial Planning Committee, 1986).

[10] Robert Bruegmann, *Holabird and Roche, Holabird and Root: An Illustrated Catalog of Works*. New York: Garland Publishing, Inc. in cooperation with The Chicago Historical Society, 1991; Vol. 1, 55.

[11] Bryan Lathrop, "A Plea for Landscape Gardening," *Journal of the International Garden Club*, Vol. II, 1918, 300-301.

[12] *A Statement of the Condition, Property, and Franchises of the Graceland Cemetery Co.*, 1872, as quoted in John Vinci, "Graceland: The Nineteenth-Century Garden Cemetery," *Chicago History* (Summer 1977), 86-98.

[13] Andreas.

[14] "Managers' Meeting," April 7, 1888, *Record Book: Graceland Cemetery Co.*, Graceland Cemetery archives.

[15] "Dean of the Cemetery Field," *The American Cemetery*, September 1930, 20.

[16] "Managers Meeting, Friday, May 9, 1879," *Record Book: Graceland Cemetery Co.*

[17] Ibid.

[18] Simonds to "My dear Whipple," November 23, 1879; SFC.

[19] David and Elizabeth Metzger Armstrong, *The Great American Medicine Show*. NY: Prentice Hall, 1991, 99-105. Research in the Sanitarium's archives in Battle Creek turned up no information about the designer of its highly-praised landscape; Simonds seemed a likely candidate.

[20] Menu in William Le Baron Jenney's scrapbook, Ryerson-Burnham Library, Art Institute of Chicago.

[21] "The Dean of the Cemetery Field."

[22] Vinci, 90.

[23] "Dean of the Cemetery Field."

[24] Philip Gilbert Hamerton, "The Chief Influences on My Career," *Forum*, Vol. 28 (December 1894): 421-22, quoted in Marie Czach, "Philip Gilbert Hamerton: Victorian Art Critic" (Ph.D. dissertation, University of Illinois at Urbana, 1985), 156. Hamerton wrote art criticism and commentaries for English and American periodicals from the 1860s on, and his later books recapitulated these views.

[25] Hamerton, *Landscape* (Boston: Roberts Brothers, 1885), 15.

[26] Hamerton, *Imagination in Landscape Painting* (Boston: Roberts Brothers, 1895), 189-90.

[27] Stanley French, "The Cemetery as a Cultural Institution," in *Death in America*, ed. and intro by David E. Stannard (University of Pennsylvania Press, 1975). 87.

[28] "Dean of the Cemetery Field."

[29] Jenney to his sister Bertha, 1855, quoted in Turak, *Architect*, 108.

[30] See, for example, his *Stones of Venice*.

[31] Quoted by David Van Zanten in "Sullivan to 1890," in *Louis Sullivan: The Function of Ornament*, ed. by Wim de Wit, St. Louis Art Museum, 1986, 59, n. 58.

[32] Bruegmann, Vol.1, 1-3.

[33] Edward Renwick, typescript memoirs, 1932, 29, SFC.

[34] Renwick, 32. His rendering skills improved and he became a partner in Holabird and Roche in 1895.

[35] "Managers' Meeting, January 16, 1885," *Records Book*.

[36] Simonds, Chicago, to W.L. Jenks, Port Huron, MI, September 26, 1928; SFC.

[37] Simonds to Charles Garfield, in "Death of Ossian Simonds," *Michigan Tradesman*, 94 [December 1931]. MA, OCS, Box 1.

[38] *New York Herald*, January 23, 1887, 3.

[39] Cohen, Stuart and Susan Benjamin. *North Shore Chicago: Houses of the Lakefront Suburbs, 1890-1940*. Acanthus Press: 2004, 19-21.

[40] "Minutes of the Meeting of the Executive Committee" (Northwestern University), October 29, 1887. Northwestern University Archives.

[41] Favretti, Rudy. *Jacob Weidenmann: Pioneer Landscape Architect*. Cedar Hill Cemetery Foundation, 2007.

[42] Historic Sheridan Park sales brochures and miscellaneous newspaper articles at the Sulzer Library's Ravenswood special collections and the Chicago Historical Society (now the Chicago History Museum).

[43] "Historical Sheridan Park," Martin Tangora, *The Chicago Rehabber*, n/d, 15-17.

[44] "Legends and Landmarks of Uptown," brochure, 1980.

[45] Miles Berger, *They Built Chicago* (Bonus Books, 1992), 127-130.

chapter 3

PROFESSIONAL AND PERSONAL GROWTH

1885-1892

Witch Hazel

O.C. SIMONDS'S BOOKPLATE featured his watermill at Pier Cove.   SIMONDS FAMILY COLLECTION

FIRST PUBLISHED ARTICLES

Simonds's professional expertise continued to expand. His published writing began in 1885 with several articles in *The Michigan Horticulturist*, a journal of the Horticultural Society of Michigan edited by his cousin and close friend Charles Garfield. These articles reflected concerns of the time, including rural and urban development, the relationship of health and sanitation to graveyards, and the study of local vegetation. In them, Simonds expressed increasing knowledge in three fields. First, he promoted the landscape gardening approach to a project, which involved the issues of "taste" and idealized nature that he had learned from Lathrop, Strauch, and the English writers. Second, he described an engineering approach, based on his university training, and set forth in his suggestions for convenience and practicality in design. And third, he considered the importance of healthy, close-to-nature environments reminiscent of his parents' and Ellen G. White's beliefs, but he developed the idea in a broader and secular context. These essays provide a glimpse early in Simonds's professional life of the landscape design principles he would employ with remarkable consistency throughout his fifty-three year career, even when they were no longer in fashion.

In the December 1885 issue, Simonds's "Planting a School Ground" article appeared on the front page. He carefully went through the different considerations necessary for planning pleasant school grounds, some of which were distinctly different from the design approach he used for other types of sites. The building, he wrote, should be placed at the rear of its lot both to keep it as far as possible from the dirt and noise of the street, and to minimize the temptation for schoolboys to bother passers-by! Simonds advised making the walk to the building "as direct as possible to insure its being used," rather than the gently curving paths he usually created to accentuate plantings and topography. He was concerned with practical matters and urged that outhouses be made inconspicuous by placement and planting, "so that timid children may not be deterred from using them by inclement weather or bashfulness." Simonds recommended transplanting from woodland edges and from along rail fences—to minimize costs. He suggested planting such native species as

Virginia creeper, bittersweet, wild grape, virgin-bower, and green brier where vines were appropriate. The native shrubs that did well in this setting included juneberry [*Amelanchier*], witch hazel, sassafras, red-bunched dogwood, sumach [*sic*], hazel, and huckleberry. He found local trees, including maples, elms, lindens, tulip trees, wild cherry, black walnut, and oaks, useful and aesthetically pleasing. He made generic, rather than specific, suggestions to allow for latitude in planting, depending on what was locally available.

In addition to larger woody plants, Simonds encouraged using wild flowers for their color. He listed hepaticas, trillium, violets, and adder-tongues for spring, golden-rod and wild sunflowers for autumn. Hardy perennial plants were more suitable than fancy flower or foliage beds, he noted, because the latter die back in cold weather. He mentioned that it was good to get some plants from nurserymen, although he did not elaborate on this thought; perhaps he did not want them to feel offended by his use of found rather than bought plants. Simonds also recommended that these native plants be arranged in as natural a manner as possible, although he was concerned because often neither adults nor children gave them the same respect as more showy exotics, picking or mutilating them without thought. People were less apt to do that with cultivated flowers, he maintained, but he hoped his advice would promote understanding and appreciation for "everything 'wild', whether plant, bird, or animal." Simonds had confidence that these suggestions "would have a moral and civilizing influence, and would add greatly to the enjoyment of life, by teaching how to appreciate the common things around us."[1] Concern for and appreciation of birds would be a continuing theme for Simonds throughout his career.

The following month, Simonds wrote about just "Twelve Good Native Shrubs," even though he regretted having to exclude many others. He made his selection following the sequence in *Gray's Manual of Botany*, rather than in order of his own preferences. He offered no explanation for this choice, but as he was writing for a horticultural/botanical publication, perhaps he was trying to fit his usual artistic approach into a more rigorous, standard scientific format. For each entry, he gave a brief description of the plant, followed by his recommendations for its landscape use.[2]

In the April 1886 issue, following an article on the moral question of keeping bees near someone else's grapevines (the little publication admirably covered a wide range of the aspects of rural living) was Simonds's next essay, "Rural Cemeteries." In it he expressed his ideas for honoring the dead, and hinted at his childhood experiences with cemeteries—and the source of his earlier concern with ghosts. In the first paragraph, he noted that children can be frightened at night by typical cemeteries, "and no wonder, for the whole thing is hideous in the day time."[3] Simonds went on to say, however, that some cemeteries could serve as models because of the "very good taste shown" by their creators. These places resembled a park more than a burial ground, with "nicely kept lawns and noble trees, interspersed with graceful groups of shrubbery, form[ing] an excellent background for monuments." Gone are the standard chains and fencing around each family plot, replaced by one flowing lawn. Gone, too, were the five to six foot high headstones "of glaring white marble, causing them to remind one of ghosts . . ."[4]

Citing Lakeview Cemetery in Cleveland as an excellent example of a properly planned burial ground, he singled out Dr. Warder's lot for special praise. A "lover of nature," Warder planted a scarlet oak, his favorite tree, at the center of his plot. This tree, he said, would improve with age and be a living monument while those made of stone would deteriorate.[*] Simonds quoted T.H. Hoskins, another landscape enthusiast, who believed that memorial money was better spent endowing a worthy institution than on buying a fancy grave marker, letting "the sweet grass over my grave grow, unvexed by costly marble or granite." Simonds added that if the cost of a monument were reduced to one-tenth of what a person intended to spend on it, and the money invested instead in a larger lot, the cemetery could be made more beautiful with additional trees and shrubs—which would "increase the value of even the most humble lot"[5]– and increase sales.

Simonds's list of physical improvements required for a decent cemetery was based on his seven years of experience at Graceland, and aimed at providing the bereaved with comfort and convenience in beautiful surroundings. The list included gravel drives passing not more than 200 feet from any spot in the cemetery, with as easy a grade as possible given the topography, and taking into account the best vistas. Walks from the drives to family plots were to be grass so

---

[*] As did the markers made of marble or limestone at the time. With the advent of new carving technologies, granite has become the standard material now and will outlast most of the longest-lived trees. This would not have changed Simonds's belief that trees were the more satisfactory monuments.

they would not interfere with the overall picture. As with the siting of schools or houses, he advised placing monuments at the rear of the lot, away from the drive—not many chose the plants-only recommendation.

Rather than separating lots with plants in lieu of fences, Simonds suggested that trees and shrubs be planted in groups to seclude monuments; a tree or a boulder, he reiterated, would make the best monument of all. He finished this short piece by praising "the late Adolph Strauch, who did more than any other man to improve public taste with regard to this subject."[6]

The May 1886 edition of *The Michigan Horticulturist* provided a look at other active members of the society. Professor L.H. Bailey submitted a short article about gardening despite the rigors of Michigan's climate. Also concerned with good taste, he believed that "The elements of attraction in landscape gardening are comparatively few and simple." He suggested the judicious use of "a half dozen kinds of ordinary trees and shrubs" planted in groups as "preferable to a thoughtless mixing of twenty rare and more beautiful kinds." These groupings could disguise any unsightly objects and provide an enjoyable view from the windows of the house, a concept gaining in popularity.[7]

Following Bailey's essay came Oliver Wendell Holmes's short piece about the seed and sapling as "A Good Investment." Next was a letter from O.C. Simonds, entitled "Take Home Lessons from the Woods." Crowding several ideas into this short composition, he mentioned the pleasure of studying woods from a train car (an activity he especially loved), the surprise of not being able to purchase red-berried elders from first-class nurseries like Ellwanger and Barry's or Parson's,[*] the sick feeling he experienced upon seeing trees trimmed of their branches twenty feet from the ground, and the lack of shrubbery for street planting. He commented as well on the ornamental value in winter (which he noted is quite long in the Midwest!) of shrubs with colored twigs. He ended his letter honoring nature:

> A great deal can be learned from the woods in regard to planting . . . in groups, . . . employment of vines, and in fact, in regard to every natural feature of which a landscape gardener avails himself. With infinite variety in detail, nature is never stiff, little or undignified in her effects.[8]

---

[*] Owned by Samuel Parsons, Sr. Simonds and Parsons Jr. will both be founders of the American Society of Landscape Architects in 1899.

HORTICULTURE AND DESIGN IN ILLINOIS AND IOWA

Simonds was, of course, not alone in learning from nature, or in enjoying and using indigenous plants. The *1856-57 Descriptive Catalogue of Fruit and Ornamental Trees* from John A. and Charles Kennicott's nursery near the Des Plaines River in northern Cook County offered 134 varieties of apple trees, fifty-six varieties of pear, thirty-three of plum, thirteen of cherry, and fifteen of peach. + Its "Ornamental Department" listed a wide selection of "native trees" including tulip trees, sycamores, willows, maples, and red buds. Curiously, European larch, European mountain ash, and Norway maple were also part of this list, while oaks, ashes, elms, hickories, butternuts, thorns, dogwoods, and basswoods were listed elsewhere. Kennicotts' also sold hardy ornamental shrubs, vines, and herbaceous perennials. They included instructions for transplanting everything they sold, from the smallest herb to the largest tree. Plants that were unavailable locally or that could not be propagated came from Ellwanger and Barry.[9] *

John Kennicott was also a medical doctor and the editor of the *Prairie Farmer*, an influential and widely circulated periodical (still published in 2011). It dealt with such agricultural issues as livestock and crop production, and as early as 1859 the magazine also carried a regular feature about native Illinois vegetation called "The Flora of Illinois," written by Dr. George Vasey. A member of the State Natural History Society, Vasey was a nationally known botanist and was compiling, with the help of colleagues throughout the state, an exhaustive inventory of each Illinois county's native plants. In his column, he described in taxonomic order plants belonging to each family found in the state, providing both botanical and common names, a brief description of the plant, and the circumstances under which it grew.[10]

Plant enthusiasts in Iowa started their horticultural society in 1869. At their fourth annual meeting, members discussed such landscape topics as beautifying their prairie homes by planting more trees, laying out walks and

---

+ The Kennicotts settled here in 1836. John's son Robert was an important American naturalist in the mid-nineteenth century, a founder of the Chicago Academy of Sciences, a scientist at the Smithsonian and an explorer along the west coast up to Alaska in the 1860s.
* This area, in what is now west Glenview, would soon be home to other nurseries, including the well-known Swain Nelson and Synnestvedt firms.

roads in "graceful curves," not obstructing "the landscape view," planting flowers and shrubbery, and managing apple orchards in the difficult Iowa climate. While the society's members were interested in Iowa's native flora, J.L. Budd's prize essay on "Prairie Home-Making" expressed their feelings about their prairie and agricultural environment. He asked if the word "home" meant

> one of the barren Iowa homes, where the years go on in the endless round of wheat and corn and hog production? Winter after winter closing around with its endless stretch of drifting snow, leafless, treeless, bleak and arctic! . . . But here and there in our travels, like an oasis in the desert, we find a tree-embowered home with its impenetrable wind-breaks, its fruit-tree surroundings, and its evergreens as symmetrical and perfect as in the rocky pastures of our early homes.[11]

The vast expanse of prairie farm fields lacked human scale without the presence of trees.

Two of Simonds's future clients were already working here to beautify the Midwestern plains with vegetation. Laverne W. Noyes, a student at the new Iowa Agricultural College in Ames, helped landscape the school's barren grounds in the 1860s. In Nebraska, the next state west, Julius Sterling Morton, future United States Secretary of Agriculture, a University of Michigan alumnus, and another tree lover, initiated "Arbor Day" in 1872. His family motto became "Plant Trees," and, with his son Joy, he visited Harvard's newly established Arnold Arboretum near Boston in 1876. With Simonds's help, Joy would make their motto a reality fifty years later by establishing an arboretum just west of Chicago.[12]

SIMONDS'S PROFESSIONAL PROGRESS

Within eight years after first learning about landscape-gardening, Simonds had begun to establish himself as an authority on the subject. His articles gave him a regional reputation. Well-situated in his position at Graceland, he was known to many men of wealth and power in Chicago. As a good friend and colleague of William Holabird, Simonds was a natural choice to design the grounds of Fort Sheridan. His cousin Charles Garfield, seven years his senior, was by this time a respected horticulturist and pomologist (a specialist in the study and growing of pome fruits, particularly apples) in Grand Rapids and southwestern Michigan. The two men now had many common professional interests and much to share with each other. Jedediah and Bryan Lathrop had taught him how to collect plants from the wild and from neighboring farms and the cemetery flourished with this local flora. They introduced him, too, to the moving of big trees, a job he learned to relish; Graceland would soon be full of beautiful mature American elms. As can be imagined, though, this kind of work was difficult, dangerous and came with no guarantee the tree would survive the trip. The *Chicago Daily Tribune* ran a piece on page nine of its December 14, 1890 edition on the "Odd Journey of a Tree; A stately elm's travels toward Graceland Cemetery," documenting one of these amazing feats. Dug from its natural home on a farm in Grosse Point (now Wilmette)—the article pointed out that "the farmer was paid a liberal price for it"—the tree was slowly moved, upright, over the course of a couple of weeks to Graceland and planted next to Jedediah Lathrop's grave. Total cost was estimated to be $2,500 and several men were slightly injured and one actually killed. That was an exception, though, and tree-moving took on a very competitive character for the next few decades.

RAVENSWOOD SOCIAL LIFE

By the mid-1880s, O.C. and Mattie Simonds had become very active in the social life of Ravenswood, the town immediately west of Graceland. Lake View and Ravenswood townships had been a big celery growing area when Simonds first moved there (including land that became part of the cemetery) and there still were many truck farms, extensive plant nurseries, and greenhouses in the vicinity. But these slowly disappeared as the neighborhood developed. One woman recalled her sentiments when Wood's Nursery was sold: "To transform it into a town seemed sacrilegious."[13]

The Simondses joined the Ravenswood Congregational Church, as did their friends the Renwicks. Simonds offered Renwick and his new wife free use of a lot on his property, suggesting that Renwick build a small house in which to live for a few years, until he saved enough money to buy his own property.

Simonds would then reimburse him for the construction cost. Due to financial complications with this arrangement, the Renwicks bought the lot instead of borrowing it. Mrs. Renwick was not pleased with its location, but her husband felt confident their land would appreciate quickly because it faced Broadway—one of two major thoroughfares leading downtown. When the Renwicks decided to sell their half-acre lot and cottage and move to Evanston, Edward was delighted that his small piece of land was worth more than Simonds's three and a half acres.[14]

Adjoining this parcel now was the estate of A.P. Brink, the same man Renwick had met on the train that evening in the fall of 1882.* Holabird and Roche designed a new house for the Brink family on this property sometime in the late 1880s; in 1900 they planned a barn for the Simonds and Brink families jointly.[15] In November 1887 the two men hosted a reception for neighbors and friends at Library Hall (later the Ravenswood Historical Society), another Holabird and Roche design.[16] Lawyer (and later judge) George DuPuy and his family lived at Hermitage and Wilson, about a mile west of the Simondses and Brinks, and became part of their social set; these friendships were to last for the rest of their lives.[17]

Dr. Wallace Calvin Abbott (1858-1921) was another neighbor who became a long-time friend. Born and raised in Vermont, he grew up on a family farm, as did Simonds and many others among this group of men. Abbott studied at the University of Michigan Medical School (about the same years that Herman Mudgett, the serial killer so vividly portrayed in *The Devil in the White City* was studying there for his medical degree) and helped bring Herbert Rumsey, the second Simonds child, into the world in 1886. Newly married in 1888, he borrowed $1000 to purchase a drugstore and medical practice in Ravenswood. Abbott became so disgusted with the available medicinals that he set up a small laboratory in his kitchen to experiment with extracting "alkaloids" from plants, from which he manufactured a type of granular pill. Much easier to swallow and assimilate than the liquid remedies then on the market, Abbott's new product was an immediate success. Within a decade, his new business, the Abbott Alkaloidal Company, sold more than $100,000 worth of pills. Charles

---

* Because Renwick had been looking for quarters closer to the train when he moved into the Brinks's home, it is unclear how this solved his problem. Perhaps living in a home that served meat (Renwick was not satisfied with the vegetarian diet at Joel and Harriet Simonds's) was reason enough; perhaps living with old family friends had been too confining, especially in light of the elder Simonds's lectures on religion.

THE SIMONDS FAMILY house on Montrose Avenue (formerly Sulzer Street) in 1880s Chicago.

SIMONDS FAMILY COLLECTION

Truax, another Ravenswood associate, filled orders for Abbott's "Dosimetric Granules." The firm continued to grow, eventually becoming the mammoth pharmaceutical firm of Abbott Laboratories.[18]

The third Simonds child, Laura May, was born in February of 1888, and died two months before her second birthday. Laura was buried at Graceland and Mattie Simonds, who had been keeping a daily journal, was unable to make another entry for more than a year. During the next decade, Mattie and O.C. had three more children: Marshall Garfield, born March 24, 1891; Donald Rumsey, April 13, 1896; and Robert Ossian, May 13, 1898.

Mattie and O.C. joined with several families in Ravenswood to start the "Ravenswood Club," a social organization that gave local families an opportunity to expand their cultural horizons. Their friends the Brinks, DuPuys, Truaxes, and a dozen other families were also original members; the Abbotts joined a few years later. The club met in Holabird and Roche's Library Hall building at Ashland and Wilson Avenues; the Ravenswood Home College (another group the Simondses participated in for many years) held lectures by club members and outside speakers, galas, and coaching parties—one of O.C.'s favorite activities. These excursions went north or west into the country-side or south along the lake shore to Hyde Park, past the World's Fair grounds, and required a coach large enough to accommodate a dozen or more people, and pulled by a team of six horses.[19] Even in his spare time, Simonds loved to look at beautiful scenery—he had found the perfect career for himself.

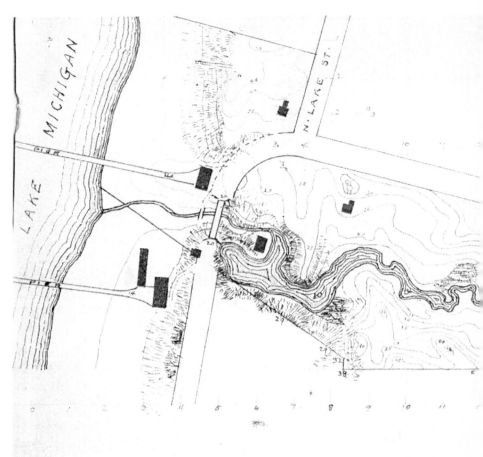

MAP OF PROPERTY
AT
PIER COVE — ALLEGAN CO·M
BELONGING TO
M⁣ᴿ·O·C·SIMONDS·
1895

Scale 1″ = 300′

Note:- Red lines show 5′ contours and figures
show elevations above lake level.

PIER COVE property map hand-drawn by O.C. Simonds in 1895.   SIMONDS FAMILY COLLECTION

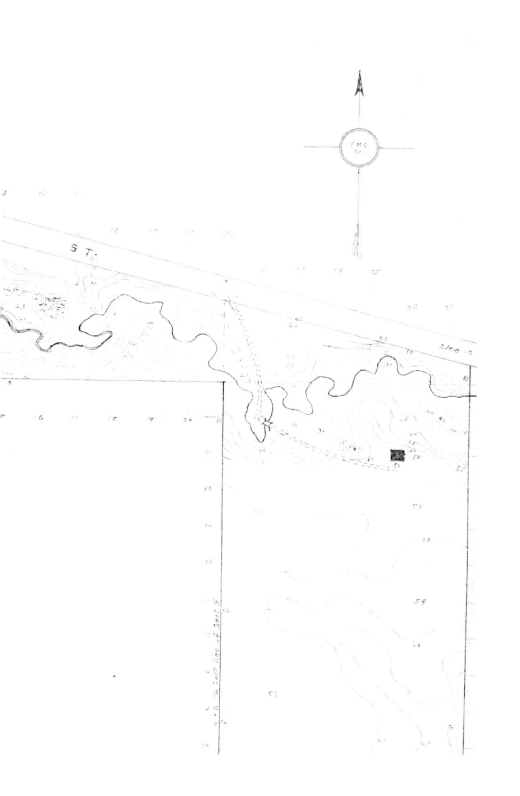

PROPERTY IN PIER COVE

In spite of their growing families and busy professional lives, neither Simonds nor J.B. Johnson, his friend from engineering school and lakes survey days, had forgotten their dream of buying lake shore property at Pier Cove, Michigan. When the two men visited the place again in 1889, the little town had almost disappeared. The railroad had come through farther inland at Fennville, and the town's few remaining business had moved or closed, causing property values to drop. So Simonds was able to buy several acres of property, the first of his holdings. When Simonds presented their new country place to his wife, she was quite surprised, as he had not mentioned his plans to her. Much to her credit, she quickly took to the new venture.[20]

On the property was a Gothic-revival frame home dating back to the 1850s and it became known as the Orchard House because of the apple trees O.C. planted to the north of it, on a dune overlooking Lake Michigan. Over the next several years, he accumulated well over a hundred acres, in an el-shaped configuration. The northern-most section included beach frontage and a sand bluff. On the east, the long leg of the el extended south, encompassing a pond with an old mill house and wheel, and a creek that wound its way out to the lake. Johnson's land lay between this rectangle and the lake.[21]

During the summer and fall, the families commuted from Pier Cove to Chicago by fruit boat. The lake effect gives southwest Michigan milder winters with more stable temperatures than the Chicago side of the lake; that, together with its sandy soil, provides an ideal climate for raising peaches, cherries, grapes, and apples. Fruit growing was a mainstay for the local farmers, with commercial boats making frequent, regular trips between Chicago and the small port towns of Michigan. Going to Pier Cove, playing in the lake, visiting with the Johnsons, and inviting other families as house guests became part of the Simonds family routine, one which continued for decades after O.C.'s death. The Pier Cove property made visiting with Simonds, Rumsey, and Garfield relatives in Grand Rapids convenient.[22]

Because he so loved his land at Pier Cove, Simonds started a journal in which he wrote the history of the town and his interest in it, then turned it into a guest book, so everyone who visited wrote a comment, a poem, a sketch, or at least signed his or her name and date of visit. The Cove Book, as it came to be known, proved to be so much fun that new books were bought as old ones were filled, and this family tradition continued into the 1930s.[23] The list of visitors over the years offers an amazing glimpse of his acquaintances. Everyone from his cousin Charlie to landscape architect Warren Manning to popular children's author Frances H. Burnett spent some time there and wrote about everything from the delicious blackberry pies to the noble benefits of landscape design.

FIRST PROFESSIONAL ORGANIZATIONS

In August 1886, Simonds was elected to membership in the Western Society of Engineers (formerly called the Civil Engineers' Club of the Northwest), his first professional organization. H.W.S. Cleveland, W.M.R. French, and W.L.B. Jenney were fellow members from Chicago, as was architect Dankmar Adler and Cook County surveyor Alexander Wolcott.[24] While his family and social lives were full, Simonds needed more professional fraternization than the WSE provided. With the growth of the rural cemetery movement in America, and its attendant increase in superintendents—with their unique responsibilities—the time had come to form an organization of cemetery professionals. In 1887, Simonds and twenty other men gathered at Spring Grove Cemetery, Adolph Strauch's influential creation, to inaugurate the Association of American Cemetery Superintendents [AACS]. At age thirty-two, Simonds was the youngest member.[26]

The AACS convened annually. At its third meeting, held in Detroit, Simonds spoke on the topic "Monuments and Headstones;" at the 1890 convention he considered "What trees and shrubs to plant in cemeteries?"[27] Meanwhile, Simonds's employer and mentor Bryan Lathrop and his uncle Thomas Barbour Bryan joined with other Chicago Board of Realtors members to lobby Congress to designate Chicago as the site of the upcoming World's Columbian Exposition.[28]

CHAPTER FOUR ENDNOTES

[1] Simonds, "Planting a School Ground," *The Michigan Horticulturist*, Vol. 1, No. 4 (December 1885), 75-76. The articles in this journal are from the files of William H. Tishler (WHT). Concern for and appreciation of birds would be a continuing theme of Simonds's designs.

[2] Ibid., Vol. 1, No. 6 (February 1886), 171-72.

[3] This was included as part of "a letter recently received."

[4] Simonds, "Rural Cemeteries," *The Michigan Horticulturist*, Vol. 1, No. 8 (April 1886), 266-267.

[5] Ibid.

[6] Ibid.

[7] *The Michigan Horticulturist*, Vol. 1, No. 9 (May 1886), 332.

[8] Ibid.

[9] *1856-57 Description Catalogue of Fruit and Ornamental Trees, Shrubs and Plans, Cultivated and for sale at the Grove Nursery & Garden, West Northfield, Cook Co., Ill. By John A. and Charles Kennicott* (Chicago: Democrat Printing, 1856). Collection of The Grove National Historic Landmark, Glenview, IL.

[10] Dr. George Vasey, "The Flora of Illinois," *The Prairie Farmer*, Vol. 19 and new series Vol. 3, 1859.

[11] J.L. Budd, "Prairie Home-Making," *Annual Report of the Iowa State Horticultural Society for 1873* (Des Moines: R.P. Clarkson, 1874), 179-82.

[12] "A Brief History of the Morton Arboretum," brochure (Lisle, IL: The Morton Arboretum, 1996).

[13] Jennie Van Allen quoted in "Romance of Ravenswood," in *A History of Ravenswood*, Ravenswood-Lakeview Community Collection.

[14] Renwick, 39.

[15] Bruegmann, Vol. 1, 217 & 290.

[16] Invitation, SFC; *A History of Ravenswood*.

[17] "Dean of the Cemetery Field."

[18] Abbott Laboratories, *The Abbott Almanac: 100 Years of Commitment to Quality Health Care* (Elmsford, NY: The Benjamin Company, 1988), 8 & 15. Courtesy of Miriam Welty, Abbott Laboratories Director of Public Relations.

[19] Miscellaneous invitations, notes, and photographs, SFC. One invitation

in particular is a hand-water colored lake shore scene, and one photo shows the coach-and-six along the shore, filled to the roof with people.

[20] Martha Simonds diary, SFC.

[21] Map and records, SFC; on-site observations.

[22] "Cove Book, Book One," 1895-1905, SFC.

[23] Ibid.

[24] *Journal of the Civil Engineers' Club of the Northwest*, October 8, 1879, i-iii, *Journal of the Western Society of Engineers*, June 1900, 33.

[26] Ernest Stevens Leland and Donald W. Smith, *The Pioneers of Cemetery Administration in America* (privately printed: Association of American Cemetery Superintendents, 1941).

[27] L.H. Bailey, ed., *Annals of Horticulture 1889* (New York: Rural Publishing Co, 1890), 92; and L.H. Bailey, ed., *Annals of Horticulture 1890* (New York: Rural Publishing Co., 1891), 152; WHT.

[28] Bessie Louise Pierce, *A History of Chicago: 1871-1893* (New York: Alfred A. Knopf, Inc., 1957), 280.

chapter 4

A SPREADING NETWORK
OF PROFESSIONAL RELATIONSHIPS

1892-1897

Polypody Fern

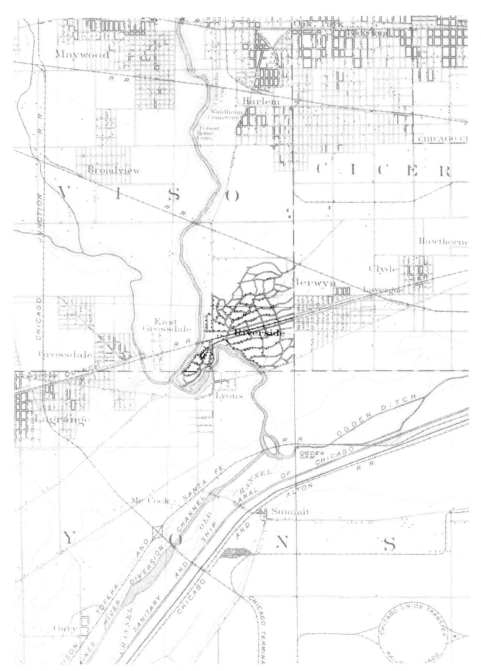

INFLUENTIAL town of Riverside, IL, built a generation before Simonds. UNIVERSITY OF TEXAS LIBRARIES

THE COLUMBIAN EXPOSITION AND OLMSTED

The Chicago Board of Realtors' efforts paid off: its city would host the World's Columbian Exposition. Bryan Lathrop served on the Board of Directors and Thomas Barbour Bryan, who had pleaded Chicago's case before a United States Senate committee, was its vice-president.[1] Despite these high-ranking connections, Simonds himself may not have been involved with the fair. Although his name does not appear in any of the Olmsted Company's scrupulously kept records, a brief look at the Olmsteds' work here helps set the stage for later developments in which Simonds would play a role.[2]

Frederick Law Olmsted and Company, of Brookline, Massachusetts, were the official landscape architects for the Columbian Exposition.[3] Working with architect Daniel H. Burnham, the fair's Director of Works, they planned the arrangement of the fair grounds, relying heavily on their representative in Chicago, Harry S. Codman. As the construction got under way in February of 1891, Olmsted arranged for his son Frederick, Jr. (known as Rick) to stay with friend and client George Glessner and his family at their Chicago residence at 1800 Prairie Avenue. The controversial stone edifice was one of the last projects of celebrated architect Henry Hobson Richardson, situated in the very center of the city's wealthiest and most prestigious neighborhood, and just a short train ride north of the fair grounds.[4] The younger Olmsted stayed in Chicago over the summer, meeting Burnham, Jenney, Codman, and Charles L. Hutchinson.[5] Rick also visited local nurseries to find suppliers for some of the 1,000,000 plus plants that would be needed to, in his father's words, "clothe several miles of newly made, raw sandy shores with a clean, graceful, intricate, picturesque green drapery, varied in tints, and pleasing in its shadows and reflections."[6]

The elder Olmsted had worked in Chicago twenty years earlier with his then-partner Calvert Vaux, first as planner for the development of the new town of Riverside in 1869, and then as landscape architect for Chicago's South Parks Commission. Working with more than 1,000 acres of land from Cottage Grove east to Lake Michigan at 59th Street (nearly 200 acres more than their Central Park project in New York), Olmsted and Vaux designed two large landscape parks on the east and west ends of their mile-long Midway Plaisance.

Under the supervision of Horace W.S. Cleveland, Washington Park on the west was mostly completed; the little real development took place at what would later be called Jackson Park on the east.[7]

Thus, having been previously well-acquainted with this low, swampy land along the lake shore about seven miles south of the business district, Olmsted was not discouraged by its drawbacks. He devised a lagoon system connecting this area with Lake Michigan, the Exposition's most dramatic feature. Olmsted created a naturalistic wooded island of many acres in the middle of the lagoon, to serve as a counter-point to the highly formal, Beaux-Arts buildings and layout of the rest of the grounds, which were punctuated by grass parterres and ornate planters, statuary, and lamps. He explained that "[f]or large, imposing buildings, the principal approach should nearly always be straight and broad."[8]

In his settings for neoclassical architecture, or any kind, for that matter, Simonds took an entirely different approach throughout his entire career, the Burnham-designed Kenosha Public Library and park of 1899 being a case in point. The Olmsteds took a dim view of this, and perhaps this explains why, despite the powerful presence of Bryan and Lathrop on the Exposition board, there seems to be no real inclusion of their landscape-gardener on this high-profile project.

GRACELAND'S CREMATORIUM

During the Exposition's planning stage, Simonds and Lathrop took a garden tour of Europe, returning home early in the spring of 1892. Mattie Simonds's diary entry for February that year said somewhat plaintively, "O.C. is still in Europe, in England somewhere."[9] When they did return, their boat was quarantined for cholera in New York harbor for two weeks. As a director of the upcoming World's Fair and the president of Graceland Cemetery, Lathrop worried about the immense problems a cholera epidemic could cause Chicago, no doubt remembering the outbreak in 1885. Because cholera is transmissible by dead bodies, it would be crucial to find a quick and clean way of disposing of them. He decided that a crematorium would be the best solution, but there were none in the city. When they were finally released from quarantine and had returned to Chicago, Lathrop asked Simonds to investigate cremation facilities in Detroit and St. Louis, but Simonds found them inadequate. Each cremation used an entire cord of wood (128 cubic feet) and took forty-eight hours to complete, causing enough damage to the retort to require its partial reconstruction. A more economical and efficient solution was required.[10]

Simonds thought about what other sorts of applications would require enduring, intense heat, and then went to visit up-to-date factories to see what kinds of furnaces they had installed. Oil was the new fuel, he discovered. It burned hot and clean, and so he recommended this to Lathrop; they proceeded to design and build a retort that burned oil. Installed in 1892 under the Holabird and Roche designed chapel, Graceland's oil-burning crematorium became the world's first.[11]* It is hard to appreciate just what a progressive, far-seeing, and perhaps radical choice this was at the time. Although cremation became more acceptable as an alternative to burial over the next several years, it was not always an agreeable choice for those arranging it for the remains of someone they loved. When Frances Willard, the leading reformer and powerful president of the Women's Christian Temperance Union (WCTU), died February 17, 1898 at age fifty-nine, she was cremated according to her specific request in the retort at Graceland Cemetery. But her assistant and close friend Anna Gordon could scarcely bring herself to comply and she left the body in a receiving vault for two months before she could commit it to fire. On April 4 she wrote to an associate that:

> On Saturday last as I renewed the fragrant 'lily censers' at her feet
> she seemed almost to chide me gently and to say 'Why do you leave
> me here in the cold and the dark away from my own? The glad
> Easter comes! Will not that hallowed day of resurrection help you
> take me <u>through the promised white path of pure refining fire</u> to the
> quiet mound . . . My heart stood still for the pain that it held while
> I reverently renewed the covenant made with her many times in life, 'it
> shall be just as you think right, dearest: I will be true "even unto this last."'

---

* More accurately, the Graceland crematorium was the first *legitimate* oil-burning crematory. Bizarrely enough, in early 1891 on the south side of Chicago in Englewood, just three miles west of where the World's Fair was being built, serial killer Herman Mudgett (a.k.a. Henry Holmes) constructed a less attractive but totally efficient retort, in the guise of a kiln for glass bending, in the basement of his World's Fair Hotel. With a double wall of firebrick and an oil burner adjusted to burn at 3,000 degrees Fahrenheit, Holmes was apparently able to completely incinerate some of his murder victims in this device, with no odor whatsoever. See *The Devil in the White City: Murder, Magic, and Madness at the Fair that Changed America* by Erik Larson; Random House, 2003, 90-93, for more details.

and:

> . . . I am pleading for strength to let this be done in the way she
> believed best—this great woman who lived more for tomorrow than
> for today.[12]

True to the last she was. On Easter Sunday (April 10) at three o'clock, Anna and others held a "loving service" for Frances at Rosehill (which, of course, did not have a crematorium) and then committed the "sacred dust" to a grave next to her mother's. Anna then wrote to her fellow "White-Ribbon Sisters" (WCTU members) to explain the disposition of Willard's body and her essay is worth quoting in full its the vivid description of the original Graceland crematorium and its expression of late Victorian era attitudes toward the subject, knowing that Gordon was not alone in her feelings. We also hear, in both pieces, the language used by women of refinement and strong Christian belief in discussing such matters. Gordon moved through her feelings of unbearable aversion to being at peace with the process and finally to encouraging others to take "the white path."

THE WHITE PATH [13]

> . . . The subject of "The White Path" had often been referred to
> by us both. When Miss Willard learned of the first building in this
> country containing a receiving room for incineration, she went to see
> it. This was many years ago, but even then she instinctively turned
> toward that method of disposition of the sacred caskets of our holy
> dead, and I believe wanted me to see it with her, hoping that from my
> more conservative mind its terrors might be dispelled. Here we first
> talked of the subject, and made the mutual promise, often renewed,
> that this method should be pursued for each by the one who should
> outlive the other, I freely admitting my conviction that it was a right
> thing to do for "humanity's sweet sake," but adding, "while I desire it
> for myself I can promise to carry out *your* wish only because I firmly
> believe that I shall not outlive you."
>   When the test came it was truly a "fiery trial," and for two
> months in my anguish I postponed the dread day. I shared the

well nigh universal opinion that in carrying her "earthly garment" to Graceland chapel I would annihilate by my own hand all that remained of that most precious earthly treasure. Religion and philosophy, I said, will come to the rescue of heart and mind if *nature*, the inevitable, is allowed to do her work for this beloved one, but if I submit her form to the white heat of incineration how unbearably pitiful will be the result. It was the torture of the inquisition—nay, it was Gethsemane—but if every human being on this round earth had disapproved I still should have been true to this heroic friend's holy wish.

The incinerating room at Graceland is of purest white. On April 9, through dear Mrs. Steven's loving thought, it was a bower of drooping palms, and with my hand upon the silver gray casket, with its encircling white ribbon and its crown of Easter lilies, I walked to the open door through which it was gently passed on into the chamber of white light. Verily no flamed kindled upon it, and after an instant's vision of it in this its last resting place, the separating slide was lowered—the doors were softly closed.

What was my experience when that noon hour had come and gone? *Peace so ineffable that its description is beyond my power of speech.* A fresh and infinite loneliness? Oh yes, yet an unutterable content, a heavenly ecstasy in the thought that the garment of such a white soul had forever escaped the touch of earthly corruption . . .

I pray that white-ribboners may not shrink from this most beautiful pure white path to the grave. I pray that none of us may hereafter hesitate to "follow that way" with those whom we love the best. The sacred white ashes are a fitting symbol to lay tenderly away in mother earth; the process of incineration is only the speedy action of the same elements that with agonizing slowness do their work in the heart-breaking grave . . .

Graceland could not have asked for a more poignant and convincing testimonial for its avant-garde crematorium. Surely Lathrop, whose conception it was, and Simonds, who found the means to bring it about, would have been pleased with such a heart-felt testimonial.

"A MORE RATIONAL VIEW OF DEATH"

While their religious beliefs may have differed greatly, Willard, J.B. Johnson, and Simonds were kindred spirits when it came to the disposal of earthly remains. When the AACS met in St. Louis in 1892, Johnson (who lived in St. Louis at the time) gave a talk on "A More Rational View of Death" at the convention.[14] Simonds shared these beliefs and discussed them "at [Johnson's] summer cottage on the eastern shore of lake Michigan, where for a number of years there has gathered a little community formed of his family and friends and where he was wont to spend his summers in quiet country life . . . [13] Johnson's objective was to encourage the funeral profession to take "a more cheerful and rational view of death itself," by thinking of death not just as a necessity but as a friend. He grounded his philosophy in the new scientific theory of human progress through evolution, believing that mortality provided the necessary motivation for life-enhancing thought and activity. Johnson "hoped the day is not far distant, when cremation, the only rational disposition of the lifeless body, will be universally adopted in all civilized communities." Like Simonds, he believed the "broken shafts" and "ghastly marbles" of graveyards ought to be replaced by flowers and foliage, "inspiring trees . . . the most restful and inviting landscapes; and in place of iron fences and stone vaults give us glassy waters and shady walks . . . " If people insisted on burial instead of cremation, then it should be done

> . . . in spots unobtrusively marked in beautiful parks, where earth
> and sky, flower and foliage, lawn and lake, birds and butterflies shall
> each and all bring healing and joy to the crushed and bleeding hearts
> which will resort thither as a thirsty traveler to rippling waters.[15]

This was the same effect Simonds was working to achieve at Graceland. However, when his father Joel died four days before Christmas in 1892, he was neither cremated nor buried at Graceland—the family returned his body to Grand Rapids and buried him at Oak Hill Cemetery there.[16] And Johnson himself, while vacationing at his Pier Cove property in the summer of 1903, was killed in a carriage accident. As a memorial, Simonds and a few close friends and fellow engineers wrote a tribute to Johnson in the *Journal of the Western Society of Engineers*, and reprinted his speech on "A More Rational View of Death." Johnson left a widow and several children; they continued to spend summers at Pier Cove.*

QUINCY PARKS

Although landscape design became a popular topic in Chicago after the World's Fair, it was still not generally viewed as a discrete occupation and architects often saw this work as being part of their domain. For example, local architect Thomas Hawkes wrote an article for *Inland Architect* in 1894 giving "Hints on the Art of Landscape Gardening", as it was still known then.[17] By the end of the century, though, landscape practitioners banded together to create their own professional title and their own organization, the American Society of Landscape Architects, as a way of setting boundaries and making clear that different skills were needed for this work.

Simonds served as President of the Association of American Cemetery Superintendents in 1895, and as his practice was expanding considerably, he took on Frank Button, the engineer from his Fort Sheridan days, as a professional associate again.[18] Coming full circle, William Le Baron Jenney designed and built a new home on Bittersweet Place in the new residential area east of Graceland Cemetery, part of Buena Park platted in the late 1880s.[19]

Going to Quincy, Illinois in 1895 to plan an expansion for Woodland Cemetery, Simonds was also asked to continue the work that H.W.S. Cleveland had begun with the Quincy parks in 1888 with the high recommendation of Frederick Law Olmsted. Thirty-two Quincy residents formed the Quincy Boulevard and Park Association that year, focusing on eight and a half acres of land that had been set aside by the city in 1867 on the site of an abandoned cemetery. Cleveland developed this into a small park. He then began simple changes for Quincy's South Park in 1891, saying "It is a park already, all it needs are a few roads through it," the highest compliment these designers could bestow on a site. Cleveland's son Ralph (a photographer) came next to plan Riverview Park in 1893. Then Simonds took on the development of the park

---

* As of this writing in 2011, Johnson's descendents continue to own a portion of this property, as Simonds's grand- and great-grand-children still own pieces of his land here. They have put Simonds's favorite section, known as the Ravine, in a trust to preserve it for future generations.

and boulevard system. He arrived on May 17, 1895 with his engineer "Fred [*sic*] Button" and set to work on South Park.[20]

Indian Mounds Park on the south side of the city became an especially favorite park. The land was slated to become a rock quarry because of its "very barren ground with deep gullies and because 'the soil was poor, no grass nor trees would ever grow there.'" Simonds and the park board thought otherwise, impressed with its river vistas and "numerous Indian burial mounds in fine state of preservation." They planted 60,000 mostly native shrubs and trees in one year alone. The development of the park so pleased Simonds that in his talks to the American Park and Outdoor Art Association (APOAA) and other civic groups he often said, "I would like to take Indian Mounds Park around the country with me as a sample of what can be done in the development of an unpromising piece of land, at a minimum expense, with native flora and other inexpensive planting." Because of the steepness of the location few recreational facilities were installed and the park design instead focused on "driving the scenic roads which afford many surpassingly beautiful views," which would have pleased Simonds.[21]

Edward J. Parker served as the park system's director from its inception until his death in 1912 and was instrumental as well in the APOAA and the Illinois parks organizations that sprang up in the early 1900s. The citizens of Quincy were profoundly grateful to him for his vision and effectiveness, believing that he was unique in his contributions to a park system. "Never in the history of municipalities has a great system of public improvements been so centered in the personality of one man as that which has had to do with the development of the parks and boulevards of Quincy." They named Parker Memorial Heights Park in his honor.[22]

Simonds was not the only landscape designer visiting Quincy. Annette McCrea (1858-1928) was also in town in 1902. A fellow member of the APOAA, Mrs. McCrea had begun her landscape career in 1892 when she took over her ailing husband's nursery in Kalamazoo, Michigan. She began to design home grounds there as well, but after her husband's death she and her two daughters moved to Chicago. She worked as consulting landscape-gardener for the Lincoln Park board, but for less than a year—a conflict with management brought about a quick departure. About 1900 she became chairman of the APOAA's Railroad Grounds Committee. When that group merged with the

A POSTCARD PRESERVES a pool scene from South Park in Quincy, IL, early 1900s.

THE SIMPLE LANDSCAPE with American elms of South Park in Quincy, IL.

American Civic Association in 1904, McCrea served as the vice president of the Department of Railroad Improvements until 1908 and continued on the executive committee until 1913.[23]

She was perhaps soliciting private projects throughout the wider Chicago region when she found a way to gain some publicity while visiting Quincy. A two-page article in the Quincy *Herald* on September 6, 1902 cited Mrs. McCrea's opinion on the opportunities the profession of landscape gardening held for her gender; she saw it as "a grand opening for young women." Apparently not aware of Beatrix Jones, Elizabeth Bullard, and other women working in the east, she wrote as though she was the lone female in the profession at the time. This does not seem to be the real theme of the article, however.

In the interview McCrea weighed in on the new Quincy park system, begun by Cleveland fourteen years earlier and developed under Simonds's direction for the past seven years, although she does not name them. The reporter slyly prefaced McCrea's statements by saying, "Referring to park work in general and with no word of criticism of local conditions except as the criticism might be felt by those in a position to know to apply to Quincy . . ." McCrea disapproved of the way the parks were maintained, claiming that the "shrubbery may languish for lack of care," and recommended that even if the caretaker claimed he did not have the time, she would "tell him to take time to spade around the shrubbery . . . and take his spade in hand and get among the bushes." This is quite different from the maintenance advice that Simonds gave, as he believed that allowing plants to flourish in natural conditions suits them much better than frequently cultivating them. It seems that she was indeed criticizing the "local conditions" as created by Simonds, whom she would have known through the APOAA and other local groups, and who would continue working with the Quincy Parks for more than a decade (the park board did not hire McCrea).

The interview continued with McCrea's unfortunately gratuitous comments (although the reporter seems to have been charmed). She found Riverview Park to be Quincy's most beautiful but thought that Indian Mounds "has the greater possibilities." However, she said, it would "never attain its full beauty until the soil has been enriched. It needs mulching and fertilizing and digging up and turning over." She would not, indeed, have approved of Simonds's rather laissez-faire approach to these matters. Without having seen any of McCrea's gardens or plans, one can at least deduce that her approach was more in the gardenesque fashion—manicured, cultivated, and plant (rather than design) based. Simonds had been at this work for over twenty years when McCrea made these comments; what her motives could have been are not apparent, other than hoping to get herself a new permanent position by discrediting the current designer, or at last getting her day in court over the Lincoln Park issue.[24]

GOLF IN CHICAGO

The World's Fair of 1893 introduced Chicagoans to a whole world of new technologies, products, and amusements—among them the game of golf. Tradition has it that four Scotsmen played the first golf in Chicago in 1887 on the very same spot, the lake and sandy soil perhaps reminding them of seaside links back home.[25] Nothing much came of it at the time. Six years later, though, the young men on the staff of Sir Henry Wood, England's Commissioner General to the Fair, golfed informally in the parks near the fairgrounds, which aroused the curiosity of several prominent locals. Hobart Chatfield-Taylor convinced his father-in-law, Senator Charles B. Farwell, to allow him use part of "Fairlawn," his Lake Forest estate on Chicago's north shore, as a small golf course. Charles Blair MacDonald, already an avid golfer and a friend of Chatfield-Taylor, designed the course. Soon dissatisfied with the few holes there, in 1894 MacDonald convinced several friends to start a golf club. Originally in Downers Grove, it moved to the 200-acre Patrick farm in Wheaton, a suburb twenty-five miles west of Chicago.[26]

The group hired Simonds to design an English landscape park setting out of the farmland and converted the farmhouse into the clubhouse. The Chicago Golf Club, as they named it, claims to be the first eighteen-hole course in the United States.[27] As Simonds's mentor and friend Bryan Lathrop lived in nearby Elmhurst and knew the club's founders (and later became a member), it is likely that he recommended his favorite landscape-gardener for the job. MacDonald laid out the actual playing course, and while he "did a splendid job", it ran in a clockwise direction with the holes hugging the perimeter. The members did not enjoy the circular scheme for long and voted to redo the basic layout within a few years.

During the early days of the Chicago Golf Club, golf advocate MacDonald went east to play in Newport, Rhode Island, with Stanford White—one of the architects responsible for the neoclassical style at the World's Fair. The two also visited the course at Shinnecock Hills in Southampton, Long Island, the first actual "designed" course (nine holes) in the United States, dating to 1891 and for which White had designed the clubhouse and Scottish golfer Willie Dunn planned the holes.[28]

The golfing movement throughout the country was the beginning of "country club life." Around Chicago, businessmen seeking something to do in the summer found that golf club membership was more convenient and much less expensive than typical Gilded Age vacations.[29] Meadows and prairies surrounded suburban Chicago and made ideal locations for the new clubs; the commuter trains from the city made traveling to them easy. Fittingly, a nine-hole course was built in Jackson Park on the grounds of the exposition after its buildings were razed, for professors from the nearby University of Chicago.

Three years after the exposition, its former Director of Works became involved with a new club, the second eighteen-hole course in the Chicago area. Daniel Burnham received credit for finding the beautiful location for the Glen View Golf and Polo Club, and for convincing Simonds to design the grounds and join as one of the one-hundred founding members. Club records mention that William Caldwell, a Scotsman and professor at Northwestern University in Evanston, suggested the idea of a golf and country club to his friend Hugh R. Wilson, who in turn discussed the notion with a few neighbors in Evanston (among them Burnham) and before long, they were looking for a piece of property to buy.[30] Northwestern was a Methodist school and a clause in its charter prohibited the sale of alcohol within four miles of its boundaries; thus the Evanstonians had to go farther afield to find the right piece of property.

According to Angus Hibbard, another founding member, the land Burnham located and the club subsequently purchased from the John Dewes family was

> on a great rolling tract of farm and woodland, and here, where experts said it was impossible, there was made the rarest, fairest golf course of them all . . . the Glen View Golf and Polo Club, six miles west of Evanston. Beyond the boundaries of the area legally prescribed as too dry for a golf club, Glen View was a venture not alone in sport, but, most of all, in good fellowship.[31]

Soon after the club acquired the land it received its charter from the State of Illinois, and by the end of March 1897, professional golfer Richard Leslie arrived from St. Andrews, Scotland to plan the actual playing course and serve as the first greenkeeper.[32] Architect William Holabird, Simonds's former partner, was another founding member and designed the clubhouse and stables complex.[33] Holabird's son William, Jr. went on to championship status a few years later.

Yet, it was Simonds (who was not a golfer) who helped make the "timeless standards" set for the Glen View Club by its founders a reality. Nearly two decades after the club's inception, Hibbard wrote:

> Names and recollections of these and many more who made Glen View come to me as I write, but one stands out for whom this beauty spot remains a monument and Nature's testimony to his artistic skill. This was O.C. Simonds, the landscape architect who planned Chicago's Lincoln Park and many another in the country, who was one of the founders of Glen View and gave to its planning his very best. Working with officers, architects, and golf experts, Simonds laid out the land, its forests, trees, and vistas, its roads and pathways. He said, "let us here create a park to serve our pleasure, a thing of beauty; do not destroy it." His word became the law and was obeyed. When Simonds said, "Woodman, spare that tree," the tree remained. Wide lanes were cut through the forest, drained, planted, and transformed into fairways. Trees and shrubs appeared where he said they should be, and Nature responded to this artistic skill and guidance, producing a landscape whose beauty has increased with every year.[34]

Contemporaries who did not belong to the club concurred. Alexis J. Colman, writing for a leisure-time periodical in 1899, remarked:

> The main club to which Evanstonians belong is the Glen View Golf and Polo Club, located on the North Branch. Here a club has been established which has won one of the first places in the galaxy of Chicago organizations. A forest innocent of an axe had to be cut out or tunneled through to lay out part of the course, and leveling, sodding, and all kinds of landscape work had to be done; but the

results of this outlay of money and labor has been one of the most picturesque courses in the country. The club-house is on a knoll in the center of the grounds.[35]

Situated on gently rolling terrain—quite rare in this region—the club's site and requirements were ideally suited to Simonds's approach to landscape gardening. Designing the course around the Dewes' seventy-five year old log cabin, a pioneer family cemetery, the west fork of the North Branch of the Chicago River, and the naturally occurring groves of trees, he incorporated the fairways, roads, and walks unobtrusively into the natural surroundings. By taking advantage of the gently rolling topography, he created "long views" down his gently curving roads, leaving as many trees intact as possible, with openings through woods onto sweeping prospects across the fairways. Simonds then situated the clubhouse near the center of the grounds, atop the highest hill, and the club was able to celebrate its grand-opening in June 1898. As Hibbard wrote, "the land responded by becoming more graceful and elegant with each passing year."

Holabird's 1897 clubhouse burned to the ground in a sensational fire on May 28, 1920. By July, a new one was being built in the same footprint, and designed again by the firm of Holabird and Roche. As with many of Simonds's projects, too, several of the club founders were also lot holders at Graceland, most prominently Burnham, William Holabird, and Simonds himself. James Patten, a residential client of Simonds's, was founder #49, and Burnham's nephew Hugh signed on as well.* It is likely too that Simonds and his associates designed landscapes for the homes of members, among them Angus Hibbard, that cropped up on the north and west perimeters of the golf course, in what became a small exclusive town known as "Golf," although no records have come to light.

Twenty years after developing his original plan, Simonds came back to the Glen View Club to create plantings around a new feature, the Jackman Fountain, a representational sculpture of a group of Boy Scouts. Holabird and Roche provided the design for the base and footing, and Simonds created a dense planting backdrop to help tie the piece into its setting.[36]

---

* Hugh Burnham had begun a small Swedenborgian subdivision called The Park five years earlier about four miles northwest of the eventual club site, and about a mile west of Swain Nelson's nursery.

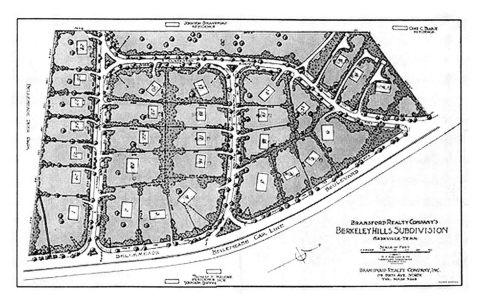

LARGE, IRREGULAR LOTS divided by plantings mark this expansion to the Belle Meade subdivision and golf course development, early 1910s. Distinctive intersections at each entrance to the subdivision distinguished the neighborhood from surrounding developments.

GOLF ELSEWHERE

The president of the Milwaukee Road railway was a member of the Glen View Club and had a rail siding next to the club where he parked his private railcar when he and his associates wished to spend the weekend there. As they approached the siding at the club, the conductor, for want of a better way to announce the stop, called out "golf!" The town that developed to the club's west was named Golf for the game, as was the road on its southern boundary. In 1906, Jacob McGavock Dickinson, general counsel to the Illinois Central Rail Road, started a similar development in Nashville, Tennessee. Dickinson formed a syndicate, chartered the Belle Meade Land Company, and then bought the Greek revival Belle Meade mansion, its outbuildings, and 2,200 acres of land. Dickinson, who commuted frequently to Chicago in his private railway car, surely dined with other railway magnates while in Chicago and quite possibly met Simonds this way.

Simonds and West began work on the Belle Meade subdivision and golf course that year. Simonds designed "numerous roads and streets" and consulted on the siting of the five to fifteen acre lots. Like other subdivisions of that era, though, Belle Meade was slow to take off. Dickinson's appointment to President Taft's cabinet took him to Washington and away from the project, further slowing down progress. However, when Bransford Real Estate stepped in Simonds had already created a plat of subdivision, and, in 1909, Bransford asked him to create another subdivision in the "red house field" of large, multiple-acre homesites. Simonds and West continued to work for this group well into the 1920s, when they designed a new area called Berkley Hills.[37]

They would do a similar development on the north shore in Winnetka, Illinois, about four miles north of the Glen View Club, beginning in 1914. The Indian Hill Club (initially called Winnetka Golf Club) lacked the rolling topography of Glen View and had flooding issues. Simonds developed a drainage tile system to solve those, and then created a subdivision of acre-plus lots around the perimeter, creating a very private enclave. A wonderful plan of one of these anonymous residential lots can be found in his 1920 book *Landscape-Gardening* on page 123 in the chapter on "Home Grounds." In Shorewood Hills, Wisconsin (for which he would also lay out the streets and home sites), Simonds was instrumental in laying out the buildings and grounds at the Black Hawk Hills Country Club, an unusual landscape laid out across historic Indian effigy mounds.

CHAPTER FOUR ENDNOTES

[1] *Elmhurst: 150 Colorful Years* (Elmhurst, IL: Elmhurst Sesquicentennial Planning and Steering Committee, 1986), 4.

[2] Olmsted Collection, 1891-1893, LOC; Olmsted Client Card File, National Park Service, Frederick Law Olmsted National Historic Site.

[3] The firm named changed to Olmsted, Olmsted & Eliot in 1893.

[4] John J. Glessner to Olmsted, February 21, 1891, FLO letters, LOC; Glessner also contributed to the purchase of land in Highwood for the construction of Fort Sheridan in the late 1880s.

[5] Hutchinson was another Fort Sheridan sponsor and Graceland investor.

[6] Olmsted Jr. to his father, June 23, 1891; Olmsted to his son, June 28 and July 6, 1891, Ibid.; and "The Landscape Architecture of the WCE" by FLO, LA, paper presented at the twenty-seventh annual convention of the AIA at the World's Congress of Architects at Chicago, August 2, 1893 (Thanks to Kathleen Cummings).

[7] Olmsted to Burnham, September 22, 1891, FLO letters, LOC; Olmsted to Codman, November 4, 1891 and subsequent letters, Ibid.

[8] Olmsted to Phillip Codman, March 3, 1891, Ibid.

[9] Martha Simonds's diary, SFC.

[10] "Dean of the Cemetery Field."

[11] Ibid.

[12] Anna Gordon to Mrs. Thompson, April 4, 1898; Frances Willard Memorial Library and Archives. Many thanks to Willard archivist Janet Olson for finding this and "The White Path" gems.

[13] "The White Path", Anna Gordon, April 1898; Frances Willard Memorial Library and Archives.

[14] It is likely that Simonds invited him to speak at the meeting. Johnson and his family had moved to St. Louis in 1883, when he accepted the chair of Civil Engineering at Washington University.

[15] O.C, Simonds, C.W. Melcher, T.L. Condron, and J.W. Schaub, "John Butler Johnson: A Memoir," *Journal of the Western Society of Engineers* (1902), 2-11.

[16] Simonds family genealogy, SFC.

[17] Turak, 19.

[18] Malcolm Cairns, *The Landscape Architecture Heritage of Illinois*; booklet, n/d.

[19] Turak, 207.

[20] "History of the Quincy Park System, 1881-1917," Quincy Park Department files.

[21] "Quincy Parks: Beauty and Utility," *The Illinois Park Board Bulletin*. November-December 1946, 81-82.

[22] *Quincy and Adams County: History and Representative Men*, David F. Wilcox, Lewis Publishing Co., 1919, 488-89.

[23] "'Annette E. McCrea" by John Gruber in *Pioneers of American Landscape Architecture*, eds. Charles A. Birnbaum and Robin Karson, McGraw Hill; 2000, 248-49.

[24] "Mrs. M'Crea and Her Work," Quincy (IL) *Herald*, Evening, September 6, 1902, no page number.

[25] Alexis J. Colman, "The Golf Clubs of Chicago," reprinted in *Golf: A Turn-of-the-*

Century Treasury, Mel Shapiro, ed. (Seacaucus, NJ: Castle Books, 1986), 112.

[26] Herbert Warren Wind, *The Story of American Golf* (New York: Simon & Schuster, 1956), 28-35.

[27] Colman, 119.

[28] Wind.

[29] Colman, 112.

[30] *The First Hundred Years*, Robert L. Snyder, ed. (Glenview, Illinois: privately printed, 1997). The Glen View Club's centennial book.

[31] Angus Hibbard, "Golf and the Glen View Club," excerpt from Chapter XXXI: *Associations of Choice*, n/d, Glen View Club files.

[32] Carlyle E. Anderson, "Glen View Club, 1897-1987" (Glenview, Illinois: privately printed brochure, 1987), 5.

[33] Bruegmann, Vol. 1, 174-75.

[34] Hibbard.

[35] Colman, 116.

[36] Bruegmann.

[37] Belle Meade National Register nomination form, courtesy of Nashville, TN councilman Emily Evans.

chapter 5

THE FOUNDING
OF THE AMERICAN SOCIETY
OF LANDSCAPE ARCHITECTS

1897-1900

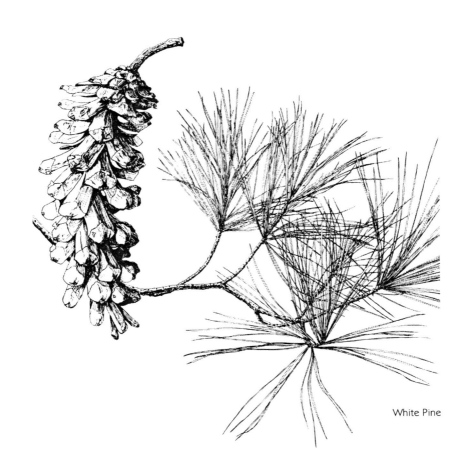

White Pine

O.C. SIMONDS ca. 1900

THE AMERICAN PARK AND OUTDOOR ART ASSOCIATION

T he popularity of golf clubs was part of a growing appreciation throughout the country for professionally designed places of recreation. In April 1897 the City of Louisville Board of Park Commissioners resolved to call

a convention of Park Commissioners, Park Architects, and Park Engineers of the United States, for the purpose of discussing such matters as appertain to park development, in order that a wider influence may be exerted throughout the country in the line of park work and in proper construction of pleasure grounds for the people.[1]

They received a good response, with thirty-five people attending the meeting, including top professionals John C. Olmsted, Warren H. Manning, and Ossian C. Simonds.

Presentations at the first convention of the Park and Outdoor Art (as the members named it initially) covered a wide range of topics.[*] There were discussions on a city-by-city basis about the number and size of public parks, costs of establishing and maintaining a park, city population and park cost per capita.[2] Thomas H. Macbride, Park Commissioner from Iowa City, spoke about "Rural Parks in a Prairie State," expressing his concern that the agricultural landscape required aesthetic consideration.[3] Manning talked about "Park Design and Park Planting," pointing out that,

The character of the native growth will often decide in favor of one piece of land over another . . . a park designer places the greatest importance upon the existing growth upon a piece of land.[4]

Olmsted looked at the bigger context with "The True Purpose of a Large Public Park," stating that public parks were the product of an educated elite,

---

[*] It is crucial to note that to this group "outdoor art" implied an idea similar to Simonds's concept of creating landscape "paintings" out of the actual environment as discussed in Chapter 2; its use of this term never referred to sculpture or other art works outdoors instead of indoors. Marianna Griswold Van Rensselaer's *Art Out-of-Doors* explains this clearly.

rather than of the people at large. The goal of parks was, he said,

> to provide for the dwellers in cities convenient opportunity to enjoy
> beautiful natural scenery and to obtain occasional relief from the
> nervous strain due to the excessive artificiality of city life,

as his uncle/step-father Frederick Law Olmsted had been suggesting for decades.[5]

Several people had written to the Louisville Parks Commission the previous winter in response to a request concerning the need for "an association of those interested in outdoor art." Before his untimely death in March 1897, landscape architect Charles W. Eliot of Olmsted, Olmsted, and Eliot, wrote that he favored an organization that could encompass everyone interested in the subject, regardless of their professional status.[6] J.C. Olmsted believed that it was not yet time to form a professional association, thus a "more comprehensive society" was in order. Marianna Griswold Van Rensselaer, architecture critic and Olmsted enthusiast, also thought that such an alliance ought to include both professional and amateur members.[7]

H.W.S. Cleveland, writing from an address in Chicago, was on the other side of the fence, preferring to "allow none but strictly professional men to become members," presaging the formation of the American Society of Landscape Architects, two years later. Both Liberty Hyde Bailey, Professor of Botany and Horticulture at Cornell University in Ithaca, New York (like Simonds, born and raised in Michigan) and Charles W. Garfield, author and horticulturist in Grand Rapids, Michigan (and Simonds's cousin) wrote that the main membership and management of such a group belonged with "bona fide landscape gardeners," and those who taught or wrote about the subject should be included within a separate membership category.[8]

Landscape-gardener Simonds and Professor William Trelease, Director of the Missouri Botanical Gardens in St. Louis, were concerned with ethical considerations. They saw the most important membership restriction as being the exclusion of those who profited from the sale of materials, especially plants. Simonds was perfectly satisfied to include professional designers, teachers, editors, writers, and those he referred to as:

patrons of the profession who are in a position to and who do influence public taste in the right direction, and by superintendents of public grounds whose income is derived from a salary.[9]

During the conference's concluding session, Simonds urged that, while the Park and Outdoor Art Association was now functioning, it was important to carefully and thoughtfully tend to its development. Executive, publication, constitution and by-laws, and membership committees were established to guide it. They included those not attending the May meeting. Manning served on three, and Olmsted, Van Rensselaer, Bailey, Garfield, Simonds, and Charles Sprague Sargent (director of the Arnold Arboretum) drafted the constitution and by-laws. Other members early on included several Chicago park employees: Oscar F. Dubuis, a park engineer in Peoria (formerly Jenney's assistant in the West Parks in Chicago; then superintendent in 1874), J. Frank Foster (superintendent of Washington Park), and James (Jens) Jensen of Humboldt Park. Simonds served as the "Consulting Landscape Architect" to the Chicago Branch of the American Park and Outdoor Art Association (APOAA), at least for the year 1903. Mrs. Frances Copley Seavey served as the group's landscape architect, a position parallel to that of Warren Manning for the Boston Branch.[10]

"THE LANDSCAPE-GARDENER AND HIS WORK"

From 1888 to 1897, Sargent published a periodical called *Garden and Forest*. A unique journal, its subjects ranged from Vermont forests to tuberous begonias to basketry of the North American Indians—in just one of its issues. *
Soon after the first APOAA meeting, he reprinted portions of Simonds's essay from *Park and Cemetery* under the title of "'The Landscape-gardener and His Work" by Mr. O.C. Simonds of Chicago, who prefers the title of Landscape-gardener to that of Landscape-engineer or Landscape-architect.'[11] Sargent printed the piece because he believed it did a good job of presenting basic elements of this "art." Only two columns long, Simonds succinctly expressed the major principles on which he based his approach to design. Gleaned from

---

* Many editions have been digitized and are available online on the Library of Congress website.

his nearly twenty years of experience at that point, these ideas were destined
to change very little over he next thirty-four years of his career, as they served
him extremely well.

Simonds explained his reasons for referring to himself as a "landscape-
gardener." "Landscape-engineer," he thought, brought to mind images of
"scars along mountain sides, of the destruction of beautiful scenery along
river banks, of the changing of watercourses into sewers . . . " and "Landscape-
architect," even though used by some of the "foremost landscape-gardeners
in this country," conjured up "summerhouses, pavilions, balustrades, fences,
hedges and things with stiff and formal lines." Despite his nomenclature
concerns, he remained active in the Western Society of Engineers and would
be a founding member of the American Society of Landscape Architects. For
Simonds, the term "landscape-gardener" was the appropriate one. He used the
word "landscape" in the sense he had learned from Philip Gilbert Hamerton,
signifying "a consistent picture." "Gardener" meant rather simplistically one
who uses the "materials . . . found in a garden."[12]

Simonds suggested reading the works of Humphry Repton, John Claudius
Loudon, Andrew Jackson Downing, Edward Kemp, William Robinson,
Frederick Law Olmsted, Samuel Parsons, and Mrs. Van Rensselaer on
landscape-gardening. He credited Mrs. Van Rensselaer with coining the term
"Art-Out-of-Doors", the name used earlier that year for the new association
begun in Louisville, and he agreed that his profession ranked among the fine
arts.[13]

The rest of the article compared the differences between what an engineer
or a horticulturist might do with the art of landscape-gardening. Simonds
made it clear that while the landscape-gardener needed to know soils,
drainage, road construction, architecture, botany, horticulture, climate, and
the "social habits of the people" who would use the locale, he also must be able
to arrange the entire construction in a pleasing manner and provide scenic
vistas. He must also be able to plan for an ever-changing work of art that
would grow and fluctuate with time. His engineering skills had to encompass
not only the materials and conditions with which he worked, but also the
convenience, comfort, and safety of the humans for whom the project was
planned.

As an artist, the landscape-gardener needed to know how to plan for colors at different seasons and at varying heights. Simonds thought it best if the designer inspected his work as frequently as possible to make the adjustments required to achieve the landscape pictures as planned. He had just such opportunities to guide the picture's development at many of his projects over the years, but especially at Graceland Cemetery, which evolved into his long-term masterpiece.

"RESIDENCE STREETS"

Continuing his affiliation with the Michigan Horticultural Society, Simonds wrote a comprehensive guide to "Residence Streets" for its *Annual Report for 1898*. In it, he explored relevant engineering features including grading, drainage, location, intersections, and width of roads. Concurrent with these practical considerations, Simonds discussed the aesthetics of streets and laid out more of his general design principles. A slight curve was more attractive to him than a straight road, but not to be used arbitrarily.* Curves could be used to reduce the grade, to preserve a tree, or to offer a view; in other words, curves needed to justify their existence. He offered specifics about many details—for example, he suggested that the width of roads without streetcar lines ought to occur in multiples of eight feet. If the road was to curve, it ought to do so "by a long gentle curve rather than a short turn." Instead of rationalizing this with pragmatic human or engineering considerations, Simonds took the plant's point of view, saying,

> We might imagine that the tree to be saved had some feeling of
> modesty, and so begin to turn long before reaching it, and thus relieve
> it of any embarrassment it might feel from occupying too prominent
> a position or appearing to be in the way.[14]

This charming description offers a peek into Simonds's personality and his approach to design. A whimsical, tree-centric way of working garnered him jobs but perhaps lost him some of the professional respect he was due from more formal colleagues like the Olmsteds.

---

* In *Landscape-Gardening*, published in 1920, Simonds explained this principle in more detail. Curves needed to fulfill a function, not just curve randomly for the sake of curving. This is one of the distinctions between his designs and those of imitators who did not fully understand the concept of "naturalistic."

A NEW AFFILIATION WITH GRACELAND AND NEW CLIENTS

The next year brought a major change: Simonds resigned from Graceland's superintendency and became instead its consulting landscape-gardener and a member of its board of managers.[15] This gave him the freedom and flexibility needed to pursue a private design practice. Not surprisingly, there would be a number of cemetery projects.

One of his first jobs after resigning the full-time Graceland position was a planting plan for Seeley Cemetery (referred to as the Sharon Cemetery) in LaCrew, Iowa. The list of plants included many of his favorites: Norway and Schwedler's maples, elms, willows, crab apples, common and Thurberg's barberries, honeysuckle, snowberry, Indian currant, rosa rugosa, forsythia, and honey locust.* The lawns on either side of the entrance drive and gate were delineated with stone curbing, a highly unusual feature in a Simonds design, and most likely a specification of the client.[16]

The cemetery was located near Farmington, about 125 miles south of Des Moines along the Des Moines River in the southeastern corner of the state, an area Simonds does not seem to have worked in otherwise. One possible link for the commission was an aunt, his father's sister Patience, who had married Hiram Selden Hunn in New York state in 1851 before moving west and settling in Des Moines. From time to time, Simonds would stop to visit them when he was traveling in the area.[17] However it came about that the Sharon Presbyterian Church retained Simonds to design their small cemetery, this was one of the few truly rural cemeteries for which his involvement is documented.

In the spring of 1899 he went north to make a topographical survey and design an "ornamental plat" for Beloit College in Beloit, Wisconsin. While he was in town, the city fathers commissioned him for a comparable project for their public parks. By that fall, the city had already implemented Simonds's recommendations and enacted an ordinance to prohibit "the beating or cleaning of carpets on all city parkland and other public grounds," a concern that even the far-sighted APOAA had not thought to address.[18]

---

* From a contemporary ecological standpoint, the many exotic (and some invasive) species in this list would hardly qualify Simonds as a strong supporter of native plants. However, in 1899 he was still among the very few recommending mostly indigenous plants.

SHARON CEMETERY (Seeley Cemetery), Henry County, Iowa   DEB COOPER COLLECTION

AMERICAN SOCIETY OF LANDSCAPE ARCHITECTS

Leaving his full-time position at Graceland also enabled Simonds to change his professional status from cemetery superintendent to landscape-gardener. While cherishing and exclusively using that professional title, Simonds nonetheless met with eleven other practitioners in Samuel Parsons, Jr.'s New York office on January 4, 1899 to establish the American Society of Landscape Architects (ASLA).[19] The group included Frederick Law Olmsted, Jr. and his cousin/step-brother John Charles; Downing Vaux, the son of Olmsted Sr.'s earlier partner Calvert; Misses Elizabeth Bullard and Beatrix Jones (later Farrand); * Nathan F. Barrett (George M. Pullman's landscape architect), Daniel W. Langton, Charles N. Lowrie, George F. Pentecost, and Samuel Parsons from New York; Warren H. Manning, formerly with the Olmsted Company; and Simonds from Chicago.+

---

* It is rather amazing that in 1897 nearly 20% of the founders were women. With the exception of Jones Farrand and a few others, by the early twentieth century women were mostly relegated to designing plantings of flowers while their male counterparts handled the larger, enduring elements of spatial organization, circulation, arrangements of structures and objects, etc. Annette McCrea, a Midwestern practitioner, apparently was not aware of Jones and Bullard (see Chapter 4).
+ Unfortunately, Simonds's reaction to the name the group chose for the profession and its society is unknown.

Within the year, "Mr. James Jensen of Humboldt Park, Chicago" asked Manning about Society membership. Manning wrote to Vaux in his role as Secretary of the ASLA to ask him to send Jensen a copy of the by-laws and constitution. (Jensen Americanized his first name from Jens to James for a few years.) Manning continued, "He is a very nice fellow and has been able to hold his position under many unfavorable political conditions. Whether his practice of the profession is such that would entitle him to membership in our Association, I can not say. I am sure that most of his work is more that of the gardener than that of the landscape architect."[20] Eventually Jensen did join, but it was a short-lived membership; his approach to the profession was not a close fit with the ASLA's.

By 1902 Simonds had at least two employees (other than J. Roy West), and they joined the ASLA as junior members that year. Frank Button had first worked with him as an engineer on the Fort Sheridan project in the late 1880s and early 90s, and again on the Quincy parks; his name was on the company letterhead until about 1916, when he moved to Coral Gables, Florida and went into landscape design on his own* (see Chapter 11 for more information about Button's Florida work). The other was Svend Lollesgaard, who was on staff until at least 1913. Button became a full-fledged member in 1913; Lollesgaard did not apply for full membership on the tenth anniversary of his junior membership, and was dropped.

The ad hoc constitution committee of 1899 consisted of Parsons, J.C. Olmsted, Manning, Vaux and Simonds; Simonds also served on the executive committee from 1899 until 1907. He managed to attend annual meetings in New York regularly for the first few years. In April and March of 1902, the ASLA held its First Annual Exhibition. Miss Jones displayed a plan, an isometric drawing, and a perspective sketch for the grounds of Anson Phelps Stokes, Esq., of Darien, Connecticut; the Olmsted Brothers brought topographical maps, designs, and planting plans for three clients.

Among the exhibiting members, only Simonds's listing in the catalog of "Plans of a subdivision. Two Plans of Drives, with Photographs of same" did not specify the location or client for his entry. Perhaps another facet of his concern about modesty—whether of trees, clients, or his own—Simonds generally used anonymous illustrations throughout his career.

---

* Button and his first wife Florence are both buried at Graceland, in the Simonds family plot.

Simonds attended a monthly meeting in February 1907, at which the Committee on Seal reported on its progress in designing an emblem for the society, and he gave a talk called "Western Notes" (Chicago was still considered 'the West'). Illustrating his presentation with photographs, he discussed country houses and their landscape designs in the Chicago area and looked briefly at solutions for smaller city lots. He discussed practical matters in road and walk construction and ended his talk with his favorite theme: designing to create landscape pictures and teaching an appreciation of aesthetics to clients.[21] As he would later write in his 1920 book on *Landscape-Gardening*, he believed his real job was to "open their eyes so that they will see the beauty around them, often the most important service that we can render."

Not every architect and landscape architect saw the world as Simonds did. Volume XII of *Architectural Record* in 1902 ran a piece by Simonds's fellow ASLA founder George Pentecost on "The Formal and the Natural Style," in which he complained that "The natural style has practically usurped the entire field of garden art, both under the conditions to which it is adapted, and under conditions to which it is utterly unfitted." Six years later, in volume XXIV, an article entitled "Chicago Parks and their Landscape Architects" expressed the writer's irritation at Chicago's spending on its parks while not tending to "its miserable pavements, ill-kept streets, slovenly municipal service." The piece went on to state that the city's independent park boards' "idea apparently has been to convert the parks into a series of country clubs for the poorer people," which also, apparently, displeased the architects. Of course, the American Society of Landscape Architects had been founded expressly, in part, to put landscape designers on an equal professional footing with architects, and they were beginning to be successful.

PROFESSIONAL ORGANIZATIONS AND CLUB MEMBERSHIPS

Over the next decade, Simonds joined several other professional organizations, including the American Forestry Association, American Civic Association (with many others from the Park and Outdoor Art Association— the two would merge in a few years), Association for the Advancement of Science, the Illinois Outdoor Improvement Association, and the Ethical Culture Society. He also became an active participant in Chicago's new men's clubs (the

Cliff Dwellers, University, and City Clubs), making new business connections, gaining new clients, and helping shape the city's cultural life.[22]

Simonds's contemporary Jens Jensen, who was known as James Jensen at this time, was a fellow member of the Cliff Dwellers, and would himself start two organizations, Friends of Our Native Landscape and the Prairie Club. Jensen also worked with community organizations. He judged flower gardens for the *Chicago Daily Tribune's* City Beautiful Contest in August 1901. Along with Mrs. Herman Hall, president of the Women's Auxiliary of the APOAA, he awarded prizes to homeowners for their gardens. An article, entitled "Begin to Judge Flower Gardens," referred to the APOAA as "an organization working zealously to make every city in the United States worth living in." It went on to describe Jensen as "perhaps, the best equipped landscape architect in Chicago. He has devoted his entire life to the study of trees and flowers and how to cultivate them . . ," as well as how he worked with the West Parks for fourteen years and planned numerous private gardens.[23]

A year later, Jensen worked with Mrs. Hall again, in her role as former president of the South Park Improvement Association. The work was well described in newspaper accounts of the time:

> "Art Scheme for Streets; Systematic Work to Beautify South Side
> Territory. District Bounded by the Midway, Fifty-fifth Street, Jackson
> and Washington Parks Will Be Made Attractive by Uniformity
> in Culture of Trees and Shrubbery—Improvement Association
> Undertakes the Work and James Jenson Will Be in Charge."

The plans were to improve each street in this district, one at a time, with a short list of street trees that included elms, honey locust, catalpa, and ailanthus,* and to plant "fancy shrubs" in vacant lots. The meeting of the organization at the end of July 1902 was held at the home of its then-president, progressive educator Francis W. Parker, and "James Jenson, former superintendent of Humboldt Park" was in charge of design and planting.[24]

Simonds and Jensen's design approaches have often been compared for their similarities, starting perhaps with Wilhelm Miller's articles in *Country Life in America*. They had similarly wealthy clients, relied (primarily) on

---

* Known as the "Tree of Heaven", ailanthus is an extremely invasive species, now the bane of many cities, but in 1902 no one knew this.

native plants, used (mostly) a naturalistic style in laying out a site and in plant arrangements, and eschewed ornate elements within their designs; they also belonged to many of the same groups and worked primarily in the Midwest. Despite these similarities, though, it is important to note that there were major differences that distinguished the careers, designs, and personalities of these two men. While Simonds often charged relatively little for his work in order to help a public client, and often worked for park districts and municipalities, he does not seem to have affiliated frequently with community organizations. Jensen, on the other hand, worked with several, including the one described above, Jane Addams's Hull House, and the groups he founded himself. Despite an aristocratic background, as an immigrant Jensen worked his way up from being a laborer and only later received the sponsorship of wealthy clients, something that Simonds had had from the start of his career. Jensen designed very few cemeteries, the north addition to Bohemian National being the best known. He did not attract the municipal and park work (other than full-time employment for Chicago's West Parks) that Simonds did, nor did he write as extensively as Simonds for both public and professional publications.

THE HOUSE BEAUTIFUL

Simonds had become nationally known by the end of the nineteenth century. He wrote two series of articles for *The House Beautiful,* a magazine with national circulation and editorial offices in Chicago (later New York) and dedicated to improving the aesthetic taste of American women. The first, entitled "Home Grounds," presented Simonds's advice for choosing a site, practical guidelines for placing walks and drives (reminiscent of the "Residence Streets" advice), and suggestions for plants that would provide winter bird food. He promoted his fundamental design principle of using painterly composition, with the sky as a canvas on which to place trees, shrubs, grass, water, and, if need be, buildings and walks.

The next sequence of articles Simonds (or the editor) called more grandly "The Surroundings of a Country House." They touched briefly on unspecified Chicago area properties and discussed general ideas for beautifying larger estates. In the October 1899 issue, Simonds took pains to refute a piece on "Formal Gardens" in a recent (but unnamed) magazine. Among other

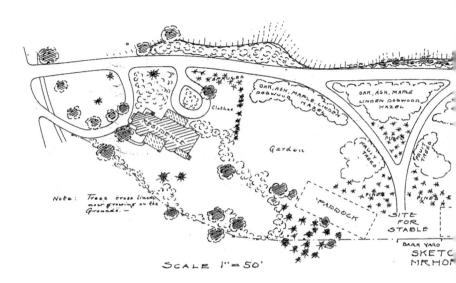

LAKE FOREST, Illinois private lakefront residence design.

comments, its author had claimed that

> Deception is a primary object of the landscape gardener and thus
> to get variety and deceive the eye into supposing that the garden is
> larger than it is, the paths are made to wind about in all directions,
> and the lawns are not to be left in broad expanse, but dotted about
> with pampas grasses, foreign shrubs, or anything else that will break
> up the surface. *

Simonds responded "Not at all!" to these accusations. He believed instead that
his objective was to create beautiful scenery, sometimes by obscuring ugly
sights. He ended the essay by saying,

> The landscape-gardener seeks first to appreciate the natural beauty of a
> place, and then makes the most of these features in his design. He has a
> reason for everything, even though it may only be that "it will look well."[25]

---

* He mentioned only three specifically: barberry, bittersweet, and buckthorn. Buckthorn (*Rhamnus
catharctica*) had not yet become the ecological problem a century ago that it is today.

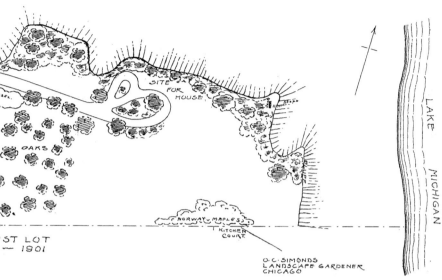

SITE FOR HOUSE

OAKS

NORWAY MAPLES

KITCHEN COURT

ST LOT
— 1901

O.C. SIMONDS
LANDSCAPE GARDENER
CHICAGO

LAKE MICHIGAN

PAUL BERGMANN / STANLEY ANDERSON ARCHIVES

Critiques of this sort from formalists, often architects, continued on and off for decades. The writers could not discern the difference between the refined work of a master landscape-gardener and that of designers casually using pampas grass and exotic shrubs. Simonds *never* attempted to "break up the surface" of a landscape. The effort he and Lathrop exerted to keep curbing and monuments from being visual obtrusions at Graceland is an important case in point.

Simonds wrote a few more articles for this series, the last one published in August 1900. Interestingly, the three photographs accompanying his article in the June issue, entitled "Lawns and How to Grow Them," show only formal gardens with tightly clipped shrubs and hedges, geometrically shaped flower beds, and walks criss-crossing the yard for no practical purpose. His article makes no reference to the pictures.[26] Because some readers could have found his lack of formal design disappointing, the magazine's editors may have been trying to appease them. This is worth noting here for two reasons. First, while Simonds himself did not like formal design, he very seldom criticized it in his writings, preferring to not address the subject at all. He accommodated formal features in his clients' designs when they so desired. Second, the formal/

informal dichotomy turns up repeatedly throughout the rest of his career.

The House Beautiful, though, was concerned about "taste" and not shy about expressing its editors' opinions. In 1904-1905 it ran a series of articles entitled "The Poor Taste of the Rich: A series of articles which show that wealth is not essential to the decoration of a house, and that the homes of many of our richest citizens are furnished in execrable taste." The pieces, published between August 1904 and February 1905, included photographs of interiors to illustrate what was meant by "execrable" and named the owners quite specifically. One of Simonds's hallmarks was never to name owners, an act he found in poor taste, even though his articles and exhibitions featured only sites he found to be in good taste and worthy of emulation.

INTERNATIONAL RECOGNITION AND A GROWING PRACTICE

Simonds and Graceland achieved an international reputation in 1900, when the Paris Exposition awarded the cemetery its Silver Medal for "the best set of twelve views in cemeteries in any country." * Spring Grove in Cincinnati—Graceland's and Simonds's fundamental inspiration—took the Gold Medal. His new private practice was an immediate success, and several important commissions originated in 1900, including the home grounds for Lyman Bement in Indianapolis and an estate for a McCormick daughter in Huntsville, Alabama.[27]

Simonds stepped in at the last minute on a high-profile project in 1899, just north of Chicago in Kenosha, Wisconsin. That January, prominent citizen Zalmon G. Simmons offered to build a new public library when the current one had outgrown its rented room above the hardware store. He offered to put it up in "the Public Square of Central Park and to place the park in condition to make a beautiful setting for the building." The site had been a "Public Common" since the platting of the town in 1838 and the early settlers had done their best to protect its ancient oaks. In 1849 Kenosha women formed a "Park Society" and sought to improve the space. The local newspaper thought the common was better used as a pasture than a park, but the Society won out and for a number of years actively maintained it as a public amenity. After the Civil War,

---

* Simonds's painterly approach to landscape design was judged by international standards, placing his work with Lathrop in what was apparently a highly-regarded genre at the time.

though, interest in the park waned and the common did indeed revert to a pasture. By the mid-1890s, the Kenosha public was again interested in making it a proper park.

Immediately upon offering to build the library and improve the park Simmons hired Daniel H. Burnham to design the building and, initially, to create a landscape plan. Burnham's firm designed a Classical Revival structure (naturally), and a plaster-of-paris model arrived in Simmons office on March 8. The Kenosha Telegraph Courier called it the "Finest Building in the State," and noted it was to be completed by September 1 of that year. The article also described Burnham's intentions for the park grounds surrounding the coolly elegant library building:

> The scheme of the architect also plans for such improvement of the park as will make it a fit place for the placing of such a building. The curb around the park is to be completed and the entire park laid out with broad walks leading from the library in every direction. The architect says that such a classic building demands a formal design for the grounds about it. The pavements are to be made of pebbles imbedded in cement and all will lead to the main entrance. Another feature of the park decoration will be the erection of a band stand in harmony with the main features of the library building. This smaller building will be placed about three hundred feet from the main building and the design will be made by Mr. Burnham.

Simmons also contributed to a Civil War memorial for the site. His preference was an Egyptian obelisk fifty-five feet tall, carved from one piece of Vermont granite weighing ninety tons. Changes behind the scenes, however, led instead to a Corinthian column topped with a twelve-foot statue of Nike, the winged victory, designed by Burnham. Then, about two weeks before the installation of the Burnham landscape plan, Simmons suddenly hired Simonds to create the park instead. Undaunted by the formal structure and its static symmetry, Simonds drew up a landscape park with gently curving walks and masses of shrubs and trees encompassing the square Beaux-Arts building, a layout that still endures. Money no doubt played a role—implementing the simpler, naturalistic scheme from Simonds would have been quicker, easier, and far cheaper to install than the formal hardscape envisioned by Burnham. Ironically, this meant that the grand allee from the monument south to the imposing library entrance that was a key part of the original plan was replaced with relatively narrow curving sidewalks, decorated with clumps of trees and shrubs to obscure any direct view of the building itself.

With their radically different design approaches, Simonds and Burnham were not likely collaborators. Yet, Burnham asked Simonds to design the grounds for the Glen View Club in 1897 and was buried in 1912 under a rough-hewn boulder on the only island in Lake Willowmere at Graceland Cemetery.[28]

CHAPTER FIVE ENDNOTES

[1] "First Report of the Park and Outdoor Art Association" (Louisville, Kentucky, 1897), 5.

[2] Ibid., 8-9.

[3] Ibid., 37-41.

[4] Ibid., 50-54.

[5] Ibid., 11-19.

[6] Ibid., 68.

[7] Ibid., 70.

[8] Ibid., 70-71, 74-75.

[9] Ibid., 72.

[10] Ibid., 4.; *Seventh Volume of [the Proceedings of] the American park and Outdoor Art Association*, Buffalo, 1903. Information courtesy of John Gruber, Madison, WI.

[11] Simonds, "The Landscape-gardener and his Work," *Garden and Forest: A Journal of Horticulture, Landscape Art and Forestry*, Vol. X (July 21, 1897), 282-83.

[12] Ibid.

[13] Ibid.

[14] Simonds, "Resident Streets," *Annual Report for the 1898 of the Michigan Horticultural Society*, 3-11, SFC.

[15] Leland, no page number.

[16] Nomination form, National Register of Historic Places, Seeley Cemetery, La Crew, Iowa, Section 7, pages 8, 13, 16. Prepared by W.C. Page. WHT.

[17] Simonds family genealogy and miscellaneous notes, SFC.

[18] Richard P. Hartung, Michael Gorecki, and David Preece, "Intensive Survey Report, Historic Resources of the City of Beloit, Wisconsin," Department of Community Development, City of Beloit, WHT.

[19] Harold A. Caparn, James Sturgis Pray, and Downing Vaux, eds., *Transactions of the American Society of Landscape Architects From its inception in 1899 to the end of 1908* (New York: American Society of Landscape Architects, 1926).

[20] Manning to Vaux, March 14, 1900, records of the ASLA, Collections of the Manuscript Division, Library of Congress.

[21] *Transactions*, 9.

[22] *Transactions of the ASLA*, 7; *National Cyclopedia*.

[23] *Chicago Tribune*, August 1, 1900, 5.

[24] Ibid., July 20, 1902, 1.

[25] Quoted in Simonds, "The Surroundings of a Country House," *The House Beautiful*, Vol. VI, No. 5 (October 1899), 227.

[26] Simonds, "Lawns and How to Grow Them," *The House Beautiful*, Vol. VII, No. 5 (June 1900).

[27] Blueprints, MA.

[28] Library Park National Reg. of Historic Places nomination written by B. Geiger; listed 2000.

chapter 6

THE PARK ERA

1899-1903

Bur Oak

O.C. SIMONDS ca. 1900

MADISON PARK AND PLEASURE DRIVE ASSOCIATION

The Madison Park and Pleasure Drive Association (MPPDA) contacted Simonds in August of 1899 to ask him to "look over the proposed Tenney Park for two days and to prepare preliminary plans for the improvement thereof."[1] Hired on a day-to-day basis, Simonds worked with the MPPDA for several years. He had already been visiting relatives and friends in Madison for years, and he likely met the MPPDA group on one of these trips. Martha, one of his father's sisters, had married in New York and moved west, as had another aunt, Patience, who settled in Des Moines. Martha and her husband Samuel Allen Warner moved just north of Madison to Windsor in Dane County, Wisconsin, to care for their grandchildren when their daughter died in the early 1860s. Other Warner children moved to the Madison area and became prominent in business and politics.[2] Another incentive for Simonds to visit Madison came in 1899, when his close friend J.B. Johnson accepted the engineering department chairmanship at the University of Wisconsin and moved from St. Louis with his family. Given these conditions, it is easy to imagine Simonds becoming acquainted with John Olin, a moving force behind the MMPDA (and other Madison ventures).

Simonds developed Tenney Park by converting a marsh to a lagoon and planting the resulting dry ground with grass, trees, and shrubs.[3] Located at the southeast corner of Lake Mendota, the park's east boundary was the Yahara River, which flowed south into Lake Monona. Simonds designed plantings and bridges over the river between the two lakes in 1903.[4] That same year Simonds completed his work for the Madison General Hospital Association, advising on building placement and grading. He also worked on plans for Vilas and Brittingham Parks and laid out the scenic wooded Lake Mendota Drive that wound its way up and down hills just west of the university. By managing to save the quarry and ridge he made the roadside scenery "far more interesting than [would] a uniformly sloping grade."[5]

The MMPDA work involved some of Simonds's favorite topographical features—bluffs and ravines, lakes and rivers, and winding roads. He must have thoroughly enjoyed his days in Madison. Beginning in 1911, he returned several times to work on at least four residential subdivisions in these same hilly sections.

The MMPDA was so well-organized and so successful in achieving its goals of providing scenic drives that within a few years its *Annual Report* was in demand across the country, as other cities and towns began to establish their own park systems. Its efforts came at the same time that the American Park and Outdoor Art Association, which promoted similar ideals, merged with the American League for Civic Improvement to form the American Civic Association.[6] Three of the ASLA's founding group were instrumental here too; Warren Manning, F.L. (Rick) Olmsted, Jr.,* and O.C. Simonds served as vice-presidents, and city planner Charles Mulford Robinson of Rochester, New York, was secretary. B.A. Parker, the group's vice-president of its Parks Department, asked Olin for a copy of the MPPDA *Annual Report* in 1904.[7] Robinson said he was "exceedingly interested" in the *Report* and in the association's pamphlet, "Madison Parks as a Municipal Investment."[8] The Manning Brothers of Boston asked for a copy of the by-laws in 1901, as did Victor Lawson, publisher of the *Chicago Daily News*, who would soon become a private client of Simonds's.[9]+

Simonds continued to correspond with Olin for several years, consulting on signs, maintenance of plantings, and even on where funds might be raised. In October 1904 he told Olin that he was trying to get Charles Hutchinson to visit Madison, in light of Olin's wish to "get some wealthy men to make the acquaintance of the land about Madison." Hutchinson, Simonds said, was "not extremely wealthy but he is intimately associated with men who are."[10] Indeed, Magnus Swenson, a sugar magnate from Chicago, became so keen on the MPPDA that he moved to Madison, and would later be involved with the development of the Highlands subdivision in 1906.

Illinois citizens were interested in park issues as well. E.J. James, President of the University of Illinois, was Chairman of the Illinois Outdoor Improvement Association (IOIA), and A.P. Wyman, also with the university, its secretary. Wyman wrote to Olin in the fall of 1909 inviting him to speak to the IOIA. Unable to do so, Olin suggested they ask Charles Brown, the MPPDA's secretary and photographer.[11] Simonds was involved with the Illinois organization as well.

---

* Olmsted, Sr. was seriously ill and in the hospital; he would die in August 1903.
+ Simonds will help Lawson develop his Green Lake, Wisconsin estate in the 1910s, and will design the plantings for his grave at Graceland in the 1920s, the centerpiece of which is a green granite statue of "The Crusader" by Lorado Taft.

UNIVERSITY OF WISCONSIN CAMPUS

The year after his initial work with the MPPDA, Simonds was asked to make a sketch plan for a portion of the University of Wisconsin campus. His good friend J.B. Johnson had become the Dean of the Engineering School a few years before—no doubt he received a good recommendation from his old surveying partner. Simonds's purview here included the area around the newly built State Historical Library.[12] The Regents explained the work, as reported in the biennial report for 1900-1901 and 1901-1902, page 56, saying that "The ground in its present condition is most unattractive and presents a bad setting for the beautiful buildings that face it." In particular they asked Simonds to place a driveway in the front of the library such that it would "not materially reduce the available area of the Lower Campus" and be a "decorative feature" as well. Not only did he tend to the driveway, but he also created a plan "by which the ground could still be used for football practice at certain seasons of the year and yet be screened by shrubbery and beautified." By April 1901 the directors of the State Historical Society were eager to plant the four elms that Simonds had designated for the front of that building. University records do not explain just how much of his plan was implemented, but it must have received professional attention as noted Boston landscape architects James Sturgis Pray and Percival Gallagher wrote to the University in 1905 to request plans showing the layout of the buildings of the Madison campus, implying that a landscape and building placement plan had been utilized. Simonds's work in Madison for the first five or six years of the twentieth century, for the school and even more so for the MPPDA, was at the center of nation-wide interest in landscape.

Simonds continued to work for the university until autumn 1906. The Regents asked him to "complete a plan for the improvement of the entire campus, including the agricultural part of the grounds and Camp Randall," and paid him $500 for the work. However, in October 1906, the Regents gave the campus planning work to Warren Laird and Paul Cret, Philadelphia architects who were designing dormitories, a Women's Building, and a commons and student union, as reported by the Committee upon the Future Constructional Development of the University. They would continue to serve as consulting architects for years to come, designing new campus buildings for liberal arts, physics, soil physics, and an engineering shop in 1913—$450,000 worth of construction (as reported in *Iron Age*, page 1142, November 13, 1913, Vol. 92, no. 20). Simonds continued to work for many other clients in Madison after his affiliation with the University ended.

LONG VIEW PARK, ROCK ISLAND

The City of Rock Island, Illinois, overlooking the Mississippi River, had set aside parkland in 1897. Other than surrounding it with barbed wire, they did nothing to improve the site until 1902 when The Long View Improvement Association was formed and, by July of that year, had asked Simonds to begin work. His first suggestion was to remove the fence so that people would no longer graze their cattle here! Then he asked that a tower be built so he could see the whole site and take "aerial photographs" from it (it was thirty feet tall). A literal approach to planning that Daniel Burnham also used a few times. Burnham arranged to have his office in a tent on the top of a high hill when working on the plan for San Francisco and in 1906 when he began the Plan of Chicago he built a small shed 277 feet up on the roof of his Railway Exchange Building. This is the first and only time, though, that there is a record of Simonds using this technique. By the time the City Council met on September 11, Simonds had presented them with a plan and they had reviewed it enough to make changes and adopt at that meeting not only his plan for the walks, a chain of lakes, planting of shrubbery, but that "the plans for the park as amended be adopted as a whole."[13]

Simonds emphasized the gently rolling hills with views to the distance through his plantings. One of the lagoons contained a waterfall, traversed by a rustic tree-limb bridge similar to the one designed for the MPPDA. Once the park was built it seems that Simonds's involvement there was completed. The park commissioners later accepted a number of *objets* which they scattered throughout the park, including fountains, statues, and shelters in a variety of styles ranging from 'rustic' to Swiss chalet. Beds of annual flowers were filled with product from the park's greenhouses. Yet, despite the addition of many features, the overall configuration of the site and the major circulation elements from Simonds's day remain intact.

LONG VIEW PARK, Rock Island, Illinois

CHARLES GARFIELD'S EFFORTS IN MICHIGAN

Simonds's hometown of Grand Rapids had its Park and Boulevard Association as well, and his cousin Charles (Charlie) Garfield (1848-1934), now president of the Grand Rapids Savings Bank, received a copy of the MPPDA's annual report each year.[14] Garfield and two other GRPBA members, the president and vice-president of the National City Bank of Grand Rapids, met with Olin and Simonds in Madison in July of 1904 so the men from Michigan could personally tour the parks.[15] By 1909, they had at least succeeded in establishing a Board of Park and Cemetery Commissioners for Grand Rapids, if not a park system.[16]

Garfield, however, was more intensely involved with the Michigan Forestry Commission, of which he was also president. He estimated that about one-third of that state had been burned or cut-over, and was now "an unproductive waste area." The commission was fighting for a permanent Forest Reserve of 6,000,000 acres to protect, among other things, "the unparalleled beauty of our state; the availability of our harbors; the safety of soil from erosion; the even flow of our streams; and our commercial fruit growing."[17]

Charlie was an enduring influence on his younger cousin O.C., whom he considered to be his best friend. He received both his undergraduate and graduate degrees in horticulture and related subjects at the Michigan Agricultural College, and stayed on to work with Professor William J. Beal at the school's botanical garden. Garfield was elected secretary of the Michigan State Horticultural Society in 1876 and served until 1888. A member of the State Board of Agriculture from 1887 to 1899, he was then appointed president of the Michigan Forestry Commission, an office he held for ten years. Among his friends and correspondents were Filibert Roth, the eminent forestry professor, and Gifford Pinchot. The two cousins (and sometimes their wives) traveled together, worked for the reforesting of their home state, and joined forces on horticultural projects well into the late 1920s (see chapter 10).

EUGENE DAVENPORT

The impressive list of Simonds's peers from Michigan who were instrumental in agriculture and horticulture included Eugene Davenport (1856-1941), Dean of the College of Agriculture at the University of Illinois from 1895 to 1922. He established a division of landscape-gardening within the College and hired Ralph Rodney Root, a recent Harvard graduate with his Masters degree in Landscape Architecture, to direct the program. The lead article in the April 1913 issue of *Landscape Architecture* quoted the dean on the topic saying, "When the University of Illinois perceives a demand for instruction, it sets about the satisfaction of that demand in the best possible way." To oversee "the propagandist work in the state for 'the country beautiful'" the department had hired Wilhelm Miller, formerly L.H. Bailey's associate at Cornell at the beginning of that academic year, thus freeing up Root and the department to focus on teaching students. A series of guest lecturers included Professor James Sturgis Pray, also of Harvard, and current president of the ASLA.

Davenport was the husband of Simonds's long-time Grand Rapids friend Emma Coats. The Michigan home of the Davenports was located in Woodland, about twenty-five miles southeast of Grand Rapids, and Simonds helped to develop a landscape at "The Maples" that gave them great pleasure. Another of Davenport's hobbies was keeping a diary of events and meetings with notable people, among whom he included Admiral Richard Byrd, the Arctic explorer, General J.J. Pershing, Daniel Burnham, and Ossian Simonds.

When Mrs. Davenport died in 1935, O.C.'s youngest son Robert O. Simonds created an addition to the little cemetery at Woodland on behalf of the Davenports, identified with a granite boulder with the inscription: "This grove is the Emma Jane Davenport Memorial to the Timberland Pioneers."

PARKS AND ENGINEERS

The June 1900 edition of the *Journal of the Western Society of Engineers* carried Simonds's written discussion of an article by A.C. Schrader, a park engineer. Schrader considered parks and boulevards from an engineering perspective, and Simonds used the opportunity to express the virtues of the softer discipline of landscape gardening.

The true use of a park is in serving as a place of rest and recreation
. . . [offering] a certain measure of seclusion while breathing pure
air, feasting one's eyes on the fresh green foliage, taking in the varied
scenery, and perhaps listening to the songs of birds is the real reason
for its existence.[18]

Rather than criticize Schrader, Simonds proposed additions to his ideas. He concluded by giving his appreciation for "men in control of parks who occupy their positions on account of their knowledge and experience and of the love they have for their work," and by expressing his pleasure that the Western Society of Engineers was interested in the topic of parks and boulevards.

ROCKCLIFFE MANSION AND HANNIBAL

Hannibal, Missouri was a booming city in 1900, just across the Mississippi River from Quincy, Illinois. The childhood home of author Samuel Clemens (better known of course as Mark Twain) and an important river port, Hannibal was home to several millionaires who sought to outdo one another in residential lavishness. Lumber baron John J. Cruikshank literally topped them all. Buying the highest bluff in the area, Cruikshank had the site's existing mansion moved to the west side of the property, and hired Barnett, Haynes, and Barnett, cathedral architects from St. Louis, to design a colossal, 13,000 square-foot brick home commanding a magnificent view of the Mississippi River and the surrounding hills to the south and east. He then hired Simonds to plan the grounds, reportedly spending $75,000 to implement the design.[19]

Simonds's plan incorporated a series of gardens within concentric circles, the groupings and borders of trees and shrubs corresponding to the edges of terraces built to accommodate the exceptionally steep (even for Hannibal) property. The large number of vines on the planting list covered Rockcliffe's almost vertical hillside. On the lowest terrace, Simonds planted a vegetable garden and orchard. For the middle level and the areas next to the house, he designed wooded walks following the hillside contours, opening onto extraordinary vistas of the Mississippi and views far into Illinois. Simonds planned the grounds for the other house on the property as an integrated part of the complete design. True to form, he enrobed the main structure with vines and shrubs to soften the architecture and blend it into the landscape.[20]

The planting list for Rockcliffe included many of the species he used in most of his residential designs. Simonds's favorites included: spirea (especially van Houteii), Indian currants, sweet briars, Rosa rugosa, and viburnums. He also used imported species—forsythia, barberry, and buckthorn. Near the veranda he preferred lilacs, climbing roses, and honeysuckle for their fragrance. To cover the steep slopes around Rockcliffe, its porches, and large veranda, he planted more vines than he typically used. These included Virginia creeper, Japan Ivy, wild grapes, clematis, climbing honeysuckle and roses, and matrimony vine (*Lycium vulgare* or *barbarum*). The *St. Louis Post Dispatch* called it the "finest country house in Missouri."[21]

John Cruikshank died in 1924 and was buried in Riverside Cemetery atop another bluff overlooking Hannibal from the southeast, and from which Rockcliffe can easily be seen. Because he spent most of his fortune (accumulated, ironically, from cut-over lumbering in Minnesota) building and furnishing his mansion, Cruikshank left little money to his widow. She closed the mansion, had it boarded up, and moved next door to the relatively smaller (though still large) house that John had had relocated earlier.[22] Except for the vandalism of local teenagers, the house was left alone for decades, and the grounds, like the

ROCKCLIFFE MANSION rises above Hannibal, Missouri with steep grades and slopes.

ROCKCLIFFE MANSION, Hannibal, Missouri, slowly being covered by the vines planted by Simonds to blend the structure into its landscape. BOTH IMAGES HAGOOD COLLECTION

house, deteriorated over time.*

The proximity of Hannibal to Quincy made it convenient for Simonds to call on clients in both towns when he traveled in that direction.

SIMONDS'S PARK EXPERTISE

Impressed with Simonds's reputation for his work at Graceland and for the Quincy parks system, the Pleasure Driveway and Park District of Springfield, Illinois (about 100 miles east of Hannibal) asked Simonds in December of 1900 to prepare a topographical map and propose a plan for Washington Park. His map showed the kind of attention Simonds gave to becoming familiar with a site. It indicated the location of individual trees, of wooded, open, and water areas, and elevations. He then platted the park grounds, including walkways and drives, ponds, and new plantings, and he recommended a construction schedule for completing these features. The Park District followed his advice, and by 1907, had implemented most of the plan.[23]

Back at home in Chicago, Simonds gave his time to the Chicago Woman's Club in 1899 and 1900, with mixed results. In the midst of the intense civic beautification trend of the early twentieth century, the club took up a small park project in a triangle of land between Rush and State Streets, on the north side of Bellevue Place (a long block west of Lathrop's town house). Simonds oversaw the landscape planning and also served on a small jury, with sculptor Lorado Taft and architect Martin Roche, to judge the architectural entries for a small shelter building at the park's south end. The clubwomen, however, continued to exhibit the entries even after the professional jury had chosen a winner, reserving the right to judge "irrespective of the finding of the jury which made the award in the competition," the *Chicago Daily Tribune* reported on page sixteen in its January 10, 1900 edition. Nearly a year later, things were still in dispute. The clubwomen had voted to build the design of Birch Burdette Long, in spite of the jury's decision to give first prize to Arthur Rouleau's design because Long's design was over the club's budget. The brick

---

* As of 1997, very little of the original plantings remained, although some of the walks and drives were intact. A local group managed to buy the property just before it was to be demolished and has slowly restored the house and provided tours. Asphalt driveways and parking lots have been added on the lower terrace to accommodate cars and tour buses. By 2010, the grounds had been improved, although not according to the original Simonds plan.

shelter house was now nearly finished but "it is not held in favor by a number of aristocratic neighbors" who had complained to the club about the removal of a tree to make space for the shelter. There were other disagreements over this miniscule but prominent landscape, too. The *Tribune* reported that "O.C. Simonds, an expert landscape gardener, offered his assistance, but a number of members of the Woman's club are considered experts in this art, and their ideas differed." The issue apparently came down to tree selection; Simonds said "oaks" and the women objected because they thought oaks would not grow there.

As reported in the *Annals of the Chicago Woman's Club, 1876-1916,* Lucy Fitch Perkins, chairman of the club's Art and Literature Department (and wife of architect Dwight Perkins, a colleague of Simonds), reported in April 1900 that they were having more than their share of problems on this little project. Difficulties getting approval from the City Council held up construction, despite approval previously from the Fine Arts Commission, which consisted of Charles L. Hutchinson, Lorado Taft, W.L.B. Jenney, and Mayor Carter Harrison, along with supervisors from the three major park districts. On a positive note, Perkins included the good news that "the authorities . . . had declared the improvement of the park and the building of the shelter . . . epoch-making events in the history of Chicago," as Bellevue Place Park was to serve as the "nucleus for establishing a system of small parks throughout the city." Despite labor strikes and other obstacles, the club managed to get its "charming little brick shelter in place" by autumn of 1900, and was waiting to install Simonds's plantings until the following spring.

By January 1901, though, there was a petition afoot for the *removal* of the shelter. The women managed to surmount that threat, but Mrs. Noyes (Ida Smith, wife of future Simonds client LaVerne Noyes) reported at the end of that October that the vandalism of the park was more than they could keep up with. A brass standpipe was stolen the first day the shelter was open; the galvanized iron one that replaced it was taken; and the iron pipe Noyes paid to have soldered in place was stolen as well. As of October 1902 the club turned the park over to the City and relinquished all responsibility.

The *Chicago Daily Tribune* next ran an article entitled "Landscape Gardening Experts Prescribe for the Rehabilitation of Lincoln Park," on April 4, 1901.[24] * It featured three essays by recognized experts on parks. E.J. Parker of the American Park and Outdoor Art Association (and director of the Quincy park system) contributed a column called "Parks A Dead Giveaway," encouraging Chicago to "take politics out of park work" and finished with a quote from H.W.S. Cleveland on creating "a fitting abode for men and women . . . who are devoted to a nobler end than money-getting." Professor William Beal of Michigan Agricultural College (former teacher of both Charles Garfield and Liberty Hyde Bailey) offered his views on the "Mischief of Ignorant Boards" and cited examples of how well things can function when knowledgeable and professional men serve on these boards. Simonds described "What a Manager Should Be" in his column, starting with such qualities as "honest, reliable, conscientious, gentlemanly—in short, be a man of good character." A few paragraphs later he continued, "The ideal superintendent should expect to spend his life with the park he cares for . . . " because the park was to last for generations and that required a superintendent's commitment to it. Two years later, when Lathrop joined the Lincoln Park board, he brought Simonds with him as consulting landscape-gardener; while neither position involved a life-long obligation, both men lived up to the principles that the three columnists had described.

THE UNIVERSITY OF CHICAGO

By early 1901, the trustees of the University of Chicago had asked Simonds to design plantings for their new, rather barren looking campus. The university's board included Charles Hutchinson, Martin Ryerson, Jr., and Adolphus Clay Bartlett—all invested in Graceland and Fort Sheridan. On April 15, the *Chicago Daily Tribune* ran an article on "Beauty Scheme for the University of Chicago Campus" with a copy of Simonds's plan on page two, showing his concept for integrating landscape and buildings with plantings and walks leading directly

---

* This article was published the year following Annette McCrea's short tenure as the first consulting landscape-gardener at Lincoln Park and the year before her interview with the *Quincy Herald* in which she expressed her views on park design. Among McCrea's proposals for Lincoln Park were horticultural displays with plants labeled as in a botanical garden. These were not the sort of displays sought by the board, and her recommendations may have precipitated McCrea's quick departure from this position. With the change in board members, and the professional assistance of Simonds and architect Dwight Perkins in modernizing the layout and buildings, Lincoln Park metamorphosed from late Victorian busyness to a simpler, less cluttered, more up-to-date style. Chicago Park District, Lincoln Park "Summary of Contributing Designers."

from building to building. Twenty-five thousand dollars of Rockefeller's "last million and a half donation" went towards the implementation that spring, with Simonds supervising planting and the construction of some drives and walkways. Adhering to his tried and true principles of using dense shrubbery to hide buildings, gently curving the intersections of paths to give a sense of intimacy and interest to a location, and creating a park-like setting to block out the surrounding city, he began transforming the campus as he had so many other sites.

To create a wooded parkland on the campus, Simonds planned to again use Chinese matrimony vine (*Lycium barbarum*), one of his favorites and an important plant in his plans for Rockcliffe, to cover the women's dorm. Apparently the idea was just too cute to resist and the *Tribune* ran a short piece on the topic, surrounding the column with a sketch of an exuberant, blossoming and fruiting vine. The "young women students" it said were "in a flutter" over the idea, and some took it as a joke. But, the article went on, "Mr. Simonds, who is superintendent of Graceland Cemetery,[5*] and of a serious disposition, announced that the report was true." It concluded by saying, "If it thrives in the learned atmosphere of the Midway it will add much to the beauty of the campus. Mr. Simonds is sure it will."[25]

Trustee Charles Hutchinson, university architects Shepley, Rutan, and Coolidge, and President William Rainey Harper, perhaps of a serious disposition themselves, had different ideas. They objected to the "markedly curvilinear system of drives and walks," and the "shrubbery plantations that had been installed." When this group complained about the location of the main entrance and the lack of a central courtyard near the science laboratories, Simonds tried to appease them by modifying his plans, but to no avail. They hired the Olmsted Brothers to examine the grounds and Simonds's plan, and provide a written report of their assessment.

John Charles Olmsted inspected the campus and wrote a very serious thirty-plus page report late in the winter of 1902. He consoled the trustees, telling them

It seems perfectly natural that the Trustees should have accepted Mr. Simonds' preliminary report, for the ideas advanced by him in that

---

* He was not technically superintendent at this time as he had resigned in 1897, but who would be able to understand the concept of a "consulting landscape-gardener"?

report certainly sound attractive and reasonable to anyone not pretty thoroughly versed in matters of architectural and landscape design.[26]

Olmsted allowed that Simonds was very good at cemetery design, but believed he was out of his depth with this campus, and that the Olmsteds were properly "versed in [the] matters" at hand. He concluded that the University of Chicago needed a landscape plan that augmented, not (in his opinion) detracted from, the English gothic architecture of its buildings (generally referred to as "collegiate Gothic"). He thought that a formal landscape with the buildings predominating the scene was the appropriate treatment for the campus. (One cannot help but wonder how things went at ASLA board meetings sometimes, with founder Olmsted critiquing the work of fellow founder Simonds.)

The Olmsted report had an immediate impact—the Trustees replaced Simonds with the brothers. Their vision was of a cloistered campus, reminiscent of Oxford or Cambridge.[27] In fact, not only had trustee Hutchinson already visited Oxford in 1900, he had taken measurements of the buildings he thought most appropriate for copying back in Chicago. The Olmsteds understood this goal and designed four courtyards and a quadrangle during their work for the university.[28] They were also commissioned by both Hutchinson and Ryerson to plan the grounds for their summer estates in Lake Geneva, Wisconsin, and installed left-over plants from these projects at the university's Yerkes Observatory, just down the road in Williams Bay.[29]

At the annual meeting of the Municipal Art League at the end of April 1901, University of Chicago professor C.R. Henderson addressed the group with criticisms about the money and attention given to the university and its front yard, the Midway Plaisance. He felt that Chicago would only be beautiful when there was "artistic spirit through the whole city." He said that the money and the resources of the city were spent where the wealthy lived, and that he "prophes[ied] that we shall not successfully raise the standard of wages until we have created an artistic spirit throughout the entire city."[30] He cited the loss of the university's telescope and Yerkes Observatory to Wisconsin because of the city's present conditions as evidence of the problem. Although no one at the meeting disagreed with Henderson, the group was taken aback at his forthright presentation. Less radical was the resolution to protest "against any act of the General Assembly of Illinois that will allow the erection of any building, except ornamental structures for park purposes, in that part of Grant Park between Michigan avenue [*sic*] and the dock line and the north line of Jackson boulevard and the south line of Eldridge court extended."

Chicago writer Hamlin Garland, a long-time critic of conditions in Chicago, said there was "no doubt that we have a badly and a cheaply built city," but "a new era is upon us." President of the League and businessman Franklin MacVeagh commented that "Beauty is the most profitable investment a city can make." O.C. Simonds addressed the issue of smoke—the city was filled with it from every conceivable, unregulated source. It killed the trees, he said, and must be dealt with. Wallace Heckman expressed faith that the "artistic conscience of the people" just needed expression. As if to prove his point, it was announced that the "residents of the block in Ewing street which is to be made a model section of street met last night at Hull House and formed the Ewing Street Outdoor Improvement Club. They have agreed to carry out faithfully the suggestions of the landscape gardener." Perhaps they had read the article about the Women's Club and the oak trees.

NEW PROJECTS WITH LATHROP

Whether or not the University of Chicago project had any effect on Simonds personally, his business continued unabated. Bryan Lathrop and his wife Helen Aldis purchased property in York Harbor, Maine. They retained Holabird and Roche to design a large vacation home for them and asked Simonds to look over the land and design a suitable setting. Lathrop also became very involved with the town by heading up efforts to beautify streets and regulate development. Back in Chicago, Lathrop became a member of the board of directors of Lincoln Park in 1903 and, with fellow commissioner Francis T. Simmons, had Simonds named Consulting Landscape-Gardener; all three held these positions for more than a decade. They simplified and modernized the Victorian elements installed by Swain Nelson and others over the past forty years—removing many of the winding little paths, the fountains, the carpet beds, and other outmoded features. They removed the Swiss gothic style structures that Jenney had designed and hired Chicago architect Dwight Perkins to design new buildings in the Prairie style; Perkins and Simonds worked together on the

Willows

Red Dogwoods

PATH

Thunberg's Barberries

Norway Maples

Thunberg's Barberry

Wild Rose

Sweet Briar Rose

Japan Privet

SOUTH LINE

Thorns

Thorns

Prickly Ash

Linden

Dewberries and other

Common Elder

Wild Roses

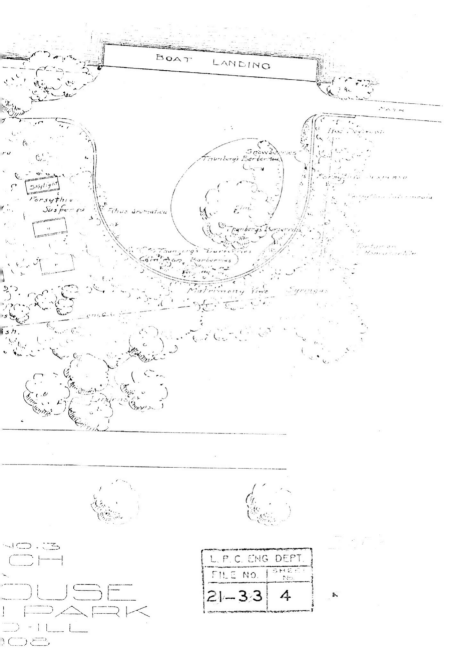

BOAT LANDING

Snowberries
Thunberg's Barberries

Skylight

Forsythia
Suspensa   Rhus aromatica

Thunberg's Barberries

Thunberg's Barberries
Common Barberries

Matrimony Vine   Syringas

PATH

L. P. C. ENG DEPT.

FILE NO.	SHEET NO.
21-3.3	4

BOAT HOUSE sketch for Lincoln Park lagoon from 1908.

rowing lagoon boathouse, which they bermed into a hill on the east side of the new zoo, to make the structure as unobtrusive as possible.* On an even larger scale, Simonds and Lathrop developed a plan to reclaim a four-mile stretch of land along Lake Michigan from Diversey Parkway north to Devon Avenue on which to expand the park, which was land-locked by development on its west side.[31] Their concept was in synch with Daniel Burnham's Plan of Chicago of 1909. This massive undertaking would not be fully accomplished in either man's lifetime, with the major portion of this land-fill project moving forward in the 1930s with Works Progress Administration funding and man-power, and finally completed in the early 1950s, ending at Hollywood Avenue on the north (not Devon). Simonds Drive on Montrose Point (landfill east of Lake Shore Drive, with the park area itself designed by Alfred Caldwell in the 1930s) commemorates his involvement.

Lathrop also served on the Special Park Commission, headed by Dwight Perkins and including Jens Jensen, Charles Hutchinson, Simonds, and reformer Graham Taylor. A remarkable study of the open-space needs of Chicagoans, many of the recommendations in the report were incorporated by Burnham and Bennett in the 1909 Plan, eventually helping to persuade the Cook County commissioners to set aside public lands as forest preserves.

Early in 1903 Simonds was off to Europe again, most likely with Lathrop. He wrote home to Mattie from Venice and she noted in her diary that he was "so far away."[32] While theirs seems to have been a stable, happy marriage, notes here and there in Mattie's journal express a wish that her husband did not travel so much. He also reorganized his business in 1903, calling it now "O.C. Simonds and Company," and began to refer to his profession sometimes as "landscape design."[33] As noted by his wife (although she did not elaborate), he traveled by train to Maine in September, probably to visit York Harbor, and to Oregon in November, perhaps to see their son Herbert who had recently moved there. He enjoyed seeing the countryside from the windows of a train, and with an expanding clientele in many states, Simonds worked this way increasingly for the rest of his career. Just judging from Simonds's commissions from 1900-1905, the first five years of the twentieth century were banner years for landscape architecture.

---

* Perkins designed many of the animal houses in the zoo and the South Pond Café, now known as Café Brauer; all of these are still standing and give Lincoln Park its distinctive character.

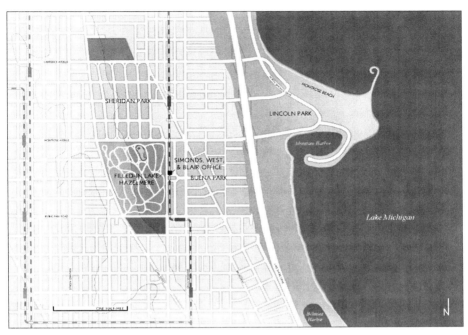

THE NEIGHBORHOOD around Graceland Cemetery **ca. 1950s**. The Lincoln Park extension from Diversey Parkway north to Hollywood Avenue, implemented mostly in the **1930s**, was Simonds and Lathrop's concept.

Alfred Caldwell designed Montrose Point in the mid-**1930s** in a style similar to that of Simonds, and the main road through the area is named Simonds Drive.

CHAPTER SIX ENDNOTES

[1] "Special Meeting of Directors," Madison Park and Pleasure Drive Association, August 7, 1899, *Records 1893-1938*, State Historical Society of Wisconsin Archives, (SHSW) Microfilm 1011.

[2] Benjamin Cole Simonds, SFC; Ernest Warner, *Genealogy of the Warner Family* (Madison, Wisconsin: privately printed, 1919), SFC.

[3] Ibid., 39.

[4] Carolyn J. Mattern, "Madison Park and Pleasure Drive Association" brochure (Madison, Wisconsin: Historic Madison, Inc., 1994).

[5] Simonds to John M. Olin, August 14 and 18, 1903, John M. Olin Papers, 1872-1924, Wis. Mss Ez and unprocessed SHSW Archives.

[6] Clinton Rogers Woodruff to Olin, March 10, 1905, Ibid.

[7] G.A. Parker to Olin, July 5, 1904, Ibid.

[8] Charles Mulford Robinson to Olin, June 22, 1909, Ibid.

[9] J.S. Graff for Victor Lawson to Olin, April 26, 1901; Manning Brothers to Olin, August 15, 1901, Ibid.

[10] Simonds to Olin, October 19, 1904; SHSW, MPPDA records.

[11] Wyman to Olin, October 26, 1909, Ibid.

[12] University of Wisconsin Board of Regents to J.T.W. Jennings, Superintendent of Architecture, June 27 and September 21, 1900; University of Wisconsin archives, Box 1.

[13] "Long View Park, Rock Island, Illinois, 1908-2008: A Pictorial History," courtesy of Diane Oestereich.

[14] Garfield to Olin, July 2, 1904, Ibid.

[15] Garfield to Olin telegram, July 3, 1904, Ibid.

[16] Garfield to Olin, April 28, 1905, Ibid.

[17] C.J. Post to the Madison Park and Boulevard Association [*sic*], May 12, 1909, Ibid.

[18] A.C. Schrader, "Parks and Boulevards," and Simonds, "Written Discussion," *Journal of the Western Society of Engineers*, Vol. V, No. 3, June 1900), 157-171.

[19] Rockcliffe Mansion brochure; National Register of Historic Places nomination form courtesy of Robert and Hurley Hagood.

[20] Rockcliffe mansion, "Plan of the Grounds for Mr. John Cruikshank; O.C. Simonds and Company, Landscape Gardeners, Chicago, Illinois, 1901," at Rockcliffe Mansion; on-site observations.

21 The page from the Sunday supplement in which the property was featured was on display in the mansion's kitchen.

22 Roberta and Hurley Hagood, *Hannibal Yesterdays* (Hannibal, MO: Hannibal Free Public Library, 1992), 167-68.

23 Himelick, 7.

24 Thanks to Harold T. Wolff for kindly forwarding a copy to me. *Annals* section courtesy of John Notz.

25 "Chinese Matrimony Vine for Coeds," *Chicago Daily Tribune*, April 20, 1901, 9.

26 Olmsted Brothers to C.L. Hutchinson, Chairman of the Committee of Trustees, University of Chicago, March 20, 1902, 4. President's Papers, 1889-1925, Department of Special Collections, University of Chicago Library.

27 Jean F. Block, *The Uses of Gothic: Planning and Building the Campus of the University of Chicago, 1892-1932* (Chicago: University of Chicago Press, 1983), 62.

28 Ibid., 64, 196.

29 Ibid., 254. Charles Yerkes made a fortune establishing streetcar lines and was another early force at the University of Chicago.

30 "Too Partial to Midway," *Chicago Daily Tribune*, May 1, 1901, 3.

31 Grese, *Jensen*, 38-39.

32 Martha Simonds's diary, March 1903, referring to her husband's letter dated February 5, SFC.

33 *National Cyclopedia.*

chapter 7

EARLY TWENTIETH-CENTURY WORK

1903-1912

Black Walnut

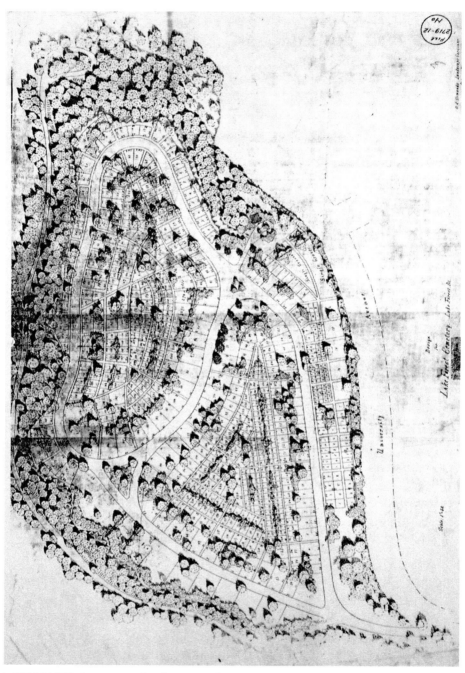

LAKE FOREST CEMETERY plan by Simonds in 1901.   LAKE FOREST CEMETERY ARCHIVES

PUBLICATIONS WITH L.H. BAILEY AT CORNELL

In 1900, distinguished Cornell horticulturist Liberty Hyde Bailey (1858-1954) began publishing *Country Life in America*, a periodical modeled partly after the popular British *Country Life*. Bailey's intention was to focus on middle-class country living, not on the great estates of the very wealthy. Bailey had grown up in South Haven, Michigan, just about twenty miles south of Pier Cove, where Simonds would buy his country property in the 1890s. As an undergraduate at Michigan Agricultural College, he studied with William Beal, a former student of the renowned Asa Gray; Simonds's cousin Charlie Garfield was here conducting experiments in apple culture at the time.[1] Bailey also received his M.S. here, and taught a course on landscape-gardening.

One of the first contributors to *Country Life in America*, Simonds wrote a piece on "The Planning and Administration of a Landscape Cemetery," and would write for or be featured in the magazine for more than fifteen years. Wilhelm Miller, Bailey's associate and former student, edited *CLiA* as well as other horticultural texts, including *How to Plant a Flower Garden* in 1903, to which Simonds contributed the chapter "Trees for Home Grounds."[2] In subsequent years, Miller would feature the work of Simonds and Jensen in the Midwest, and become a fervent promoter of their regional design styles. Bailey published the ground-breaking first edition of the *Cyclopedia of American Horticulture* in 1902; he later edited a *Manual of Horticulture* in 1910, which included a number of pages on drainage written by Simonds. Bailey's Rural Science series for Macmillan Company would publish Simonds's only book, *Landscape-Gardening*, in 1920. It was through Bailey's numerous publications, in part, that Simonds continued to contribute to the horticultural world throughout his career.

President Theodore Roosevelt appointed Bailey to be head of the Country Life Commission, and when Bailey published the commission's findings in 1911, it was to his long-time colleague Charles Garfield that he dedicated the volume. Gifford Pinchot, then head of the U.S. Forest Service, served on the Commission as well, and shared Garfield's strong interest in reforestation.

MORE MIDWEST PROJECTS

The next year brought Simonds many more projects. He planned a campus for the Central States Normal School in Mount Pleasant, Michigan, some seventy miles northeast of Grand Rapids.[3] He designed a small park in Springfield and handled new projects in Ann Arbor and Quincy, as well as calling on clients in LaSalle, Illinois, Dubuque, Iowa, Lake Geneva, Wisconsin, and Mackinac, Michigan.[*] In 1905, Simonds designed Vilas park, with its zoological garden, for the MPPDA, and he returned to Madison the following year to work on Brittingham Park, on the shore of Lake Monona. Traveling around the Midwest, he designed home grounds for Thomas R. Kackley in Indianapolis, R.P. Murdoch in Wichita, Kansas, and E.K. Hardy in Akron, Ohio. In the metropolitan Chicago area, he planned a small urban campus for the Academy of our Lady and designed small estates for J.L. Stack and Mrs. E.L. Gaylord in south suburban Midlothian, the site of a new eighteen-hole golf course.[4]

LAKE FOREST

In 1900-1901, Simonds had the unique opportunity to advise the trustees of Lake Forest Cemetery at the north end of Lake Road and at the same time to design a simple park a mile south, over looking Lake Michigan.[5] He worked on two residences in between the public sites during this same era as well. After working for the Graceland trustees for nearly twenty years, he knew how to express his ideas to the men on the cemetery board, many of whom would have been associates of the men at Graceland. He put his initial, specific recommendations for the cemetery in a two-page letter (his letterhead now read: "O.C. Simonds, Landscape-Gardener, Buena Avenue, Chicago, Ill") accompanied by a plat, re-working an earlier Jenney design by simplifying the roads and plantings, and taking advantage of the lake views and ravine. First, he suggested moving the cemetery entrance to the southwest corner of the site, a more attractive area and closer to the town itself. Then he described how to position and grade the drives, how to place the sewers most effectively, and

---

[*] See the project catalog in the Appendix for a listing of projects.

FOREST PARK in Lake Forest, Illinois.

offered suggestions for other improvements to enhance the utility and beauty of the cemetery, as well as protecting and making the most of the ravines.[6] Simonds planned Forest Park at the other end of Lake Road to make the most of its location on the top of a bluff and the dramatic natural scenery of the lake and a ravine. The plan featured a ring road near the edge of the cliff so residents could ride out for views across the water. In 1901 he created a simple plan with few specific for Horace Martin's new residence overlooking Lake Michigan, siting the house, driveway, and major plantings (either in place already or to be added). Simonds next planned the grounds for the Colvin sisters' Halcyon Lodge, located just a few blocks south of the cemetery, making the most of the natural forest, the dramatic ravine, and views across the street to Lake Michigan.[7]

In the western part of Lake Forest, J. Ogden Armour began developing his extravagant estate Mellody Farm* in 1905, and hired Simonds to design parts of the broader landscape and a bridge to cross his railroad tracks. Jens Jensen created the plantings within the Arthur Heun-designed gardens around the house.[8] This is one of very few, if not the only, project on which Simonds and Jensen both worked; whether they worked separately or collaborated is not known.

Residents in Lake Forest and throughout Chicago's northern suburbs were actively involved in the outdoor improvement trend. The *North Shore News* reported on the front page of its December 17, 1904 issue that J. Horace McFarland of the American Civic Association spoke to the Women's Outdoor Art League, telling them that "apples, peaches, plums, cherries should be grown on grass plots along thoroughfares" and also recommended "foliage for downtown." The article went on to say that McFarland, from Pittsburgh, "would

---

* Not to be confused with the Cuneo family's Hawthorn Melody Farm in nearby Libertyville.

transform Chicago into a great orchard." The members of this group worked hard to bring their ideas to fruition. Down in the city, the *Chicago Daily Tribune* reported on March 9, 1906 that Mrs. Frederick C. Anderson, the director of the Chicago chapter of the Women's Outdoor Art League, "...Wants Chicago to Be a Garden City."* To that end, Mrs. Anderson would distribute vegetable and flower seeds to children to plant in their various city neighborhoods. However far the group got with its beautification projects, Chicago's parkways were not planted with orchards. McFarland and Anderson would no doubt be surprised and pleased to see the emergence of a renewed interest in their ideas today with "urban agriculture" in Chicago a century after their endeavors.

CLIENTS FROM GRACELAND

In tragic circumstances, wholesale grocer William Hoyt commissioned Simonds to create a garden setting for the church he built in memory of his daughter Emilie Fox and her three children, who perished in the Iroquois Theater fire in 1903. Situated on a steeply sloping, triangular piece of land on Sheridan Road in Winnetka, Christ Church's Memorial Church was designed by local architect William Otis and built of stone with a Celtic cross at its apex, resembling an old English parish church. Simonds created a verdant park around the building and its existing graveyard, fencing off the grounds from the road and the neighbors with thick plantings of snowberries, viburnums, wild crabapples, native hawthorns, barberries, and black locusts. At the northeast corner of the garden, inside the trees, he planted a perennial garden of helenium, Joe Pye weed, golden rod (one of his favorite plants), and wild asters. He filled in the parkway between the sidewalk and Sheridan Road with aromatic sumacs.[9]+

The Hoyt family is buried at Graceland Cemetery. As Simonds's private project roster grew, he designed for many families both at the cemetery and at their private estates and other projects. A number of plots on the east side (the section of the cemetery developed during Simonds's years there) were also individual Simonds projects. Among other family plots to Simonds's credit, or

---

* Chicago's motto has been, since its incorporation, "Urbs in horto," or "City in a garden."
+ Forty years later, the church hired landscape architect Ralph Rodney Root to convert part of the garden into a columbarium. Only Simonds's driveway and a few large trees remain from his original scheme; the new churchyard, while visually striking, is a very different style.

to designers working for him, is the Kranz plot, a unique, rounded triangular-shaped lot at the intersection of three roads that contains a large group monument with dense plantings of Rosa setigera, Thunberg's barberries, Spirea van houttei, Indian currants, and Philadelphus coronarius, all favorites of his; there are also peonies, lilies, German iris, hostas, and – yucca. The plantings hug the neoclassical marker, blending it in to its setting. On the road second back from the lake is an enclave of Chicago's most powerful and influential residents, with a contiguous landscape created over time by Simonds. The McCormicks, the Marshall Field family, Henry Field (Florence Lathrop's first husband), Bryan and Helen Lathrop, Jedediah and Mariana Lathrop, and Owen Aldis and his wife occupy this densely planted row.[10] Simonds's primary job, though, was to oversee the entire cemetery landscape. He made sure it was well-planted with mature trees, creating a forest that blocked out views and noise from this flourishing micro-climate.

Harriet Simonds, O.C.'s mother, died in 1906 at the age of eighty. She and Joel had never felt at home in Chicago, and so she was interred with her husband at Oakhill Cemetery in Grand Rapids, rather than at Graceland.[11] Herbert, Simonds's eldest son, wrote many years later that he and his grandmother had a warm and special relationship and, even though Herbert's memory seems to not have always been accurate, his childhood recollections of going next door to visit her after school for cookies and attention stand out among his early remembrances.[12]

THE CARPENTERS AND THE HOUGHTELINGS

In 1906, Simonds designed the surroundings for Reheboth, the Lake Geneva, Wisconsin summer estate of the Hubbard Carpenter family from Chicago. The long, narrow lot ran north from the lake to the state highway. Under Simonds's direction, more than three-fourths of the property was densely planted with an extensive list which included oak and maple seedlings, bladder nut, hazel, wild cherries, witch hazel, and wild flowers; Wichuriana roses, Indian currant, hawthorn, and barberry. His entrance drive gently wound through these woods, finally arriving at the mansion with a framed view of the lake—right through the glassed-in entrance hall in the middle of the house. As spectacular as this approach was, it caused confusion for carriage drivers unfamiliar with the layout, especially in the dark. One night, a fire-truck almost drove into the hall, but was turned away in the nick-of-time by one of the Carpenters' servants.[13] Simonds's devotion to curving roads and to the use of dense plantings to serve as a link between structure and landscape sometimes had its limits.

Around this same time, Simonds designed the grounds of an entire block around four large summer homes. Across the street to the south of Christ Memorial Church, the enclave belonged to four related families. The largest, a shingle style house on the top of the bluff, belonged to James Houghteling, a prominent Chicago businessman and member of the Commercial Club; the Francis Peabody (a business associate of Houghteling's), Butler, and Crowell families owned the other three. Wilhelm Miller featured the property in the August 1, 1911 edition of *Country Life in America*, pages thirty-four to thirty-six, under the heading "How to Multiply Your Grounds by Four." With his typical dramatic flair, Miller started the article saying, "Blind and stupid! If we had only a little imagination, and a little give-and-take, what wonders we could perform, simply by a little cooperation!" The article described how these four families "wisely engaged Mr. O.C. Simonds, the celebrated landscape gardener of Chicago, to design their places as a single whole," thereby enjoying all of the block and variety of gardens, paths, vistas, and outdoor rooms. The block encompassed the bluff and its steep drop, as well as flat property at the bottom, affording an exciting range of topographies. The grounds were spacious enough to accommodate large lawns, tennis courts, and stables. Simonds designed a driveway with turnaround for each house individually. The Houghtelings' drive was the longest and curved from street to house; Simonds planted a woodland so that even in the winter the house was not visible from the street.

Miller especially liked the privacy that a Simonds design incorporated, the most important thing being "the irregular boundary of trees and tall shrubs around the whole property." He took the opportunity this article offered to share his comments on "what barbarians we Americans are" by citing the story of a Pittsburgh millionaire who wanted his terraces very low so he could watch the cars go by. Simonds preferred privacy for the residents, their grounds presenting quiet, beautiful landscape pictures for them as they looked out windows or walked in their gardens. His wealthy clients had no need to show off, preferring discreet properties in "good taste."

THE BRUCEMORE LANDSCAPE by Simonds and West in its prime.   BRUCEMORE ARCHIVES

BRUCEMORE AND CEDAR RAPIDS

Simonds's first projects in Cedar Rapids, Iowa were a neighborhood plan for the Ridgewood area in 1907 and a plan for the Grand Avenue Land Company to extend Grand Avenue to Bever Park. J. Roy West managed most of the Cedar Rapids projects beginning in 1908 when he introduced macadam paving to Cedar Rapids, using it there for the first time at Ellis Park. Simonds and West's best-known work here, though, was for Brucemore. In 1906, Simonds had begun what would become a twenty-year affiliation when the Douglas family asked him to create a grounds plan for their property in Charlevoix, Michigan. Founders of the Quaker Oats Company, the Douglases then acquired their Cedar Rapids estate from Caroline Sinclair, an elderly widow who wanted a smaller home in town. At Brucemore, as they called their new property, Simonds worked with the existing features to customize the site. He altered the expansive front lawn by planting additional groups of shrubs and small trees, thereby adding visual interest while increasing privacy. The back drive was expanded and turned into the main entrance.[14] Working here intermittently for two decades, Simonds and West gradually changed the look of the property. They set aside space near the house for flower gardens, and West took over much of the ongoing client work, as he did with many of their projects. As West and Simonds began their re-design of the Douglas property, they also submitted a plan to the City for May's Island, the civic center of Cedar Rapids—as did Edward Bennett, fresh from serving as Burnham's right-hand man on the development of the Plan of Chicago.

In 1926, near the end of Simonds and West's involvement at Brucemore, West arranged for the purchase of enormous urns from E.E. Soderholtz in Maine, which he placed for dramatic effect at one end of the pond, near the southeast corner of the estate.[15] West and several new staff designers had branched out from the strictly naturalistic style that Simonds himself always practiced, bringing the firm up to date and enlarging its client base.

It is with Brucemore that Helen Agnes Dupuy, a heretofore unknown member of the firm, was discovered. The Smith College *Catalog of officers, graduates and non-graduates for 1875-1910* listed her as "landscape gardener, O.C. Simonds & Co, Chicago." Born in 1885, she was the daughter of O.C. and Mattie's good friends George and Mary Dupuy in Ravenswood and a contemporary of the Simonds's children.[16]

Miss DuPuy visited Brucemore by herself several times from 1910-1912 to prepare the planting plans, staying with her aunt, Mrs. J.R. Van Pelt, in Mount Vernon, Iowa. While working for Simonds, she met and married Charles Deusner in 1912. Deusner had won a "Garden Scholarship" in 1896 to study at the Missouri Botanical Garden, and, sometime after receiving a certificate from this program, Deusner went to work for Simonds. Within a year or two after marrying, the couple moved to Pasadena, California (where Helen's parents had relocated and her father George had become a prominent judge[17]) and ran

THE FORMAL GARDENS at Brucemore, the Douglas family home in Cedar Rapids, Iowa are not visible from beyond the grounds. BRUCEMORE ARCHIVES

their own landscape practice there for two years. The Deusners then moved back east to Batavia, Illinois and "engaged in horticulture" until they returned to Pasadena in 1920; they returned again to the Chicago area when Charles worked as a superintendent for Simonds on the initial work at the Morton Arboretum in late summer 1921. Charles would also be involved with the inception of the Boyce Thompson Arboretum in Arizona, a project Simonds may have been invited to consult upon as well. Helen was a founder of the Women's National Horticultural Association (May 1914) and continued to be active in this group and others for years to come. She was an early twentieth-century landscape practitioner when, for a time, women were advancing in this new profession.

Another Simonds project in Cedar Rapids was Oak Hill Cemetery. H.W.S. Cleveland had worked on plans for the cemetery circa 1870, if not earlier; Simonds planned additions and new roadways over the course of eight years, from 1911 to 1919. He and his colleagues also worked on Mound Farm, North View, Bever Woods, and Eastland Manor Neighborhoods from 1914 through 1919; Belmont Park Neighborhood followed in 1923 (concurrent with Simonds's own work on subdivision in Madison).[18]

COUNTRY ESTATES

In the early years of the twentieth century Simonds and Company had a number of estate projects. At the ASLA meeting on February 5, 1907, Simonds discussed some of the issues he was resolving at these sites in his "Talk on Western Notes." As he would reiterate throughout his career, Simonds explained that the client was best served when he called the landscape architect in early on to consult—not only on placement of the house and outbuildings—but on the placement of rooms and siting of windows and views. "There are many architects, especially young ones, who think they know best about all these things," he said, pressing the point that the landscape designer's role was far broader and more important than providing plants. Simonds continued by talking about several specific estate projects of his (none of them named). One was located on a bluff overlooking Lake Michigan that required dense planting to hold the slope in place. Another house was situated on a ravine but the effect had been ruined by the placement of the road and the use of the ravine as a dump. Simonds moved the stable, re-routed the drive, and had the ravine restored. A third client owned a large farm on which trees had been planted in a scattering. Simonds found this "an excellent opportunity to demonstrate the value of mass-planting by grouping them as a background to the house."

Landscape painters Corot and Daubigny were invoked as the standard for the aesthetics of a landscape design, and Simonds thought that the real pictures being created by the landscape architect were better than those on canvas. He concluded by encouraging his listeners to not only create satisfactory work for their clients, but to educate them as well. "The most perfect success will not be attained until good work is understood and appreciated by the public."[19]

CRANBROOK

George G. Booth was the very wealthy publisher of the Detroit Daily News and, like many of his economic peers, he began to buy property in the country with the intention of creating a gentleman's farm. Booth's initial purchase

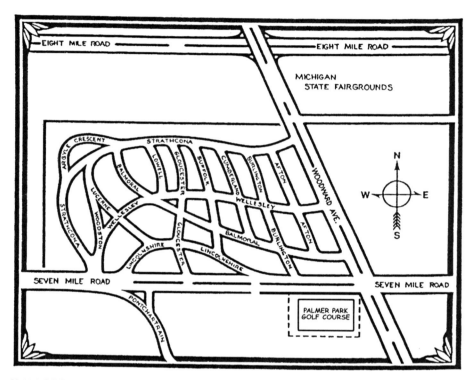

PLAN OF PALMER WOODS, Detroit, MI. Winner of the Michigan Horticultural Society's 1938 Award of Merit, its curvilinear street layout is distinct from the surrounding grid.

around 1905 was 225 acres of worn out farmland just outside of Birmingham, Michigan, in what would become Bloomfield Hills. Booth did much of the early landscape planning himself, assisted by his son and by Englishman H.J. Corfield, a horticulturist and designer who would continue to be involved with the project for many years. Booth modeled his approach to the estate on the current English Arts and Crafts tenets of using local materials, creating unique and aesthetically pleasing decorative elements, and using handcrafted rather than factory-made objects; his hands-on involvement was quite in keeping. By 1908, he hired Simonds to assist with road design at first. By 1910, though, Simonds was involved in the overall estate planning and was ordering trees—nearly 4,000 from the Geneva Nursery alone in April that year, to enhance the scenery and seclusion of Cranbrook, as Booth called his estate. Booth asked Simonds to supervise the planting of all these, but Simonds wrote back, "I shall try to help you out, but we have been driven with work and I have not yet decided as to just who I can send. If you have a competent foreman, do you not think that I could give him enough instructions in one day so that, with your help and that of your son, he could arrange the planting?"[20] Simonds and Button's names are the only two listed on the firm's letterhead at the time. West of course was a trusted employee, and Charles Deusner and Helen Dupuy may have been on staff, as well as several young men learning the trade, but apparently no one who was both experienced and expendable enough to make the trip. Although Booth managed to have his own crew heel in the shipments of plants as they arrived, he still needed help with the actual planting because there was just so much of it.

In March 1915, another order went in to Geneva Nursery for 4,000 hemlock seedlings (at one and a half cents each), about 3,300 other tree seedlings, and 700 Wichuriana roses. In late 1915, Simonds suggested "a planting of several thousand small pines on the hills to the south of the main road and around the locality where the Greek theatre is located." Booth also intended to plant "several hundred feet of arbor vitae hedge" around the theatre *per se* as a green wall, and wondered if Simonds, who had begun his own small nursery at Pier Cove by this time, could provide any or all of the material. He could not, so the plants came from Ellwanger and Barry in New York instead. This time Simonds sent a new man, Erle Blair, to make a topographical and tree survey before they began the planting. Simonds's letterhead now included Button, West, and George Cone. They continued to work with Blair's 1916 map, using it as late as 1922 when they began a reforestation project. Inspired no doubt by the inception of the Morton Arboretum and by the botanical gardens he had visited in Europe, Simonds wrote to Booth that what he "had in mind for the forest was to use trees suited to the soil and situation, using trees of different species in colonies. This would be a valuable experiment in forestry growth showing the comparative growth of different species and their adaptability to the soil and climate of Oakland County." He also consulted with his colleague Filibert Roth, a forester with the University of Michigan, who agreed with the "general idea." Simonds then went on to list nearly four dozen species he thought would be suitable, including a few imports such as Norway maple, gingko, and European beech. Most of the recommendations were native species such as hackberry, wild black cherry, several types of oaks, sassafras, and a number of evergreens. Booth and Simonds were still working out the forest plans in January 1923.

Simonds's work here had a strong impact because of the large scale and the immense number of plants he installed. The estate became the campus of the Cranbrook Academy of Art shortly after his affiliation ended. In 1925, Booth hired architect Eliel Saarinen to design buildings and landscape, marking the beginning of a new design era at Cranbrook, yet one that continued the original arts and crafts ideal of an integration of all aspects into a cohesive whole.[21]

ANN ARBOR PARKS

The Ann Arbor, Michigan Park Commission resolved in May 1905 to "get Mr. Simonds to draw a plan for developing and laying out the Boulevard Park, provided that such a service can be obtained for a sum not to exceed $100." It probably could, as that was Simonds's day rate, and he could have junior staff do the drawing to his specifications. Yet again an Olmsted was in the vicinity and visited Ann Arbor on June 8 as a guest of the Ypsilanti Civic Improvement Society. He visited again on the sixteenth and admonished the park superintendent not to ruin what nature had already blessed them with. In particular, he warned that, "By all means the park should not be too much cut up with roads, and, in fact, said Prof. Olmstead [sic], no road at all should be built through the tract. This decision he based on the steepness of the rise, which will necessitate a very winding path and will cause considerable territory to be used."[22]

In the meantime, Simonds apparently continued to consult as well. He wrote to the park commissioners on June 30 congratulating them on acquiring such a beautiful piece of land along the Huron River. He enumerated the native plants that were flourishing there without human help, and related that when he had visited William Robinson at his home thirty miles from London several years previously, Robinson proudly showed him the sixty acre tract of original forest he owned. This was something rare and "prized very highly" in England. * Ann Arbor had its chance now to preserve some of its natural forest.

Simonds's comments on how little work would be required to make a park

---

* William Robinson (1838-1935) was an Irish plantsman working in England in the second half of the nineteenth century. He was one of the first garden writers to recommend the use of native plants in his book *The Wild Garden*, although he was fond of exotics throughout his career.

here echo Olmsted's (and William Saunders's comments in 1861 upon seeing the Graceland site in Chicago!) Simonds disagreed, though, regarding the road. He wrote that ". . . those who drive or walk should be enabled to reach the points of interest with ease and comfort. I find it is quite feasible to make a driveway with easy grades connecting the river drive with the Boulevard at the top of the bluff."[23] As the work commenced, however, "objections were raised to the road as laid out by Simonds that would necessitate a cut in the bank," reported the Park Commission minutes on July 17. Although Olmsted Jr.'s high profile and non-negotiable comments had had an impact, Simonds proceeded with the work. Ann Arborites must have been pleased overall, as Simonds continued to develop parks there and in 1906 began work on what would be called the Nichols Arboretum.

THE ARBORETUM AT THE UNIVERSITY OF MICHIGAN

As Simonds concluded his work for the University of Chicago in 1902, the school was installing Botany Pond under the direction of John Coulter, first head of its botany department. Eminent early ecologist Henry Cowles was a recent graduate from and currently teaching in this department and helped to develop botanizing in the field (with colleague Jens Jensen), as well as installing plantings at the pond for study. Professor Beal, of course, had instituted such a garden at Michigan State Agricultural College as long ago as 1871. Travel to actual locations was vital, but sometimes having the plants close at hand was more useful. Thus in 1907 the University of Michigan at Ann Arbor established an arboretum for this purpose on twenty-seven and a half acres donated by alumni Walter and Esther Conner Nichols. Fellow alumnus Simonds was asked to plat the general layout of the site in 1906. The plan clearly shows his input. For this very steep site sloping down to the Huron River Simonds created wide grassy meadow paths that wind gently down from the street to the river, obscuring any sign of the river itself until the last curve—then a visitor can see it glinting through openings in the vegetation. Simonds used native plants "to emphasize and enhance the Arboretum's rolling topography and breathtaking overlooks . . . [when he] designed the sweeping vistas and intimate coves."[24] Under his direction, the arboretum provided both a delightful landscape experience and a study in the plants themselves.[25]

Simonds's associate Aubrey Tealdi (ca.1881-ca.1979) served as Director of the Arboretum (as well as Chairman of the Department of Landscape Design) from 1916 to 1934. Although not formally trained in landscape design, his engineering experience at the Italian Naval Academy and subsequent training in the subject in England gave him enough ability that Simonds hired him in 1907 while Tealdi was visiting relatives in Chicago.[26] He subsequently recommended Tealdi for an instructorship when the University of Michigan began its landscape program two years later. Over the years Tealdi taught studio courses with George Cone, from Simonds's office back in Chicago.[27] He also found time to serve as ASLA vice-president and to work with yet another organization, the Illinois Outdoor Improvement Association, as a director. The aptly-named Edward J. Park was the original president in 1909, and Dean Eugene Davenport of the Agriculture School at the University of Illinois (and friend and fellow Michigander of Simonds) served as first Vice President.[28]

UNIVERSITY OF MICHIGAN LANDSCAPE GARDENING PROGRAM

Simonds was a natural to help start a landscape program at his alma mater. He was already mentoring young people starting out in the profession at his office, he enjoyed lecturing and writing about landscape-gardening, and after those remarkably busy years of 1900-1905, he could see the need for more and properly trained practitioners. He had participated in such an experiment himself in 1877-78 when the school offered Jenney's architecture courses and he had developed a career beyond his expectations because of it. Now it was Simonds who would take the train from Chicago to Ann Arbor to deliver lectures in this new series.

In his initial lecture, given February 1909, Simonds described the benefits of studying landscape-gardening even for those who would not follow it as a career. That landscape-gardening helped people see and appreciate the world around them and that it required a wide range of skills was a core belief he enjoyed extolling. In fact, Liberty Hyde Bailey had begun the country's first such program in 1885 at the Michigan Agricultural College when he implemented a Department of Horticulture and Landscape Gardening. Frederick R. Steiner and Kenneth R. Brooks describe the integration of schools of agriculture and early landscape-gardening courses, and Bailey's direct influence, in "Agricultural Education and Landscape Architecture" in *Landscape Journal*, Volume 5, Number 1. Not only had Bailey intended to train students who might go on to design professionally, but in particular he hoped to give rural students an appreciation for what they could do back home to improve the appearance of their farms and towns. He brought this approach with him when he moved on to Cornell.

Simonds gave his second lecture that March and talked about the "making of plans [as] perhaps the most important work that one can do" with landscape. He explained that the plan focuses things, helps the designer gain a clear understanding of the conditions, gives him the opportunity to walk the land to be improved, and provided "knowledge of the soil, the plants, engineering, etc. and above all, picture-making."[29] He combined specific advice for drainage, plant selection, and road construction with general suggestions for creating landscape pictures to provide a pleasing environment; he illustrated his instructions by projecting images from glass lantern slides.[30]

The first year's lectures were given at the request of botany professor Dr. Burns, who had no intention of creating an ongoing design program. They were well received and enough interest was sparked, though, that by the time Simonds began the second series in February 1910, the regents and faculty had already approved a program. He found it "very gratifying." An untitled, undated manuscript in the Simonds file of "Reprints and Articles" at the Bentley Historical Library at the University of Michigan reiterated what he said in his first lecture, and expressed his feeling in more detail.

> It gives me pleasure to meet so many young men who are trying to
> learn to appreciate nature. Nothing can add more to the enjoyment of
> living in this world than to learn to see beauty in it . . . I believe there
> is no study that leads one to as full an appreciation of nature as the
> study of landscape gardening.

He did acknowledge that perhaps landscape painting might give one some of the same sensibility, in regards to the "study of form and color of natural objects, their aspects at different hours and seasons, but landscape gardening also has intimate knowledge of trees, shrubs, and flowers."

VIEW OF THE MISSISSIPPI from Mark Twain statue in River View Park.

MARK TWAIN STATUE installed in River View Park in 1910, Hannibal, MO.

RIVERVIEW PARK, HANNIBAL

Eight years after he had finished John Cruikshank's landscape at Rockcliffe Mansion, Simonds came back to work in Hannibal again. Wilson Pettibone, another lumber magnate, donated a few hundred acres of land on bluffs above the Mississippi River to the city for park and recreational use. Naming it Riverview Park, he established a governing board of nine citizens (including Cruikshank), provided an endowment to maintain the park, and paid for Simonds's design services. Because this land had already been cleared for farming, Simonds was able to incorporate magnificent views of the river into the park's layout. He planned the drives through the park with as minimal incline as the steep terrain permitted.* Complaints that it would only be accessible to carriage and horse owners motivated Pettibone to have Simonds provide a concrete stairway into the park for pedestrians.[31]

Hannibal native Samuel Clemens/Mark Twain died the following year, in 1910, and the state of Missouri commissioned a memorial at Riverview Park as a tribute. While Pettibone had stipulated that the park was to be as "primitive" as possible, with no man-made objects such as toilets, tables, or benches, he made an exception for the monument. Simonds designed the setting on the highest point in the park, before the design of the statue was selected,

> for the guidance of the competing sculptors, and the final choice of the [sculpture] design was influenced as much by its particular fitness for the locality selected as by the sculptor's conception of the man to be commemorated.[32]

The model made by Frederick C. Hibbard, of Chicago, won the competition. A life-like statue of Twain looking off into the distance of his beloved Mississippi River, it fit perfectly into its location atop the high bluff in Riverview Park. *Park and Cemetery* featured the memorial in its December issue and included a copy of Simonds's site plan and section. Sculptor Hibbard was a Missouri native who had studied at the Art Institute of Chicago under Lorado Taft.

Hannibal Too recounts an earlier writer's imaginative conclusion that Simonds's roads through the park turned to the left in what that writer believed was "the English style," (perhaps because of the reverse traffic direction of English roads) and that therefore Simonds was English.

In 1924, when Pettibone donated additional land to Riverview Park, he asked Simonds back, and when the city of Hannibal developed another new park along its river front seven years later, it was to Simonds the city turned.[33]* Nipper Park was partly a project to help put people to work in 1931, and it took 225 part-time workers to construct the site. Simonds's suggestions were carried out, although he continued to work on the plan, which was on his desk when he died in November 1931.[34]

SIMONDS IN EVANSTON

About the same time that Simonds was planning Hannibal's Riverview Park, financier Charles Gates Dawes hired him to redesign the grounds of a mansion he had recently purchased on the lake in Evanston, Illinois. Dawes's new home was just a block from Daniel Burnham's and a short distance from that of William Holabird. He was also an acquaintance and correspondent of Kenoshan Zalmon Simmons, for whom Simonds had created Library Park (and Burnham the library). Like Simonds, Dawes was a member of Delta Upsilon. Architect Henry Edwards-Ficken (who designed Gifford Pinchot's family home "Grey Towers" in Pennsylvania) had created the chateauesque, red brick house for Dr. Robert Dickinson Sheppard, treasurer and business manager of Northwestern University. Completed around 1896, the house was built on the northwest corner of a nearly two-acre lot overlooking Lake Michigan. A turf-covered terrace ran along the library on the east side of the house, facing the lake; a lawn dotted by trees and shrubs covered the rest of the grounds in a Victorian gardenesque collection of visually unrelated plants.

When he began working at the Dawes house around 1910, Simonds drew a site plan to inventory existing vegetation and structures. He noted diseased or dying trees and shrubs, as well as obtrusive sights to be blocked with foliage. This evolved into a second-stage plan with proposed additions and changes. Finally, by 1912, he prepared a new plan for the site, documenting the actual changes and conditions of the property as he had altered it.

---

* The *Courier-Post* story credits "W.T. Lengue and a Mr. Cohan of Chicago, both with the firm of architects who planned the improvements . . . same landscaper who designed the lawn of the Cruikshank home, with directing the work at Riverview Park in 1908-09." The source of this information is unknown. George Carroll Cone, a lecturer at the University of Michigan and an associate of Simonds, was quite likely the "Mr. Cohan" mentioned in the *Courier-Post* article. This is the only mention of Lengue.

Simonds developed his design to frame the lake view. Unlike the steep bluffs he had covered with vines in Missouri, this land was flat, except for the slight artificial incline leading up to the terrace. Taking this topography into account, Simonds made changes on the Dawes grounds that incorporated his ideas of what made a house beautiful and a landscape artistic, while accommodating client requirements and climate limitations. He added plants along the driveway fences between the west and north neighbors to establish a dense foliage screen. New trees along the front walk softened the entrance and the roses and shrubs along the side of the front steps diminished the façade's severity. He introduced foundation plantings around the house's perimeter, placing snowberries on the north side. Roses, honeysuckle, and Virginia creeper filled in the east side of the terrace, giving a visual transition from the house to the lawn and then to the lake. A new front terrace along the south side was partially hidden with flowering shrubs such as Indian currant, forsythia, and weigela, and he planted hydrangeas under the windows of the east side parlor. The Dawes family entertained frequently on their terrace during the 1910s, with a backdrop of Simonds's exuberant plantings.[35]

At the back of the house, on the north end of the property, hemlock, dwarf mountain pine, and a trailing juniper filled the empty spot east of the carriage house. A cement balustrade delineated the perimeter of the terrace (quite similar to the one on the east side of Burnham's property), and a winding path lined with hostas led from the north side of the terrace to the service drive and carriage house, replacing the grass that had been there. Northeast of the house, just south of the service drive, Simonds put in a "wild garden" of native plants and grape vines, and he transformed the drive into one of his favorite landscape features: a slowly curving, densely planted road, that made a mystery of whatever lay beyond it—even though in this case it was only a half-block long. He added trees and shrubs to existing plantations through the grounds, creating a lusher look and a more cohesive planting out of the previously unrelated groupings. The privet hedge around the edge of the property remained, a rarity in Simonds's plans. Trimmed to a height of two to three feet, the hedge kept the public from cutting across the Dawes lawn on its way to the public beach across the street.

The Daweses lived here graciously until their deaths in the 1950s; Mr. Dawes was a Vice President of the United States, American Ambassador to the

O.C. SIMONDS out of doors, 1920s.
SIMONDS FAMILY COLLECTION

Court of St. James, and developed the Dawes Plan for the Allied Reparations Committee in 1923, for which he shared the Nobel Peace Prize of 1925. Currently the mansion is the home of the Evanston Historical Society, and the plantings have been greatly simplified for ease of grounds maintenance by the City of Evanston and the Society.

ELSEWHERE IN EVANSTON

Throughout the first few decades of the twentieth century, O.C. Simonds and Company had many residential commissions along Chicago's north shore, including several in Evanston. James Patten, famous as the "Wheat King" for nearly cornering the market in 1909, built a new house on Ridge Street. Designed by George Maher in 1901, the house was made of heavy rusticated stone and was decorated with a thistle motif Maher created specifically for the stained glass and woodwork. The grounds were enclosed with iron fencing purportedly salvaged from the World's Fair. Simonds and associates created an appropriate setting for the massive structure, which was razed just a few decades later.

A mile farther north along the lake, Simonds provided the landscape design for Charles Deering's small Evanston estate. Charles and his brother James Deering were the heirs to the Deering Harvester Company (combined with the McCormick Harvesting Machine Company in 1902 to form International Harverster). Chances are Deering and Simonds worked exceptionally well together. In *Charles Deering: An Appreciation* (privately printed, 1929), Walter Dill Scott and Robert B. Harshe explicitly describe Deering as a naturalist who, in the right season, could be found in his yard waiting for migratory birds to return. Birdhouses, food, and masses of vegetation for habitat were all in place. Throughout his career, Simonds referred to the importance of providing shrubs for protection and for fruit for birds. The essay described Deering's personality as being such that "In his lawn in Evanston he had planted in profusion flowers, shrubs, and trees. These served as objects of delight for himself and his friends, but those who knew him best realized that in his planting he had provided for the needs of bees and birds."

Simonds and Company also consulted on Charles Deering's property "Buena Vista", north of Miami, and may have consulted on the naturalized areas at his brother James's famed estate, Vizcaya, just south of Miami in Coconut Grove. David Fairchild, plant collector and close colleague of Bryan Lathrop's brother Barbour, began his botanical garden there about the same time, 1916. (See chapter twelve on the Lathrops for further information.)

VICTOR LAWSON'S LONE TREE FARM

The first two decades of the twentieth century brought, among other things, the gentleman's farm of the very wealthy. Publications such as *Country Life in America*, with its first issue printed in November 1901, showcased rural life as befitting the refined and the comfortable. When Liberty Hyde Bailey first conceived of this magazine, he intended that it feature middle-class, modest living in the countryside. Readers, though, were more interested in the estates of the truly wealthy and soon those appeared as well. Simonds had at least two of these gentleman farmer clients, Frank and Florence Lowden at Sinnissippi Farm (beginning about 1901) and Victor and Jessie Lawson at Lone Tree Farm, 1912. Lawson was the owner of the *Chicago Daily News* and his city home was at Lake Shore Drive and Burton Place, just four blocks north of the Lathrops on Bellevue, and about two blocks north of the Noyeses

CHARLES DEERING family home on Sheridan Road, Evanston, Illinois, ca. 1920.
NORTHWESTERN UNIVERSITY ARCHIVES

(another Simonds client also on Lake Shore Drive; the Lowdens lived on Prairie Avenue when they were in town). The goal of both the Lowdens and the Lawsons was to make their retreats self-supporting through the sale of farm products.

The Lawsons had bought ten acres at Lone Tree Point in Green Lake, Wisconsin for their country home. The lake is about 180 miles north-northwest of Chicago and their parcel was on the north side of the lake on Norwegian Bay. They continued to add to their holdings over the years until they owned 1,100 acres. They first called in Simonds in 1903 to design roads; George Cone served as the supervising engineer. According to later Green Lake residents, the roads were exceptionally well built and still serviceable after more than sixty years, with twelve to fourteen inch roadbeds filled with a series of materials embedded in tar.[36]

After several years of slowly improving the property, in November 1912 Lawson hired a Chicago engineer named William Merigold through the

John M. Ewen Company. Merigold moved up to the farm and functioned as the superintendent of construction. From the start, he disagreed with what Simonds was doing. The correspondence between Merigold and Lawson does not make it clear whether he and Simonds just did not get along, or if Simonds was being as negligent as Merigold accused; in any case, Merigold did not appreciate Simonds's approach. One of the first assignments Lawson gave to Merigold was to confer with Simonds about his plan to use muck from Norwegian Bay on Lawson's golf grounds. Simonds had explained that it would be "sour" at first and needed to dry in the sun and air and then be treated with lime. Lawson was not clear about the process and wanted his man-on-the-grounds to understand it; he did not understand it either and found Simonds's idea less than useful.

By October 1913, Simonds recommended extensive underground drain tiles, "3,700 feet of trench four feet deep to be dug into sand, deeper than a man's waist" to drain the eighty-acre marsh on the Lawson property. Merigold wrote to Lawson that not only did they not have the man power to tackle such a project, but that the water would then drain on to their neighbor Mr. Parker's land and they had no such agreement with him. Simonds continued to order materials, with Merigold reporting "Plants and bushes arriving in great quantities and Parsons is putting then along Link Rd., at entrance, and elsewhere."

Merigold wrote to Lawson (traveling through Europe and now in France) in November, saying that Simonds had been out again to talk about draining the eighty-acre marsh. According to Merigold, "He seems to have no idea of the work involved or what it means and no regard for what the neighbors might do. He has given Parsons orders to go ahead with it just as soon as he is through planting." On top of that, the plant orders placed by Simonds were for tiny new plants (as at Cranbrook) and as Merigold reminded his employer, "I know you are opposed to planting anything but fair sized things."

A report on November 24, 1913 from Simonds on the eighty-acre drainage system followed. In the meantime, though, Lawson had written to Merigold from Lausanne, Switzerland, telling him, "Your treatment of this situation has been entirely right . . . I am writing Mr. Simonds that we must . . . let the matter rest until next year . . ." Simonds then asked Parsons to stop work for the time being, and things calmed down. In March of the following year Simonds developed plantings for a bird refuge on the property. Merigold still did not understand his approach and wrote to Lawson on August 24, 1914 that "I have tried to check over Mr. Simonds list of planting, but as there are no specific number of plants given on the list I cannot give you the quantities. If you will write to him and ask him to complete . . ."

By 1915 the farm was producing enough to sell eggs, milk and apples, as well as buckwheat flour (ordered at least by a Mrs. C.B. Wright, who lived just a few blocks from Simonds in Chicago, if not by other customers). Despite the disagreements with Merigold, Simonds seems to have maintained a presence on this project for several more years because in 1923 the Lone Tree Farm stationery listed A.A. Penfield as assistant manager, surely the same Penfield who the following year would be in touch with Charles Deusner regarding the Boyce Thompson Southwest Arboretum.[37] Penfield's position did not last long, however, as Lawson died in 1925, and the estate was purchased by developers. They intended to create a private, high-end "community of summer homes within a great country estate," which they called Lawsonia.[38] Since then, the site has gone through a number of iterations; it is now the Green Lake Conference Center of the American Baptist Assembly.

ILLINOIS AND MICHIGAN CANAL ROAD

Cemetery work, Fort Sheridan, the Quincy parks, and other large-scale projects had given Simonds a great deal of experience in road design and construction and he was well known for it. With the advent and steadily increasing popularity of the automobile, drivable roads were more and more a necessity. Simonds, always on the go visiting clients, was eminently aware of this need. In early 1910 he recommended using the right of way next to the defunct Illinois and Michigan Canal as an excellent location—pretty much ready-made—for installing a road. "The automobile will soon be in universal use and with it, the people of the city in great numbers will desire to reach the country." He went on to say that "The Illinois [River] valley contains many flourishing cities which would be greatly benefited by such a road and it would form a desirable way of reaching the country from Chicago."[39] Simonds's belief in bringing nature to the city or bringing people out to nature was finding new and expansive landscape outlets.

CHAPTER SEVEN ENDNOTES

[1] Wilhelm Miller, ed., *How to Plant a Flower Garden: a Manual of Practical Information and Suggestions* (New York: Doubleday, Page and Co., 1903).

[2] Plan at MA.

[3] Martha Simonds's diary, SFC.

[4] The greenkeeper at the Midlothian Club finds no reference to Simonds in the club's history, unfortunately.

[5] Plans on file with the City of Lake Forest.

[6] Letter from Simonds to the Trustees of the Cemetery of Lake Forest, November 27, 1900; courtesy of Rommy Lopat.

[7] Plan at MA.

[8] Plan at MA; information also found at http://www.lib.lfc.edu/special/Mellody_Farm.html, with research from Arthur Miller and Shirley Paddock.

[9] Plan at MA and at Christ Church.

[10] Plan in SFC.

[11] Benjamin Cole Simonds.

[12] Herbert R. Simonds, *Memoirs* (unpublished typescript, undated), SFC.

[13] Plan in Warren Manning Collection, Special Collections, Iowa State University, Ames.; *Lake Geneva History*, 15-17, local history collection at the Lake Geneva Public Library. Thank you to John K. Notz for access to the property.

[14] Cecelia Rusnak, *Historic Landscape Report for Brucemore, Cedar Rapids, Iowa*, Vol. 1 (State College, PA: March 1997), WHT.

[15] Rusnak.

[16] The information about Helen Dupuy and Charles Deusner has been generously shared by Deb Engmark, Head Gardener at Brucemore Estate, from her research on Dupuy as a significant designer in Brucemore's history. This material fills in heretofore mysterious gaps. Her research took her to the Missouri Botanic Garden's *Annual Reports*; *The American Architect*, Vol. CXVIII, No. 2324, July 7, 1920; *Garden & home builder*, Vol. 28, October 1918; and other periodicals of the 1910s and 1920s.

[17] Election flyer and miscellaneous correspondence in the Sulzer Library local history collection and the Simonds family materials.

[18] Thank you to Deb Engmark for the expanded Cedar Rapids project list found here.

[19] "Synopsis of Talk on Western Notes" by Ossian C. Simonds, *Transactions of the American Society of Landscape Architects for 1907*, 90-91.

[20] Simonds to Booth, April 1, 1910; Cranbrook Archives.

[21] Diana Balmori, "Cranbrook: The Invisible Landscape," *Journal of the Society of Architectural Historians*, 53 (March 1994), 30-60.

[22] *Ann Arbor Daily Times*, May and June 1905. Courtesy of Robert Grese.

[23] *Ann Arbor Daily Argus*, June 30, 1905. Courtesy of Robert Grese.

[24] "Nichols Arboretum" informational brochure (Ann Arbor, Michigan: University of Michigan, 1996).

[25] http:/www.umich.edu/~snrewww/arb/arbmis.html

[26] Walter A. Donnelly, Wilfred B. Shaw, and Ruth W. Gjelsness, eds., "Landscape Architecture," *The University of Michigan, An Encyclopedic Survey*, Vol. III, Parts VI and VII (Ann Arbor: University of Michigan Press, 1953), 1312.

[27] Sally Linvill Bund, "The Life of Aubrey William Tealdi and His Design of the Estate Grounds of Arnold H. and Gertrude E. Goss," unpublished paper, Department of Landscape Architecture, University of Michigan, 1992.

[28] Organization letterhead.

[29] Simonds's typed lecture notes; University of Michigan Bentley Historical Library.

[30] Simonds's "Lecture Notes," files of Robert E. Grese, Department of Natural Resources, University of Michigan, Ann Arbor.

[31] Roberta and Hurley Hagood, *Hannibal Too* (Marcelline, MO: Walsworth Publishing, 1986), 228-30.

[32] "Mark Twain Memorial and Its Setting," *Park and Cemetery*, Vol. 22, No. 10 (December 1912), 236-38.

[33] "Strolling was a pleasant pastime," *Hannibal Courier-Post* (June 20, 1908), 9; Simonds to Pettibone, October 31, 1929.

[34] Tuesday, January 8, 1931 page from O.C. Simonds's desk calendar, "Sent letter to Roy [J. Roy West] enclosing one to Mr. Pettibone to be copied and sent to Hannibal with plan of park." SFC.

[35] Sources for information on Dawes and the house include Margery Blair Perkins, *Evanstoniana: An Informal History of Evanston and Its Architecture*, Barbara Buchbinder-Green, ed. (Chicago: Chicago Review Press and Evanston Historical Society, 1984). Thanks to Mark Burnett, EHS archivist in the 1990s, for access to photographs, plans, and miscellany in the collection of the Evanston Historical Society.

36 *A Heritage History of Beautiful Green Lake, Wisconsin* by Robert W. & Emma B. Heiple; Ripon: Macmillan, 1976, 212-216.

37 Merigold-Lawson correspondence, Victor Fremont Lawson collection; Newberry Library Special Collections.

38 Sales brochure, n/d.

39 "Says Turn Canal into Road; Landscape Gardener Enthusiastic Over Old Ditch Scheme," *Chicago Daily Tribune*, February 25, 1910, 20.

chapter 8

CONTENDING WITH THE "PRAIRIE SPIRIT"

1911-1916

Jack Pine

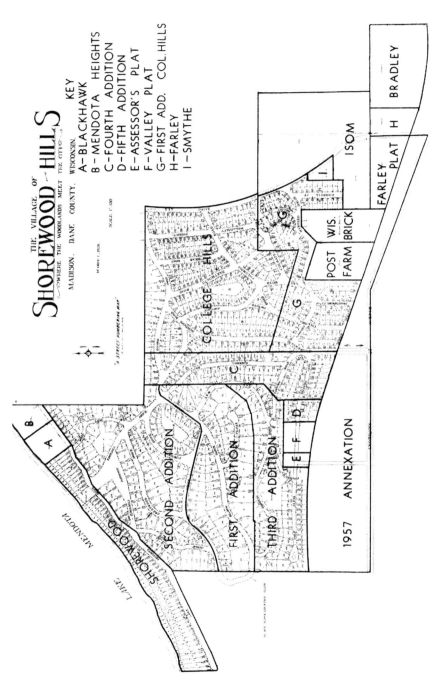

SHOREWOOD HILLS subdivision, Madison, Wisconsin.

MADISON SUBDIVISIONS

Simonds went back to Madison in 1911 to plat a new subdivision called the Highlands, just to the west of the city. His cousin, Ernest N. Warner, was president of the land company. Because the property had been grazed, there were no shrubs or trees; but it was hilly with splendid views of Lake Mendota to the north, pastoral vistas in two other directions, and Madison to the east. Simonds laid out the roads following the site's topography, as he had for the MPPDA's projects a few miles away. He installed plantations of his preferred trees and shrubs: indigenous maples and oaks, Indian currants, hawthorns, barberries, and elms.[1]

Despite the developers' good intentions, the thirty-seven multi-acre lots did not sell quickly and many who bought did not build.[2] Among the few who did were Thomas Brittingham and Edith and Frederick Davis, people with strong ties to the MPPDA.[3] Brittingham had donated land along Lake Monona out of which Simonds had created a park in 1906. Edith Davis's father, Magnus Swenson, was a wealthy sugar processor who had moved from Chicago to Madison, quite likely because of his involvement with the MPPDA. Both families built large, unique homes on their estates, setting the standard for subsequent lot buyers.[4]

In 1912, after thinking it over for many years, Ernest Warner also subdivided his farm a mile or so northeast of the Highlands into Spring Harbor.

> He would walk over his land with his cousin Ossian Simonds, widely known landscape architect from Chicago, and visualize proposed roads and homesites. He pictured a development for his farms . . . [that was] quiet and exclusive.[5]

Simonds followed the contours of the hills to lay in the roads and created a wooded setting for the lots carved out of his cousin's farm. Like his cousin the landscape designer, Warner enjoyed witnessing the processes of nature and weather. For his subdivision, he thought that living on a hill, with great uninterrupted views of sky and clouds "and all the wonderful changes that are continually taking place out of men's reach" was something special.

That same year John McKenna, another real estate developer, bought fifty-seven acres of farmland a few miles farther east, adjacent to the University of Wisconsin campus. He named his new subdivision "College Hills" in hopes of attracting professors and their families and gave it the slogan, "Where the Woodlands Meet the City;" he then hired Simonds to plat his subdivision.[6] This was to be more intensively developed than the Highlands, with three lots per acre. Lake Mendota Drive, which connected the city and the campus with College Hills and neighboring Eagle Heights (a wooded park on a hill with panoramic vistas), was part of the MPPDA road system that Simonds planned several years earlier, and thus he was already familiar with the area. He replaced old roads within the new town, first finding optimal home sites and then locating the roads to reach these spots, once again following the contours of the hill to provide gentle slopes.[7]

College Hills, like the Highlands, was slow to develop. It was outside the bounds of city services and there was no transportation to the capitol, and, during World War I, McKenna lost his investment. Undaunted, by 1922 he purchased fallow farmland on the west side of College Hills, named the new area "Shorewood," and again asked Simonds to design roads and plantings. This time, his timing was right and Shorewood (which soon merged with College Hills to become "Shorewood Hills") was an immediate success.[8] Mrs. McKenna had moved against her will into the first of her husband's College Hill houses in 1913, but she grew to love the area and had a special appreciation for Simonds's work there. In her reminiscences of the early days, she wrote

> . . . he accentuated the relationships of hills and lake shore and produced innumerable, often breath-taking vistas. These landscapes present infinite variety during the passage of daily shadow and sunshine and the seasonal transformations from leafless trees to full foliage and the bloom and green of gardens and lawns.[9]

The landscape-gardener would have been most gratified to have someone understand his work so well.

In the years between McKenna's two projects, Simonds helped design Nakoma, another new Madison suburb, in 1915.[10] On the southwest corner

CURVING ROAD in Lowell Park, on the Rock River in Dixon, Illinois.   AUTHOR PHOTO

of Lake Monona, Nakoma was less hilly and picturesque that the other new developments, but it too was a subdivision for Madison's upper-middle class. Landscape architect Franz Aust, who had just begun teaching at the university, became involved with Nakoma, laying out streets and lots and developing its planting plan. Aust had studied with Simonds at Michigan and worked with Wilhelm Miller at the University of Illinois Landscape Extension Service.

ROCK RIVER PROJECTS

The small city of Dixon on the Rock River started its park system in 1906, a little later than some other Midwestern cities. Carlotta Lowell donated not only the beautiful hilly site along the river but also paid for an initial report created by the Olmsted Brothers. The property had belonged to her parents,

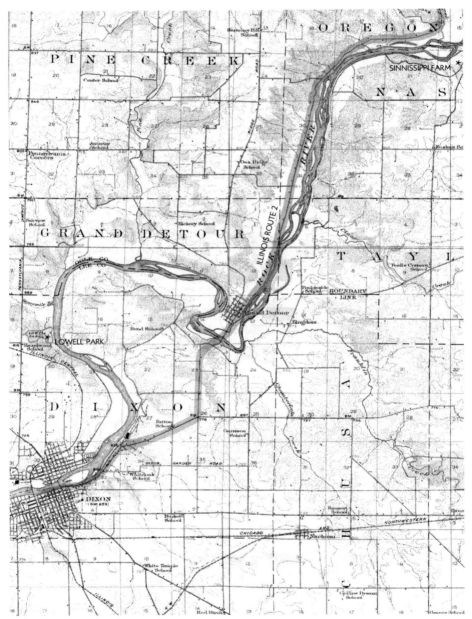

SIMONDS'S WORK along the Rock River area included Lowell Park on the west bank of the river, just north of Dixon; Sinnissppi Farm (shown in the upper right corner of the map), and Illinois Route 2, the scenic highway Simonds helped lay out (the current route of which is outlined in light gray).

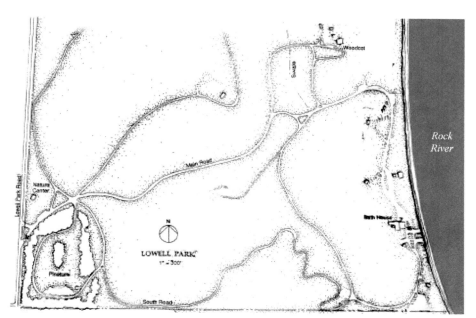

Rock
River

THE INFLUENCE OF TOPOGRAPHY is evident in the meandering roadways Simonds employed in his design for Lowell Park in Dixon, Illinois.

and her mother Josephine, who lived in New York City and knew Olmsted Sr., envisioned it as a park but never developed it as such. The year after her mother's death, Miss Lowell decided to create a park in her parents' memory.[11]

In her transfer of title of the park property to the city, Lowell stipulated that the park not be enclosed, specifically so that it would be free and no one could charge an entrance fee; that there be no zoo; no structures beyond the basic necessities; no intoxicating beverages; and no removal of trees for any purpose other than developing the park itself. John Charles Olmsted came to Dixon to assess the site and project, staying at the home of E.N. Howell, a prosperous local hardware merchant who was a strong supporter of the park. Olmsted's proposal to develop a park plan came in at $3,600, which was beyond the park commissioners' budget. Instead, at the suggestion of the Olmsteds, they decided to find someone who could serve multiple functions. They hired a young man from Pennsylvania named Arthur Comey early in 1908. Comey had had some professional training at Harvard and for the salary of $100 a month was to serve as "superintendent, caretaker, police, tree surgeon and laborer." Given the Olmsted connection with the Harvard landscape program, Comey would have

CHIEF BLACKHAWK, a concrete statue created by Lorado Taft ca. **1910**, on a bluff overlooking the Rock River in what is now Lowden State Park, Oregon, IL; made of poured concrete and about thirty-five feet tall. author photo

seemed an admirable choice. Nonetheless, he spent only a fraction of a $500 donation from Lowell on the plantings for which it was intended, spending most of it on plans for a house. This led to his resignation in less than a year. Comey had created recommendations for the further development of the park, however, and even after accepting the position of superintendent of parks in Utica, New York the following year, he wrote with further thoughts, strongly encouraging the use of native rather showy exotic plantings.

By the end of 1912 the commissioners had worked out a new agreement with O.C. Simonds. His firm would provide planning and "general supervision" of the parks (Dixon now had a second park and was improving other city properties along the river) for $150 year plus expenses. Bryan Lathrop had recommended him, and Simonds was already acquainted with Howell, as well.[12] As Simonds had been landscaping Sinnissippi, the huge estate of the Lowdens just up the river at Oregon since 1900, he would have been a known and respected landscape designer in this region before the Olmsteds had come to Dixon. This perhaps explains the exceedingly low price for his firm's park work—his men could easily include visits here on their trips out to the Lowdens, with Roy West managing both projects. The Dixon park commissioners could also have been familiar with Simonds from his publications, such as his article in the *Chicago Daily Tribune* in April 1901 (see Chapter 6). Here at Lowell Park, Simonds would have been his element, following the natural contours of this hilly site with his curving roads, creating openings in the forest to provide glimpses of the river sparkling below, and making the most of the indigenous limestone.

Once Simonds and his team became involved with the Dixon parks, they developed a lasting relationship, working on a total of eight parks there between 1912 and 1939, according to the "Survey of the historic Dixon Parks" (by which time it was Simonds, West, and Blair, with West at the helm). The citizens of the town, too, continued to be very active in the beautification movement of the first part of the twentieth century, and when a section of the Lincoln Highway was built through Dixon in 1915, the Women's Club planted crabapples along side it.

After Simonds's death, Roy West continued the company's affiliation with the park until the late 1930s, as he did with a number of on-going projects. There was little active management though, perhaps because of a lack of money, and the park became very overgrown. Simonds's son Robert O. Simonds considered consulting in the 1940s but decided against it.[13]

MAIN DRIVEWAY at Sinnissippi Farm.

SINNISSIPPI FARM

One of the most notable of Simonds's projects was that of Mr. and Mrs. Frank Lowden's "Sinnissippi Farm," just south of Oregon, Illinois. He was a lawyer, future governor of Illinois, presidential candidate, and on the cover of *Time* twice; she was Florence, George Pullman's favorite daughter. Pullman had developed the first luxury railroad sleeping car and had made a vast fortune with it. From 1880-84, he had developed the town of Pullman south of Chicago, and had been internationally lauded for providing factories, stores, and residences designed by architect Solon Beman and surrounded by ASLA founder Nathan Barrett's thoughtful and attractive landscaping—at a time when most factory workers lived in squalor. But despite Pullman's good intentions, the inequity between wages and prices during the recession of the early 1890s reached a climax in 1894 when, due to the still-deepening financial depression, Pullman reduced wages but did not reduce workers' rents in his company-owned housing. This, combined with his refusal to negotiate, led to the infamous Pullman strike. The rancor of workers and union organizers continued unabated in the following years, such that he feared his grave and corpse would be desecrated after his death, and so Pullman left explicit instructions for his burial: eight feet deep in a lead-lined casket wrapped in tarpaper, covered with inch-thick asphalt, all enclosed with steel rails, and encased in concrete. When Pullman died in October 1897, Simonds, still Graceland's superintendent, would have been there to oversee his midnight burial (an additional precaution), one of history's most famous interments. Beman designed a towering neo-classical column and exedra for a monument, its elegance and calm belying the turbulence at the time of Pullman's burial. The Lowdens and their descendants are buried at Graceland, behind the Pullman tomb, with modest markers.

With some of Florence's impressive inheritance, she and her husband began purchasing property along the Rock River in 1899, eventually acquiring about 4,800 acres according to their daughter Florence (Miller). They asked Simonds to help develop the property into a 'gentleman's farm,' popular in the early years of the twentieth-century with wealthy families looking for a rural retreat that would pay for itself through farm production. Simonds sited the structures,

HISTORICAL IMAGE of front gates to Sinnissippi Farm with Simonds's massing
of various sizes and species of plants that created a naturalistic transition, blending
gate posts into the landscape.   PHILLIP L. MILLER COLLECTION

CONTEMPORARY IMAGE of the same gates illustrates how the lack of plant massing
and layering makes a less integrated composition.   AUTHOR PHOTO

THE MANSION at Sinnissippi, designed by Irving and Allen Pond.   PHILLIP L. MILLER COLLECTION

THE MANSION at Sinnissippi, with landscape by Simonds and West, ca. 1910.

PHILLIP L. MILLER COLLECTION

FRONT HALLWAY of the Lowden's Pond and Pond-designed mansion at Sinnissippi.

PHILLIP L. MILLER COLLECTION

POND AND POND-designed stable at Sinnissippi Farm.   AUTHOR PHOTO

GARDEN BENCH framing
a landscape picture
at Sinnissippi Farm.

BOTH PHILLIP L. MILLER COLLECTION

A GROUPING of Pond and Pond-designed farm buildings at Sinnissippi Farm.

BIRD'S-EYE VIEW of Sinnissippi Farm.   PHILLIP L. MILLER COLLECTION

AERIAL VIEW of Sinnissippi Farm and the Rock River.   PHILLIP L. MILLER COLLECTION

CURVING ROADS wind through the fields of Sinnissippi Farm. PHILLIP L. MILLER COLLECTION

THE FAMOUS WHITE PINES (*Pinus strobus*) planted by Simonds and West AUTHOR PHOTO
at Sinnissippi Farm.

LAWN AND VISTA of Rock River at Sinnissippi Farm. PHILLIP L. MILLER COLLECTION

CONTEMPORARY VIEW of Rock River from Sinnissippi Farm. AUTHOR PHOTO

laid out roads, and developed tree plantations for forestry experiments.*

The Lowdens hired architects Irving and Allen Pond to design the main house, servants quarters, barns, and other outbuildings. Irving had interned in Chicago with Solon Beman and no doubt already knew Mrs. Lowden. Simonds's Sinnissippi collaboration with the Pond brothers may have been one of several joint ventures. Irving had attended the University of Michigan also and was an old friend of Simonds. In fact, when they both first moved to Chicago, they shared living quarters with Clarence Arey, a third Michigan alumnus. Pond later wrote of these days in his memoirs, describing how Arey met John Edelmann (who had previously worked for both Dankmar Adler and William Le Baron Jenney as a draftsman) and brought him home for conversation. Pond wrote, "At any rate Edelmann discovered Simonds and me. With Simonds he talked transcendentalism of a sort, with me he talked anything . . . "[14] Many years later Chicagoans George C. Cone (of Simonds's office) and Irving K. Pond contributed chapters to *City Residential Land Development: Studies in Planning; Competitive Plans for Subdividing a Typical Quarter-section of Land in the Outskirts of Chicago*, published in 1916. The book summarized the competition entries from 1913 and included as well the name of Arthur Comey, now an associate of Warren Manning's, as taking second prize.

The Lowdens, the Pond brothers, and O.C. and Mattie Simonds were part of Lorado Taft's Eagle's Nest colony, located on a bluff on Walter Heckman's property, above "Ganymede Spring," so named by transcendentalist Margaret Fuller in 1843. She found this area along the Rock River to be "enchanting, beyond any I have ever seen, from its fullness of expression, its bold and impassioned sweetness," as poet Harriet Monroe quoted her in *The House Beautiful* in 1904. The artists and friends of the colony concurred. Taft completed his nearly fifty-feet tall, poured-in-place concrete statue of Chief Blackhawk on the bluff overlooking the river and an unveiling ceremony took place on July 1, 1911, with Frank Lowden presiding. The Ponds designed several structures for the camp and a public library (still standing) for the town of Oregon; Taft sculpted a war memorial for the town square.

The Lowdens' Sinnissippi Farm was featured in the April 1913 issue of *Country Life in America*. Wilhelm Miller described its attributes in "A New Kind

---

* Lowden family correspondence, photographs, and memorabilia indicate that the family thoroughly enjoyed Sinnissippi Farm, and Governor Lowden much preferred life here to the city. Materials courtesy of Phillip Lowden Miller.

A CANOEIST on the Rock River at Sinnissippi Farm, with its two signature pine trees.

of Western Home," in his typical extravagant phrasing as being "Better Than the Fast Life of a Great City—Better than a Mere Summer Dwelling—Better than Spectacular Scenery—Better than a Show Place." He had been "looking for a great country estate in the Middle West that stands for something better than present-day ideals," and he found it, he said, at Sinnissippi Farm. Miller praised its working farms, its ornamental landscapes, and most of all, its scenery. He credited Colonel Lowden's foresight in hiring "first-class landscape gardener" O.C. Simonds, before building. Simonds located all the buildings, placed the roads, and developed "how to approach the house; where visitors can first see it to the best advantage; how much of each building to reveal and how much to hide; how to get the full benefit of sunlight; how to get shelter from the winds; how to manage the vistas, so that each window of the most important rooms has a different picture; how to have stables and other subsidiary buildings near at hand, yet screened."

Amongst all of Sinnissippi's charms, Miller's favorite was its vistas. He devoted nearly a page of text and included several photos to explain just what he meant—how to show a river to best advantage, how to make the most of bluffs, and how to create pictures framed by plantings. Again Simonds received credit for orchestrating many of these views. Miller wrote, "But when a man like Mr. Simonds goes into such woods he knows what are the best things outside and the direction in which they lie. So he will always try to give you a panorama of your own farm." Oddly, Miller ended the article with the faint praise of saying that "While one can always see something to criticize, I have no serious fault to find with Sinnissippi Farm." His heart, however, "crave[d] more of the Western element or local color," and referred the reader to his companion article in the same issue on "How to Heighten Western Color." The gist of this piece was that at least ninety percent of the plants in landscapes ought to be local and indigenous species, and that Sinnissippi Farm was exceptional for its use of native plants—despite Miller claiming that to be its one weakness. He was pleased with the Lowdens' massive white pine plantings over the past several years, as he found the typical Midwestern scene lacking in evergreens.

A couple of years earlier Roy West had sent Lowden a list of evergreens planted at the farm from 1902 to 1910—a total of 128,800 that included red, white, Austrian and dwarf mountain pines, larches (deciduous, but coniferous, and included in the count), and "various kinds of evergreen." The Lowdens especially loved the white pine (*Pinus strobus*) and continued to plant them until World War I, according to their daughter Florence Miller. Just two miles west of Sinnissippi, in Mount Morris, Simonds and others had discovered around 1900 what they considered to be the southern-most stand of white pine in the country and the residents of Ogle County had lobbied the state legislature to purchase the property in 1903. The measure was vetoed, and White Pines State Park was not established until 1927; the trees flourished on the sandy soils of Sinnissippi Farm for those intervening twenty-four years, helping to maintain the affiliation between *Pinus strobus* and Ogle County.

Simonds contributed to a number of other projects in the Rock River area, among them Howell's residence in Dixon (seventeen miles south of Oregon), which he featured in photographs in *Landscape-Gardening*. Simonds instructed highway engineers in laying out Illinois Route 2 along the west side of the Rock River from Dixon up to Byron, showing them how to best take advantage of the river views and hilltop vistas, creating one of the first scenic highways in America.

PRESIDENT OF THE ASLA

Simonds served as the president of ASLA 1913-1914, the first Midwesterner to do so. At the February 1913 meeting, he "gave an interesting talk on topics of general interest and Mr. Nolen spoke on the 'City Planning Committee.'"[15]* The monthly meeting for May was held in Chicago, the organization's first meeting in that city—the ASLA was very much oriented to east coast practitioners. Gathering at the Hotel LaSalle, members attending included Simonds, Frank Button, Aubrey Tealdi, and Svend Lollesgaard of O.C. Simonds and Company, as well as Warren Manning, John Nolen, and John Charles Olmsted. There were two guest speakers that evening: W.M.R. French, Director of the Art Institute of Chicago, who gave a talk on his work with H.W.S. Cleveland (who had died in 1900), and Wilhelm Miller, now of the University of Illinois, who explained what the Extension Service was doing in the field of landscape-gardening.[16]

At the first meeting of 1914, Simonds spoke on extension work in Illinois,

---

* John Nolen was a landscape architect and city planner from Boston. He re-designed some of the Madison parks immediately after Simonds's affiliation ended, and devised a comprehensive plan for the city, in a formal Beaux-Arts style reminiscent of Burnham's recently published plan of Chicago.

Wisconsin, and Michigan. The Smith-Lever Act of that year created the extension service, a result in part from Bailey's Country Life Commission report. Rural improvement was a popular topic in the Midwest at this time but it may have been somewhat more of a novelty for landscape architects from the east, where land-grant colleges did not have the same significance. Simonds also addressed the need for a common name for their profession, with his own preference of course being "landscape-gardener."[17] During Simonds's tenure as president, the ASLA was actively involved with the many other civic improvement organizations flourishing at the time. One joint meeting alone, planned in June 1914, involved the American Civic Association, the American Forestry Association, the American Scenic and Historic Preservation Society, the National Conservation Congress, the National Housing Association, and the Playground and Recreational Association of America.

By autumn of that year, Warren Manning was elected the new ASLA president and the ASLA Executive Committee became involved with the American Institute of Architects' commission on "plan and scope for the Lincoln Highway." There were very few trans-continental highways in 1914, and care was taken to plan this one well. Correspondence between Manning and A.R. Pardington, vice-president of the Lincoln Highway Association, indicates the strong interest in the project from landscape designers in Illinois. Many of the civic organizations the ASLA had worked with over the years were equally enthusiastic. Pardington was in Chicago to meet with the General Federation of Women's Clubs of America on November 21, 1914. Simonds was to have been the ASLA representative at the meeting, but, as Pardington wrote to Manning the following week, "We were sorry indeed that Mr. Simmonds [sic] was unable to be present in order that your Society might have been represented in each step." Jens Jensen, as President of Friends of our Native Landscape, and Professor Wilhelm Miller, University of Illinois, did attend, though, and "Either one of these gentlemen stand high, and both of them have contributed much effort to the Society's work already."[18]

Miller and landscape architect Franz Aust (who would shortly leave the University of Illinois for the University of Wisconsin) had developed a draft of what they called the "Lincoln Planting Motive: A Scheme for Beautifying Any or All the Four Roadside Projects Known as the Lincoln Way" that summer. The ten-page document analogized their approach to the roadway designs to Wagner's approach to a grand opera, using planting units as leit-motives (borrowed, perhaps, from Jensen's use of Mendelssohn's *Spring Song* motif for the waterfall at the Garfield Park Conservatory). Each indigenous plant and each native planting group would express some aspect of Lincoln's character. For example, the white oak (*Quercus alba*) would express Lincoln's national appeal, as well as symbolize his "far-sighted ideals since the white oak cannot be transplanted in large sizes," but had to be grown from seed in its intended location. The red cedar (*Juniperus virginiana*) would "suggest that mellowness which we feel in Lincoln's character." Miller and Aust recommended about a dozen trees and shrubs, describing the physical attributes of the plant and then comparing it to Lincoln's character in a similar manner. Certain sections of the highway were to have Kentucky plants, those that would have been familiar to Lincoln's family during its years there.* They were aware that this approach to highway planting was walking a fine line, and looked to outside editorial assistance. "In all such matters it is easy to carry analogy too far and provoke ridicule or contempt; therefore the Lincoln motive should be submitted privately to many people for criticism before it is published, an account of it should be written by a firm and sure hand and accompanied with the best possible illustrations."[19] Miller's enthusiasm continued to expand, until his creation of the "Prairie Spirit in Landscape Gardening" in 1915 crossed the fine line (see The Prairie Becomes a Style, below). How much further involvement Simonds had with the project is unknown.

INDIAN HILL CLUB

Throughout his career Simonds worked on several golf clubs, including Chicago Golf and the Glen View Club, already discussed. In 1913-14 he consulted on the development of a new club initially called the Winnetka Country Club, but changed by 1914 to the Indian Hill Club. At first "the famous landscape architect" Simonds was asked to "criticize the plans made by golf architect H. H. Barker," and "to consider the problem of landscaping the additional lots which were for sale" around the club's perimeter. He also took on the task of designing a drain tile system because, unlike the Glen View

---

* This is the same theme that Jens Jensen will use at the Lincoln Memorial Garden in Springfield in the 1940s. He will also be responsible for the design and planting of the "Ideal Section" of the Lincoln Highway outside of Dyer, Indiana.

Club about four miles southwest, this land along the Skokie marsh was so low and flat it flooded regularly. As part of this system, he created or expanded an existing pond to absorb the overflow.[20]

Simonds's 1914 plan shows tree and shrub placement on adjoining residential lots, as well as on the golf course proper. In his typical rendering style, the vegetation is portrayed as miniature cabbage roses on the plan. No planting list is attached and many areas seem rather sparse compared to other Simonds designs. As with most of his projects, there are no records indicating the duration of his involvement with this landscape. There is, however, a wonderful illustration of his subdivision work around the golf course in his 1920 book *Landscape-Gardening*, on page 123.

Daniel Burnham and Edward Bennett's *magnum opus*, *The Plan of Chicago*, was published in 1909 amidst the nation-wide city planning movement of the Progressive era. It was a natural shift for many architects and landscape designers to broaden their businesses to include large-scale design. O.C. Simonds and Company was already designing subdivisions, and continued to do so throughout its life, although it was never a focus of the firm. City planning quickly became its own profession, with organizations and texts and standards immediately following.

KINCAID, ILLINOIS: THE COALECTRIC CITY

Francis S. Peabody (Houghteling's Winnetka neighbor and business associate) founded the town of Kincaid in 1913, adjacent to his Peabody Coal Company mines in central Illinois.[21] He had acquired mineral rights to 40,000 acres in that region ten years earlier, for the mining of bituminous coal. His vision was of "a new city, the spotless, the electric town," and he had begun discretely acquiring property there through the services of James Kincaid of Springfield (for whom the town was named). Peabody intended to start the town with 6,000 residents—quite a jump for a town that currently had only one house that doubled as the post office. His plan was to "erect an immense electric plant in the heart of the Illinois coal field, at the very mouth of the mine. Bringing the electric plant to the coal instead of shipping the coal long distances to the plant. Supplying light, heat and power to almost numberless towns and villages in Illinois."

SPRINGFIELD ROAD

IL 104

CHICAGO & ILLINOIS MIDLAND R.R.

MODERN HIGHWAY

RESIDENTIAL

SCHOOL

BUSINESS DISTRICT

RESIDENTIAL

RAIL DEPOT

CHICAGO

KINCAID

ST. LOUIS

CHANGE IN ELEVATION	CITY PARK SURROUNDED BY STREETS	BRIDGE OVER CREEK OR RIVER	RAILROAD CREEK DAM AND LAKE
STREET INTERSECTION AND ALLEY	RAILROAD STATION	HIGHWAY SPLITS FROM O.C.'S DESIGN	TRIANGLE SPLIT INTERSECTION

104

THE COALECTRIC CITY was one of several towns in the Midwest that Simonds designed.

South Fork of the Sangamon River

KINCAID LAND ASSOCIATION
(GARDEN PLOTS AVAILABLE
FOR RESIDENTS)

SPRINGFIELD STREET

TAYLORVILLE STREET

OAL MINE NO. 7

MODERN HIGHWAY IL 104

TAYLORVILLE ROAD

N

W. M. WALKER

Simonds platted the 640-acre town site, creating curved streets and irregularly shaped lots, with civil engineers Alvord and Burdick supervising construction.[22] Sixty acres of bottomland along the river were reserved for garden plots for miners so inclined.* Architect George Maher designed five commercial structures, including the Chicago & Illinois Midland Railroad depot, and eighty-five residences, using simple, white enameled brick facades; the commercial buildings and a few homes were completed by 1914.[23] The 6,000 residents never materialized, nor did the shining future the Kincaid publicity had promised when it was incorporated in 1915. Several mines continued to operate successfully for several more decades, until Mine #7 and #8 closed in the 1950s.

THE PRAIRIE BECOMES A STYLE

Wilhelm Miller, formerly Bailey's assistant at Cornell and now editor of *Country Life in America*, had become a booster of the naturalistic landscape designs of Simonds, Jensen, architect Walter Burley Griffin, and a few other Midwesterners. He promoted their work heavily in *CLiA*. Bailey's, and subsequently Miller's, involvement with rural beautification evolved into work with the Country Life movement. President Theodore Roosevelt asked Bailey in 1908 to head a Country Life Commission to find out what life was like for rural Americans. In part he wanted to know what farming families needed to make living in the country fulfilling enough for them to stay down on the farm. Bailey continued this work under President Taft and the Commission released its findings in 1909 (interestingly, the same year as Burnham's city plan) as *Report of the Country Life Commission: special message from the President of the United States transmitting the report of the Country Life Commission*. Bailey continued this research and published *The Country Life Movement* in 1911 (with The Macmillan Company, which would later publish his Rural Science Series). Bailey began this book "TO Charles W. Garfield [none other than Simonds's cousin], Seer of Visions, Prophet of a Better Country Life, I dedicate this budget of opinions." Although Bailey, Garfield, and Simonds may not have

---

* Among the remnants of Simonds's papers held by the family are a number of photographs, professionally taken in 1910, and received from the Olmsted Brothers, of the backyards of National Cash Register factory workers in Dayton, Ohio. They had held a garden competition and used the photos for judging. It would seem Simonds was studying these for similar ideas in his own projects. According to Thomas Schlereth in *Victorian America: Transformations in Everyday Life* (Longman, 1997), the Olmsteds worked with L.H. Bailey in planning model gardens for 2,500 workers in Dayton, with the intention of preventing labor agitation.

collaborated on projects during the 1910s, individually they continued to work towards similar goals of a high standard of living for farmers, an aesthetically pleasing countryside, and appreciation and conservation of our natural resources.

Within a year of the book's release, his passion for this work (and the passage of the Smith-Lever Act) led Miller to accept a job as "Head of Division of Landscape Extension" at the University of Illinois (under Simonds's friend Dean Eugene Davenport). In this position he traveled and lectured throughout the state and published circulars under the auspices of the Agricultural Experiment Station and the Department of Horticulture (his dissertation at Cornell dealt with dahlias). Miller hybridized the idea of rural beautification with the naturalistic landscape-gardening style and the use of native prairie plants into something he eventually named "the prairie spirit" and "the prairie style." Over the few years of his employment at the university he focused more and more on how things were done in Illinois. Judging from responses to his campaign, it appears to have been a one-man mission, but his term "prairie style" would have long-lasting effect into the twentieth-first century.

In Miller's 1914 circular, *The "Illinois Way" of Beautifying the Farm*, he gave several directives for improving rural scenery, most of them based on principles of landscape painting similar to those that Simonds had employed for more than thirty years. Now Miller called these precepts the "Illinois Way"—including the "'Illinois Way' of Planting a Lawn," the "'Illinois Way' of Sheltering Livestock," and the "'Illinois Way' of Screening Unsightly Objects."[24] He was unstinting in his praise of the men who "no longer fear or despise the prairie; they love it and are opening our eyes to its true wonder and beauty." Many belonged to the Cliff Dweller's Club and believed in "local color." He listed sculptor Lorado Taft, writer Hamlin Garland, architects Louis Sullivan and Frank Lloyd Wright, and landscape-gardeners O.C. Simonds and Jens Jensen as the primary examples.

By the following year, Miller had developed his Illinois concepts further and published *The Prairie Spirit in Landscape Gardening*.[25] This circular, like the previous one, was offered "Free to anyone in Illinois who will sign a promise to do some permanent ornamental planting with a year." In it, he expanded upon earlier ideas, tying Midwestern architecture and landscape design together, perhaps the first writer to do so. Miller thought the predominant feature was horizontality and began using the word "stratified" to describe characteristics he thought were specific to Illinois prairies, applying it to almost anything that had a horizontal aspect.* Although Miller's writing was energetic and stimulating, and some writers and designers adopted his terms and ideas, not everyone was swept along.

Early in 1915 Miller sent two questionnaires to people on his list of "local color" proponents. One included "Two Definitions" for his terms "Prairie Style of Architecture" and "Prairie Style of Landscape Gardening" (the third revision of terms per Miller).[26] The other form queried his respondents regarding the history of the term "Prairie School," and asked whether or not they would sign their names to accept the phrase. Frank Lloyd Wright wrote back saying he was "unwilling to wear any tag which will identify me with any sect or system." Miller had positioned Louis Sullivan as the progenitor of this "school" of architecture and Wright rebutted that Sullivan could not "figure in any form other than grotesque as the founder of a 'Prairie School of Architecture,'" and that as far as he knew, Sullivan had never found the prairie to be an influence. Neither, of course, had Simonds, whose work showed quite clearly that he felt the same way those early pioneers in Iowa did about the vast open plains (see Chapter 3) and did his best to plant trees, shrubs, and vines to tie buildings into the land, not leaving them "naked and defenseless," as he described buildings out on the prairies.[27]

Resolute, Miller submitted most of his new publication, including proposed photographs and captions, to Simonds for suggestions before going to press. Receiving the package on July 19, Simonds wrote a six-page response the next day, and returned it all to Miller by express. He began by saying "The 'Prairie Spirit' and 'Prairie Style' do not appeal to me as to some." "Boasting" was not Simonds's way. He went on to give specific criticism or praise for each of the sections and photographs. He did not get enthused about the "Illinois Way," saying that "I think I have a stronger feeling for Michigan than for any other state." Regarding plants, "Prairie Rose is a suitable and appropriate name . . . why should we call it the 'Illinois Rose?'"[28]

Although Simonds found the illustrations of Jensen's work "very satisfying," (Miller jotted on the letter, "generous praise to a rival") he thought Miller's attempt to connect Jensen's planting design in the Garfield Park [Chicago] Conservatory "with the prairie . . . rather far fetched. It is beautiful and well done, but the lessons from nature which would inspire it might have been learned in a mountainous region."

---

* The word "stratified" means "in layers'" and most often describes sedimentary rock or a method of germinating seed. When Simonds pointed out that some of the plants Miller called "stratified" did not in fact branch horizontally, Miller responded that they were "stratified when old." (Simonds to Miller, July 20, 1915).

Simonds was not comfortable with Miller's Illinois obsession. "As I read over your manuscript, I sometimes wonder if you do not try to make facts fit a theory rather than theory fit the facts." Miller did not think so. He noted on the letter (although not in his reply to Simonds), "But these combinations are Nature's own, as cited by Cowles in the Plant Societies of Chicago!" Simonds just did "not yet feel that here is a distinct 'Prairie Style.'" His own approach was to "simply do that which . . . will make the most beautiful effect."[29]

Despite these reservations, however, Simonds ended his letter apologizing for not being able to spend more time reviewing the material Miller had sent. He also "hope[d] that my skepticism regarding the 'Prairie Style' will not give you any offense. I fully approve of the spirit of your work and believe it will be of great benefit to the state."

Miller wrote back thanking Simonds for his comments, taking into account "that your point of view about the 'Prairie Style' is very conservative," and while he worked on his circular, "felt the restraining influence of Mr. Lathrop [who had expressed his reservations on the subject as well] and yourself." "Mr. Jensen's criticisms," on the other hand were "more radical, and show[ed] more feeling." Miller found Simonds's comments "couched in such amiable and gentle spirit that I cannot possibly take any offence." He was deeply satisfied with Simonds's closing remark about the benefit of his work.

As well he should have been. The big boys on the east coast, never fanciers of Simonds's and Jensen's low-key, follow-what-nature-does approach, found Miller's writings laughable, referring to him in a review of *The Prairie Spirit* as the "Billy Sunday of horticulture." * Miller, in a letter to Jensen, warned him of "the polar express" from Harvard when the chilly review arrived. Miller left the university and Illinois the following year to establish a private design practice in Michigan, and the "Prairie Style" issue subsided for the time being.

In the 1960s Chicago preservation architect and Wilbert Hasbrouck began publishing a journal called *The Prairie School Review*, which featured photographs and essays about the work of the Midwestern architects of the early twentieth-century. They had changed the face of design from Victorian and historic revival styles by creating buildings whose exteriors reflected the open, flowing spaces of their interiors. Frank Lloyd Wright, Walter Burley

---

* Sunday had been a famous baseball player with the Chicago Whitestockings who underwent a conversion experience in 1886 at the Pacific Garden Mission in Chicago and subsequently became a nationally known evangelist during the great age of revivals.

Griffin, Dwight Perkins, and a dozen or so of their peers were the subjects. In 1972, H. Allen Brooks published his now-classic study, *The Prairie School: Frank Lloyd Wright and His Midwest Contemporaries*. With this renewed interest, University of Chicago art history student Mara Gelbloom wrote a master's paper in 1974 entitled "Ossian Cole Simonds: 'The Prairie Spirit in Landscape Gardening.'" It was published in *The Prairie School Review* two years later, the only significant essay on Simonds since his death more than forty years earlier. It also strengthened interest in the Prairie School renaissance begun by Hasbrouck's journal and Brooks's book. +

CHAPTER EIGHT ENDNOTES

[1] Norman K. Risjord, *Madison's Highlands A Community with a Land Ethic* (Madison: The Highlands Association, 1988). WHT.

[2] Jon Kollitz, "The Highlands: A Landscape History" (unpublished paper, Department of Landscape Architecture, University of Wisconsin-Madison, 1988), WHT.

[3] Risjord.

[4] Ibid.

[5] Elizabeth Warner Risser, unpublished biography of her father, Ernest N. Warner, 1930. Courtesy of Susan O. Haswell.

[6] College Hills advertisement, Village of Shorewood Hills archives. Thank you to Professor Thomas Brock, Village of Shorewood Hills historian, for access to archival materials.

[7] Marcia Nickels McKenna, "The Birth of College Hills," in *The Story of Shorewood Hills* (Shorewood Hills Village Board, 1958), 7 & 14.

[8] Thomas Brock, unpublished history of Shorewood Hills. Courtesy of Dr. Brock.

+ While presenting well-researched background information about landscape-gardening, Gelbloom seems to have accepted Miller's thesis that Simonds based his style of landscape design on the horizontality and open spaces of the prairie, as well as Miller's description of Simonds's "sylvan rooms." I disagree with this assessment, as I do with her conclusion, based on her analysis of the plans for the Quincy Parks from 1895 to 1913, that in general he increased his use of native plants over the years. Research into several other sites does not confirm this trend. Gelbloom also credited Simonds with designing twenty-eight sites in Winnetka (which he may well have done), but does not cite a source for this information or enumerate the sites. Although Gelbloom's article provided excellent information, it applied the "Prairie Spirit" label to Simonds's work despite his own rejection of the term and the actuality of his designs. Some essay writers over the past few decades have continued to do the same.

[9] McKenna, 14.

[10] Tricia Canaday, "The Story of Nakoma" (unpublished paper, Department of Landscape Architecture, University of Wisconsin-Madison, 1992), WHT.

[11] The Lowell Park history material can be found in "Survey of Dixon Parks; Dixon, Illinois;" IHPA Project No. 17-90-50102.509, Illinois Historic Preservation Agency; prepared by Dean Scheaffer, Landscape Architect; November 1990 and September 1991.

[12] Ibid.

[13] Author's conversation with Robert C. Simonds (son of Robert O.), Pier Cove, Michigan, July 1997.

[14] Quoted in David Van Zanten, "Sullivan to 1890," in *Louis Sullivan: The Function of Ornament*, ed. by Wim de Wit, St. Louis Art Museum, 1986, 34.

[15] *Transactions, 1909-1921,* American Society of Landscape Architects, February 18, 1913.

[16] Ibid., May 8, 1913.

[17] Ibid., January 13, 1914.

[18] Manning to the ASLA Executive Committee, n/d (late November 1914), Records of the American Society of Landscape Architects, Manuscript Division, Library of Congress.

[19] Wilhelm Miller and Franz Aust, "Lincoln Planting Motive," July 30, 1914. Records of the American Society of Landscape Architects, Manuscript Division, Library of Congress.

[20] Original drainage plan in the greenkeeper's office at Indian Hill Club. According to David Schlagetter in conversation with the author July 1997, he had found the plan in a ditch on the golf course. He reclaimed it and had it restored.

[21] *History of Christian County, 1880-1968.* Courtesy of Wilda Q. Cooper, former editor of the *Taylorville Breeze-Courier*. Thank you to Christopher Vernon for bringing Kincaid to my attention.

[22] John S. Garner, "The Garden City and Planned Industrial Suburbs: Housing and Planning on the Eve of World War I," in *From Tenements to the Taylor Homes: In Search of an Urban Housing Policy in Twentieth-Century America*, Bauman, Biles, and Szylvia, eds., Pennsylvania State University Press, 47-forward.

[23] "Creating a Model Town," *George W. Maher Quarterly* 1 (April-June 1995), 1-11; and "Kincaid—the 'Coal-Electric City' by Wilda Q. Coper, *Taylorville Breeze-Courier*, n/d. Courtesy of Wilda Q. Cooper.

[24] Wilhelm Miller, *The "Illinois Way" of Beautifying the Farm*, Circular 170 of the Agricultural Experiment Station (Urbana: University of Illinois, Department

of Horticulture, 1914), 1, 3, 4.

[25] Wilhelm Miller, *The Prairie Spirit in Landscape Gardening*, Circular 184 of the Agricultural Experiment Station (Urbana: University of Illinois, Department of Horticulture, 1915).

[26] Correspondence, Department of Horticulture, University Archives, University of Illinois.

[27] Simonds, *Landscape-Gardening*.

[28] Simonds to Miller, University Archives, University of Illinois.

[29] Ibid.

chapter 9

COLLABORATION
WITH TWO PROMINENT CLIENTS:
MORTON AND NOYES

1915-1925

Douglas Fir

DIGGING LAKE MARMO at the Morton Arboretum.　　　STERLING MORTON LIBRARY

WORKING WITH NOYES

L aVerne W. Noyes (1849-1919) was a self-made man, an inventor, and the founder and president of the Chicago Aermotor Company, the world's largest manufacturer of windmills at the turn of the century.[1] Noyes and his business partner perfected the steel-blade windmill in the 1880s, to the derision of the traditional wooden mill manufacturers; Noyes had the last laugh. By 1890 the steel mills began to take over the market because they cost a fraction of wooden ones, were smaller, lighter, far more efficient, and more adjustable. To keep up with his expanding business, Noyes built a two-acre factory in Chicago at Rockwell and Twelfth Street and was given a place of honor in the windmill exhibit at the World's Columbian Exposition in 1893.

He and Simonds first worked together in 1907 when Noyes and his wife Ida donated a new $18,000 residence cottage to the Illinois Industrial School for Girls. The school relocated from Evanston to a forty-acre farm in Park Ridge and Simonds was involved in planning its new campus.[*] When Ida died five years later, Noyes privately published a book of her poetry; he and Simonds knew each other well enough by then that he gave a copy to Simonds.[2] Ida E. Smith Noyes (1853-1912) was an unusual woman for her time. By all accounts she was exceptionally bright, finishing high school two years early and winning admittance to Iowa State Agricultural College at seventeen by petitioning the school president directly. She and LaVerne met while students there, marrying a few years later. Eventually they moved to Batavia, Illinois, and then to Chicago to accommodate their expanding business. The Noyeses had no children, and as their fortune grew, Ida enrolled in the School of the Art Institute of Chicago to study painting and photography, and her husband became a governing life-member. An independent spirit, Ida began to travel by herself, first studying painting in Paris for nineteen months and then making several European journeys throughout the years. She took up poetry in the early twentieth-century, making something of a name for herself in cultural circles in Chicago.

As well as publishing Ida's work, Noyes also created two substantial

---

[*] Holabird and Roche designed several buildings for the school, which received endowments from the Julius Rosenwalds, Potter Palmers, George Strauts, and James Pattens (another Simonds client in Evanston), as well as from the Noyes. (Bruegmann, Vol. 1, 336-37.)

memorials in her honor. He donated $25,000 to Fourth Presbyterian Church on Michigan Avenue (about a mile south of their home on Lake Shore Drive) to build the cloister connecting the church and the "manse." He further donated about $500,000 that year to the University of Chicago to build a women's social center in the University's preferred collegiate Gothic style. Across Woodlawn Avenue from the eventual site of Rockefeller Chapel, the structure faced the Midway Plaisance at the south end (at the time) of the campus. Noyes asked Simonds to design a plan for the small front and back areas, giving him another opportunity to utilize his design approach on the campus. Ida Noyes Hall opened in 1916. While on site, the two men also proposed a re-design of the Plaisance based on Olmsted and Vaux's original 1871 plan and Burnham's 1909 plan. The canal shown in the two earlier versions was a long, sunken, formal waterway, flowing from the lagoon in Washington Park on the west down the Midway east to the lagoons in Jackson Park.[3] In their version, however, rather than a canal, they drew a lake with irregular boundaries, from two hundred to four hundred feet wide, and fully visible from the surrounding streets. They submitted their plans that April to the University of Chicago Board of Trustees, which turned the matter over to the Committee on Buildings and Grounds.[4] Neither the board nor the committee were enthused and the following year reported that "an informal conference with the South Park Commission (the actual owner of the property) reveals that there is little likelihood of the adoption of Mr. O.C. Simonds' plan for the improvement of the Midway Plaisance." They moved to cease "further consideration" of the matter.[5]

Noyes also hired the landscape-gardener to accompany him to Iowa State University, his alma mater, to re-design parts of the campus in 1915. Donating money and time to Iowa State was a labor of love. Noyes, who graduated in 1872, had worked with the school's first president, Adonijah S. Welch, on his campus-beautification plan. Welch, like Lathrop in Chicago those same years, had cultivated a passion for pastoral landscapes. Iowa Agricultural College, as it was called then, was brand new, its one building standing alone on the barren, wind-swept plains, in need of a little campus planting. At the time the school required three hours of work daily from its students; Welch had a group of student workers dig, haul, and plant. Noyes's expertise transplanting trees was duly appreciated and he was made a foreman. Subsequent administrators, though, did not share Welch's vision, and his landscape was never completed.

His goal had so impressed young Noyes, however, that, forty-five years later when in a position to help, he went back to revitalize Welch's plans, bringing, at his own expense, his landscape designer with him. Iowa State bestowed on him an honorary Doctor of Engineering while he was there.[6]

Once again, as at Lowell Park and the University of Chicago, John Charles Olmsted was also on the scene. Hired in 1906, Olmsted visited the campus to assess the site. His twelve-page report at least convinced the trustees not to install the electric railway across the grounds as they had planned; he compared the idea to the open sewers of New Orleans and the board got the message. He also thought that the engineering and main buildings were situated in too casual a fashion to match their formal style. That was as far as Olmsted's involvement went, but, as the campus grew, the school did use his idea of making a strong symmetrical axis to organize further building, with a large square quad-like courtyard.[7]

Most of Simonds's work on the Iowa campus was concentrated at the southwest corner. At his client's request, he designed a small lake, to be modestly called "Lake LaVerne," with wooded areas of small trees and shrubs. Rather than making drawings for others to follow, Simonds, as was his preference, personally directed the construction and planting. He was also responsible for softening the look of the formal buildings around the square grass courtyard by adding vines, foundation plantings, and larch trees.[8] Simonds worked with L.H. Pammel, Professor of Botany, in acquiring species that interested his students and in finding inexpensive plant labels.[9] He continued to advise on campus landscape matters until 1923 but, less than ten years later, the lake was reworked and the masses of vegetation were removed, under the direction of P.H. Elwood, Jr.[*]

With no direct heirs, Noyes used his fortune and his time for an ever-growing number of philanthropic projects, especially after Ida's death. When he died in 1919, he bequeathed $2,500,000 to an eponymous scholarship fund for World War I veterans and their direct descendents, to be dispersed among fifty different colleges and universities, including the University of Chicago, Iowa State, and Lewis Institute.[10] LaVerne and Ida were interred at Graceland Cemetery, on a grassy hill overlooking Lake Willowmere.

---

[*] Elwood was a younger ASLA member responsible for producing the first photographic record of works of ASLA members in 1924; he later became the chairman of the ISU Department of Landscape Architecture.

SIMONDS'S CAREER AND HIS MENTOR BRYAN LATHROP

While Simonds was in the midst of these projects, his mentor Bryan Lathrop died on May 13,1916. Lathrop, and later his wife Helen, were buried at Graceland. They could have had any spot in the cemetery; they chose a plot on top of the ridge of the Graceland spit that runs north and south through the site. For markers, nothing more than simple flat stones with their names and life dates, made of a special granite from the east coast. For ninety years after Bryan's death, their plot had a large grassy lawn with a simple shrub boundary; the cemetery has since subdivided the area and sold off several new plots. Nonetheless, the elegant, less-is-more landscape of the Lathrops' graves is in tact. Simonds treasured his relationship with Lathrop for the rest of his life, continuing to follow the landscape precepts he had learned from him in the early days at Graceland. He often quoted or mentioned Lathrop in his writings, and in an interview when he was seventy-five, recalled his mentor's kind and cultured demeanor.[11] When *Landscape-Gardening* was published in 1920, Simonds began the book "Dedicated to the memory of BRYAN LATHROP to whom all fine arts made a strong appeal and whose influence has been felt in each page of this volume and in all the professional work of the author." He included two of Lathrop's pieces on landscape-gardening in the appendix. They had worked together for thirty-eight years. (See chapter 12 on the Lathrops and Bryans for further information.)

WORLD WAR I YEARS

The two eldest Simonds sons, Herbert and Marshall, both served overseas during the war. These must have been difficult years for the family, with great joy and relief when both men returned home from the European conflict unharmed. Herbert had no interest in his father's work, but Marshall became a landscape architect and later worked as the park superintendent for the Green Bay, Wisconsin park system. Simonds *père* continued his trips to Ann Arbor as a non-resident lecturer in the Department of Landscape Design. George Cone, from Simonds's office, was teaching there by now as well, and Aubrey Tealdi had been promoted from instructor to assistant professor. During this time, Simonds visited clients in Grand Rapids and Madison and, in October of 1918, accompanied by his wife, went out to the Glen View Club again to plan a setting for a new fountain and sculpture.[12] Club member E.S. Jackman commissioned sculptor Andrew O'Connor to create a statue of a group of four Boy Scouts and their dog as a memorial to Theodore Roosevelt, who had been a supporter of the Scouts. Jackman donated the piece to the club. Holabird and Roche designed the base and a fountain in front of it; Simonds created the setting and devised a planting plan.[13]

INTERNATIONAL GARDEN CLUB

The *International Garden Club* carried two articles by Simonds in 1918. He illustrated the first, "Landscape Gardening in its Relation to Roadside Planting," with a photograph of "An English Lane," lined with shrubs and trees, slowly curving around out of sight, inviting the pedestrian or rider to follow. On the next page, there was a picture of Wildwood Drive in Graceland Cemetery, which was remarkably similar to the English road. At the end of that issue, in "Notes and News," Simonds submitted a short introduction to Bryan Lathrop's article, "A Plea for Landscape Gardening."[14] In a subsequent edition he wrote about the "Care of Woods and Ravines," urging restraint in raking leaves from the woods and offering a glimpse into the source of his motivation for naturalistic design:

> Doubtless nearly everyone remembers the pleasure of a day spent
> in the woods. The first wild flowers, the new leaves, the element
> of mystery, the chances to make new discoveries and the perfect
> freedom, give more pleasure than is usually received from a visit to
> the most cultivated and well-cared-for park.[15]

Simonds maintained that ravines were especially sensitive to the removal of leaf litter, and he listed eight management considerations. Noting that "brown leaves are not objectionable in appearance," he mentioned Hamerton's belief that an oak leaf was the best subject for practice drawing.

The next year (1919) Simonds was on the road again, traveling to Ames, Omaha, Springfield, and Dixon. In April he went to Lansing, perhaps to design the state capitol grounds,[16] and in May on to Akron. Another trip west in November took him to Dixon for the third time that year, and to near-by Grand Detour.*

LANDSCAPE-GARDENING

After years of writing articles and booklets, lecturing and educating, Simonds wrote his only full-length book. *Landscape-Gardening*, as he simply called it, was published by Macmillan in 1920, part of the "Rural Science" series edited by his long-time colleague L.H. Bailey. Three-hundred thirty-one pages long, it covered such topics as "The Saving of Natural Features and Resources," "Land," "Planting Materials," "Water," "Home Ground," and "Landscape-Gardening for Arid and Semi-Arid Regions." In the first chapter, "The Aims of Landscape-Gardening," Simonds began by saying "The purpose of this book is to help make our country more beautiful."[17] Not only was the landscape-gardener called upon to achieve that goal by actively working on "home grounds, roadsides, river banks, [and] parks," but also he must "open . . . the eyes of those who fail to see such beauty as already exists."

For his first illustration, Simonds chose a photograph of a landscape painter at work under a bridge. (The frontispiece of the book was a copy of an old painting of Mount Vernon with its lawn rolling gently down towards the Potomac.) The picture itself resembled a landscape painting, and recalled Constable's statement that for him, "art could be found under every bridge."[18] Simonds's text compared the art of landscape-gardening to that of the landscape painter very directly:

> His canvas, the background for his work is the sky . . . Nature
> indeed is a most helpful and willing partner in all the real work of
> a landscape-gardener, and also his best teacher . . . The landscape-
> gardener . . . must wait years for the picture he conceives to develop
> fully.[19]

He directly explained his preference for the title of "landscape-gardener" over

---

* Holabird and Roche designed a house for E.J. Brundage, Attorney General of Illinois, at Babson Farms in Grand Detour. (Bruegmann, Vol.1, #960.) There is no mention of Simonds, but it is possible that his trip there in 1919 included a visit with Brundage; Grand Detour is a tiny village.

that of "landscape architect," stating

> The work of the landscape-gardener is largely with things that are alive, growing, changing. As Bryan Lathrop has said, 'It is not the name so much as the idea behind it which is objectionable.' To use the word 'architect' tends to take away that freedom and gracefulness that should go with the development of beautiful landscapes.[20]

The landscape-gardener needed to have "a love and appreciation of natural beauty." He had to be conversant in world history, astronomy, geology, physiography [physical geography], botany, zoology, and chemistry. He needed not only to be skilled in construction but at the same time possess artistic talent. In addition, he ought to be willing to serve the betterment of humanity, and while he should be paid equal to other men in professions, Simonds believed that the personal satisfaction derived from creating beautiful landscapes, being out-of-doors, and making spaces for pleasant and convenient living meant that "no [other] profession can vie with this new art."[21]

The book received good reviews from a number sources and Simonds later sent several of them from the *London Times*, *The Gardener's Chronicle* (also a British publication), and some unnamed American periodicals to the *National Cyclopedia of Biography* as background information about himself.[22] One notable and rather surprisingly harsh exception was an unsigned review in *Landscape Architecture*, the ASLA's own journal. The anonymous author warned that "Three things should be borne in mind by the landscape designer who picks up Mr. Simonds' volume." First, it is part of the "Rural Science Series," which the reviewer believes "sets a certain atmosphere . . . especially suited to the expression of Mr. Simonds' naturalistic ideals," obviously something for which this self-proclaimed expert had little use. Second, he objected to the idea that a designer ought to "protect the appearance of the great out-of-doors," as Simonds encouraged. And last, that it would be all right to recommend this book "as first reading for rural clients, women's clubs, and men engaged in outdoor work . . . " i.e., what this nameless reviewer saw as an unsophisticated and unprofessional population.

Quoting a long passage about the landscape-gardener's approach to beautifying the "country as a whole," the reviewer nonetheless concluded that

"We thus see the field for Mr. Simonds' landscape gardener is far smaller than that generally understood to be covered by the landscape architect of today." He found the chapter on city planning "entirely superficial," and the idea of "embellishment by planting" equally disappointing. He did appreciate the high quality of the photographs, and noted that the chapter on arid and semi-arid regions "show[ed] a keen appreciation of the esthetic value of land forms." But in the end the reviewer did not even like the actual physical book itself, saying it was "most uncomfortably heavy to hold . . . the index is very poor." He concluded lamely by saying "Whatever we may find to criticize unfavorably, we realize that we are reading the sincere words of a man who knows and believes in the greatness of the landscape art."[23] What the anonymous reviewer failed to mention was that Simonds not only "believes in the greatness of the landscape art," but that he had been demonstrating it for over forty years by the time he wrote this book, and that he was one the ASLA's founders. The review was in fact a sign of the times. The naturalistic style had fallen out of favor with younger and newer practitioners a decade before, and the war had, paradoxically enough, brought intense new interest in historic revivalism in architecture and landscape—this despite radical departures from tradition in the art world.

SARGENT AND THE ARNOLD ARBORETUM

However, many others — older, conservative, traditional — found Simonds's approach to landscape design as set forth in his book to be quite agreeable. *House & Garden* featured him in its August 1923 issue, along side notable designers Ferrucio Vitale and James L. Greenleaf, ASLA president at the time. The year *Landscape-Gardening* was released, Simonds and his wife visited Mr. and Mrs. Charles Sprague Sargent and toured the Arnold Arboretum with them.[24] Sargent had been the arboretum's director since its inception nearly fifty years before in 1872. The two men had been acquainted since the 1890s—if not earlier—when Sargent edited *Garden and Forest*, the popular publication in which Simonds's important essay "The Landscape-gardener and his Work" was reprinted from the more narrowly focused *Park and Cemetery*.

Wealthy and well-educated, Sargent came from a prominent New England family, and had been interested in horticulture since childhood. His cousin

Henry Winthrop Sargent was a friend and client of Andrew Jackson Downing, which gave Charles first-hand experience with Downing's work and philosophy.* Turning the arboretum's twenty-five acres of hilly farmland into a "tree-garden" to go with Harvard's botanic garden, Sargent used principles similar to those J.C. Loudon followed in 1840 for his plan for the Derby Arboretum. These included a museum-like collection of plants arranged in logical order, placed so that they also formed a pleasing landscape.[25] Frederick Law Olmsted, Sr. strengthened the overall design of the arboretum in the 1880s.[26]

JOY MORTON'S ARBORETUM

Forty-nine years after the inception of the Arnold Arboretum, and while he was still its director, Sargent received a letter from a Chicagoan named Sterling Morton in December 1920. Morton wrote to ask where he could purchase books about the Arnold, and was modest enough to enclose a self-addressed, stamped envelope for the reply. He also mentioned his grandfather Julius Sterling Morton, founder of Arbor Day in the United States in 1872 and a former Secretary of Agriculture.[27] In the exchange of correspondence, Sargent learned that Joy Morton, Sterling's father and chairman of the Morton Salt Company, was ready to realize his lifelong vision of establishing a midwestern arboretum. He had been dreaming of this since 1876 when, at the age of twenty-one, he had visited the then-new Arnold Arboretum with his father Julius.

Joy Morton soon took over the discussions with Sargent, and in June of 1921 he went to see the Arnold again and to meet Sargent. At some point during these early letters and meetings, Sargent recommended Simonds to Morton.[28] Morton took Sargent's advice and within two weeks of his visit to Jamaica Plain, he wrote to Sargent that Simonds "will aid in the preparation of a tentative plan, if his health permits."[29]

The next day Morton met Jean Cudahy, his daughter, and Simonds over lunch to present his "scheme for establishing an arboretum" on land he owned twenty-five miles west of Chicago. Mrs. Cudahy was as enthusiastic and committed to the project as her father. Morton had thought about this project

---

* Downing (1815-1852) was Calvert Vaux's first American business partner. A horticulturist with wide ranging interests, he published a popular periodical called *The Horticulturist*. Downing's work helped lay the groundwork for Olmsted and Vaux's extensive landscape oeuvre and for the entire profession of landscape architecture in America.

for nearly fifty years and wanted an arboretum that "would rival or surpass Kew Gardens in London or the Arnold Arboretum at Boston." Knowing full well how much this would really cost, he was prepared to provide "plenty of money to develop" it. This garden would remain in Morton's private ownership, with restricted public admittance. Simonds responded later that he was very pleased that Morton had asked him to work as consulting landscape-gardener—for the rest of Simonds's life.[30]

On June 18, Simonds and Morton walked around the site together, and seven days later Simonds sent Morton a three-page letter, "to be filed away as a record of the early days of the Morton Arboretum." He outlined their preliminary plans, clarified Morton's stated intentions, and described the condition of the lands. Simonds recommended that in addition to securing "specimens of all the trees and shrubs which will grow in Northern Illinois" it was equally important "to preserve forever some native forest without molestation." He had often written about the long time span to be considered when designing a landscape, and this concern would be exemplified at the arboretum. He told Morton that "In considering the arboretum one must think of the people who will visit it fifty, one hundred, two hundred or more years in the future." The size of the arboretum Morton was proposing impressed his landscape-gardener, who pointed out that it would be twice as large as the Arnold or Kew, and he reiterated the importance of an artistic arrangement as well as one showing different species.[31]

The collaboration amongst Morton, Sargent, and Simonds created a synergy and enthusiasm that achieved a great deal in a short time. By June 23, 1921 Bartlett and Blair of Simonds and Company had competed a topographic survey and established the boundaries for the new arboretum.[*] Simonds was out on the property again the next day, staking out the center-line of the main drive and walking through the woods to find suitable places for lakes. He was already designing as he walked, choosing appropriate tree species for low areas near the DuPage River. In a letter to Joy Morton, the first of a series he would write over the next few years documenting the progress of the arboretum's development, he suggested that the arboretum drive go underneath the highway (then called Joliet Road, now Route 53, it runs north-south through the middle of the property)

---

[*] Erle O. Blair joined the firm by 1914 as a young practitioner. He brought new energy and a more formal design approach to some projects. He became a partner and the firm was renamed Simonds, West, & Blair in the early 1930s. Blair spent the rest of his career here, perhaps being the one to finally close the company.

between the eastern and western sections of the grounds.[32] This allowed visitors to explore the entire property without having to cross the public road.

Morton and Simonds developed a relationship of mutual trust and respect almost immediately, based on their ability to express honest concerns to one another. Morton wrote to Simonds, asking him to look at farm buildings on his next visit and to give his opinion on their suitability for housing the "local working force." He also noted that they had a "good general understanding" of each other's views.[33]

Early in July, Sterling Morton expressed doubts to his father in writing about the proposed scope of the arboretum, and Joy Morton passed these on to Simonds. He responded to Joy in a letter, explaining in no uncertain terms the values that he believed the arboretum would provide, basing his ideas on his more than four decades of landscape-gardening experience. Despite his earlier interest in the project, Morton's son felt that financial resources ought to be put to better use finding cures for diseases and creating the nation's monetary wealth. Simonds's rejoinder acknowledged the worth of those goals, and then eased into the elder Morton's qualms by discussing the underlying questions.[34]

He began by asking what an arboretum was and what purpose it would serve. Webster's definition, as quoted by Simonds, was "a place where trees and shrubs are cultivated for scientific or educational purposes; a botanical garden of trees." From this, he inferred that a wide range of places could be included, from Kew Gardens to small collections like Luther Burbank's garden, because they both added to the "food supply and the beauty of our surroundings." He suggested that providing benefits to those who are "well and strong" is just as noble an effort as helping those who are suffering.

While an arboretum's basic function was to display a variety of trees and shrubs for educational reasons, Simonds also believed that the scope of an arboretum included forestry, horticulture, and landscape-gardening; among these, forestry was most important. He had been concerned for many years with reforestation and the value of woodlots to agriculture, establishing a tree nursery on his farm in Michigan as a practical way of encouraging tree planting.* Horticulture's value, he believed, could not be called into question.

---

* He and his cousin Charlie Garfield communicated often about Garfield's dearest interest, reforesting the cut-over areas of Michigan. Simonds's library contained many books on the topic, including an English translation of the 1886 French treatment of the subject, *The Forest Waters the Farm*, a treatise on the necessity of woodlands to absorb water in an otherwise plowed/bare soil region.

As for landscape-gardening, he knew that many considered it "a useless and wasteful art, if they [gave] it any recognition. But, he continued, it should rank higher than art or music because it alone satisfies all of our senses—echoing the earlier sentiments of his mentor Bryan Lathrop. Considering the opinions of both Morton men, Simonds recommended that the arboretum contain "all hardy trees and shrubs which are useful in the production of food, production of lumber, and the creation of scenery . . . also . . . a collection of medicinal plants."[35]

This arboretum, he concluded:

> should exceed all previous efforts. It should contain a thousand
> pictures more beautiful than any that have been painted by the best
> painters, and varieties that will be hardy and happy at the arboretum
> should be used. It should, in fact, be a temple where religion is felt
> rather than expressed in words, or if given vocal expression this ...
> should come from the throats of song sparrows, robins, thrushes,
> redbirds, and feathered warblers.

Joy Morton was convinced, and proceeded to develop the arboretum at full speed.[36]

Sterling apparently relaxed his attitude, and went to visit the arboretum at Tervuern, Belgium in August of 1921. Involved with a Chicago firm that manufactured steel labels, he was now interested in how he could use them to identify plant names at his father's arboretum, and in doing so adding the didactic element needed to make it a museum and educational facility. His father and Simonds were involved in designing labels, too, and they consulted with Sargent regarding the Arnold's plant labeling system.[37] Sargent made a special trip to visit Morton's new arboretum that autumn and Morton, grateful for Sargent's continuing interest and advice, donated $2,500 to the Arnold Arboretum in October.[38] The next month, Morton sent Sargent a draft of the arboretum's purpose and goals; Sargent responded by revising a paragraph to describe his idea of a scientific arboretum.[39] It should be "equipped with an herbarium, a reference library, and laboratories for the study of trees . . ." so that the plants themselves and their economic potential could be explored. Much to Morton's credit, he spared no expense in incorporating these suggestions.

In the meantime, Simonds hired a photographer to document the changes as the land was re-shaped and planted. Photographer Jun Fujita made enough images to submit a handwritten invoice for $758.34.[40]* *Park and Cemetery* later reported that

> Joy Morton, president of the Morton Salt Company, has given 400 of his 2,000 acres to what will be known as the Morton Arboretum. It will be to the scientific forester and gardener what his laboratory is to the chemist, and to the everyday nature lover a spot where he can see both his own native trees and trees imported from foreign lands.[41]

Surprisingly, it does not mention Simonds's involvement, even though he was a founding member and past-president of its sponsoring organization, the American Association of Cemetery Superintendents.

Later that month Simonds again went to Jamaica Plain to visit Sargent, tour the arboretum, and interview a "young Austrian" there, perhaps Heinrich Teuscher, as a possible superintendent for Morton.+ Sargent was satisfied that they had "fully discussed the Arboretum" and he compiled a list of trees he thought would grow well in Illinois.[42] It was just a year since Sterling had sent his first letter to the Director of the Arnold Arboretum.

By January of 1922, Simonds was staying overnight at Thornhill, Morton's estate adjacent to the arboretum, and supervising a young landscape architect named Clarence Godshalk, who had been hired the previous fall.[43] Simonds ordered most of the plants himself, many from Naperville Nurseries, one of his favorites and just a few miles away. On December 14, 1922 the Morton family and other board members signed the formal indenture for the Morton Arboretum. It named the trustees and successors, gave the legal description of the institution, and provided an indenture clause stipulating that the land could not be sold and would remain forever intact.

---

* Fujita was born near Hiroshima in December 1888 and studied math at the Armour Institute in Chicago. To make money to defray school expenses, he took a job as a newspaper photographer at the *Chicago Evening Post* (later merged with the *Chicago Daily News*). He later opened his own studio, taking on commercial projects. Fujita's love of nature made him a good choice for the Arboretum assignment. He is quoted as saying, "My dream . . . is to go far away from civilization some day and lose myself in the wilderness." Instead, he died at home in Chicago in 1963 and his remains were cremated and interred in Graceland Cemetery. Information from *Wikipedia*.

+ Teuscher later worked at Morton Arboretum as its botanist.

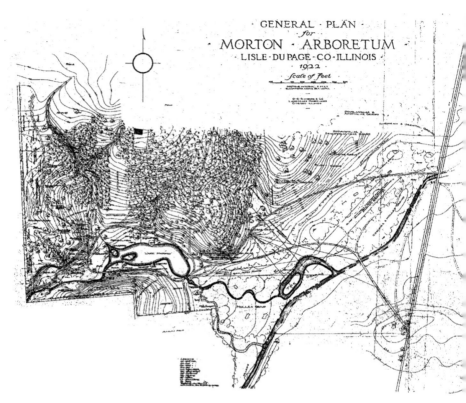

O.C. SIMONDS AND COMPANY'S 1922 survey and general plan for the property on which the Morton Arboretum would soon be created.

Simonds's network of colleagues was useful again at the arboretum's inception. Two and a half years preceding the work for the Thompson arboretum in Arizona (see below), Charles Deusner had worked for Simonds again, as superintendent at the very beginning of the transformation of farm fields into the Morton Arboretum. Clarence Godshalk had been a student in the Landscape Department at University of Michigan, graduating in 1921. While visiting relatives in Chicago that summer, he went to see Simonds about a job—he would have known Simonds from his lectures in the department. Simonds said he had no openings, but that he would keep an eye out for him. Just two weeks later, Simonds sent Godshalk a telegram asking him to come to Chicago immediately. Simonds and Company was just breaking ground on the Arboretum project and they needed workers. Deusner supervised; Godshalk

STERLING MORTON LIBRARY

started, as he put it, "grubbing out Hawthorns with pick and shovel, which I can assure you did not please me much after spending five years studying landscape." After just a few weeks, though, he moved into a crew management position and by the spring of 1923 he was the overseeing the work.˙ He took over the directorship from Joy Morton when Morton died in 1934. The arboretum staff was still farming 1,070 acres on land adjoining the Arboretum as late as 1943 and he managed these properties as well.

Simonds continued his involvement for the next several years, and Godshalk sent him updates from time to time, especially later in the decade

---

* For these first few months, payroll was handled through O.C. Simonds and Company. Albert Roehl, Godshalk, Herman Reich, and Deusner are listed under "labor and superintendence"; Blair, Olson, and O.C. Simonds are listed in a different category; no mention of West. O.C. Simonds and Company invoice to Mr. Joy Morton, November 1, 1921 (MA).

when the grounds were well along. He had given Godshalk a subscription
to *National Geographic* in his early days at the Arboretum, published by
Simonds's Maryland client Gilbert Grosvenor. Godshalk wrote to thank him
in February 1928 for renewing this again, saying "The *Geographic* is such a
splendid magazine and it is a constant reminder of the many things you have
done to get me established here. Even though I am a poor correspondent I
do hope you will realize I appreciate what you have done and are doing for
me."[44] Simonds's interest in Thompson's venture in Arizona motivated him to
share with Morton, in October 1924, a pamphlet called the "Weather Vein" in
which "Colonel 'Facts' Thompson" had an article. And Simonds's first partners
and long-time friends Holabird and Roche* designed several structures for
Morton Arboretum—Administration Building, Superintendent's House, and
an addition for the library, swimming pool, and its cottage.[45]

Heinrich Teuscher was hired after the project was underway. His role in part
was to conduct reforestation experiments. As he wrote in an early Arboretum
Bulletin, "One of the most interesting aims and perhaps *the* foremost feature
of the Morton Arboretum is and always will be the experimental plantings
of forest trees. It was indeed more than anything else the realization of the
urgent need of practical reforestation experiments which induced the founder
to establish this Arboretum." Simonds then would have been most empathetic
with Morton's intentions. He contributed a piece himself, describing the layout
of the grounds, the views, and the special places to watch for, and Godshalk
wrote descriptions of the wildflowers to be found there.[46] Further continuity
came with John A. Holabird serving as a Trustee.

On the eighteenth of that month, Simonds wrote his third report for Morton,
reviewing the progress to date. The first lake was completed; the second nearly
so. His men had platted the roads and surveyed newly acquired land, sickly
trees had been removed, and Godshalk was now in charge of pruning. Alfred
Senn from Chicago was hired as superintendent and was ready to go to work
as soon as the ground thawed. Sargent expressed his "hearty approval" while
visiting and encouraged Morton to plant the "largest collection of hawthorns
in the world" on one hundred acres of the arboretum.

Simonds and Company had drawn planting plans for the different sections,

---

* William Holabird died in 1923; Martin Roche in 1927. The successor firm was Holabird and Root,
headed by sons of Holabird and John Wellborn Root.

THE BEGINNINGS of one of Simonds's roads in the Morton Arboretum; note how it curves around the trees and winds over the subtle topography.

STERLING MORTON LIBRARY

AN EARLY ROAD at the Morton Arboretum.

STERLING MORTON LIBRARY

including a pinetum in the southwest corner. While the Mortons vacationed in Honolulu, Simonds prepared a general plan for locating 2,200 to 2,300 species and varieties of trees and shrubs. He intended to plant first on the west edge and east sides of the property because the central areas were still in agricultural use. Species that were more difficult to find would be sent to him from the Arnold's collection. He planned a lilac garden near the highway, with two hundred varieties—lilacs were one of his favorite plants, loved for their sensational fragrance. Simonds set aside different collection areas, including one just for viburnums and another for roses, and he placed willows, alders, and poplars along the river and stream banks. He felt by now that the "Arboretum is gradually taking on a definite shape and character."[47]

Joy Morton wrote to Sargent in May that "Mr. Simonds is spending four nights a week at my house and most of his daylight time in the Arboretum. It is coming along splendidly and its development is most satisfactory. We are both delighted."[48]

That summer, Simonds and his wife Mattie, along with his cousin Charlie Garfield and his wife Emma, took a trip abroad. As Simonds wrote to Morton while onboard ship, the trip was

> partly for the ladies, partly for rest and relaxation, and partly to take another look at Kew, see the arboretum at Brussels, and to visit various other collections of trees and shrubs in different parts of France and Great Britain.[49]

The rest of the six-page letter dealt with progress at the Morton Arboretum, including an inventory of 138,160 plants set out that April and May. Areas had been named, such as the Ozarks; Hemlock, Evergreen, and Pine Hills, and Sargent Glade. "Marmo," a contraction of Margaret Morton, was being considered as a name for the first lake.* He listed fifteen projects needing attention, including such items as building a bridge, constructing a propagating house, erecting more fences, and starting the lilac garden.

At the end of July, the Simondses and Garfields visited the arboretum at Brussels and met with Professor Bommer, its director. In a letter to Morton, Simonds described the tour and the layout of the garden. He had been puzzled

---

* The lake is still called "Marmo."

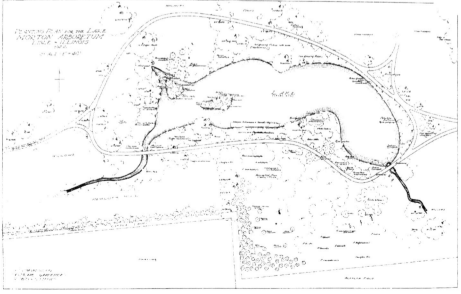

LAKE MARMO'S site (top) and Simonds's plan (bottom).

AN EARLY GAS-POWERED tractor in use at the Morton Arboretum.   STERLING MORTON LIBRARY

by the lack of labels, but was satisfied when Bommer explained that, because of free public access, vandals had destroyed them. Simonds felt that this "show[ed] the wisdom of [Morton's] ideas in regard to fences and the limited admittance of visitors." He signed off hoping the arboretum would keep the Mortons "young and interested for the next twenty-five years."[50]

Designing and planting continued at the arboretum that fall. The Rochester, New York, Parks Department sent plants that were unavailable locally or from the Arnold. Simonds shared his ideas about landscape-gardening and his goals for the Morton with Godshalk, who had already been promoted to arboretum superintendent.[51] Holabird and Roche's library, swimming pool, and cottage for the Morton estate were all completed in 1924.[52] Meanwhile, Simonds investigated sources for herbarium cases. In July of 1924 he wrote to Morton with planting recommendations and adjustments. That August, Morton asked for his comments on a proposed arboretum booklet. His involvement did indeed continue for several more years, slowly tapering off through the end of the 1920s. A few letters were exchanged in 1928 and 1929, with the last written in November of 1931, the month of Simonds's death. In a letter to Michigan landscape architect Genevieve Gillette in 1943, Godshalk reminisced about his former professors Tealdi and Whittemore, and closed by saying he had had a number of graduates from the Landscape Department at the arboretum and hoped to continue to do so, as well as wishing that the Department would visit the arboretum for field trips.[53] Under his direction, the arboretum continued to expand its collections and to become a community resource. Today, it is one of the premier cultural institutions of Chicago's western suburbs.

BOYCE THOMPSON SOUTHWESTERN ARBORETUM

Academic botanical gardens and arboretums flourished in the first decade of the 1900s; by the early 1920s private and public gardens were in favor. Shortly after Simonds and Company began its work on the Morton Arboretum, a copper mining magnate named William Boyce Thompson (1869-1930), of Yonkers, New York and Superior, Arizona, endowed both the Boyce Thompson Institute for Plant Research at Cornell University ($10,000,000)[54] and the Boyce Thompson Southwestern Arboretum in Superior ($5,000,000),[55] now part of the College of Agriculture and Life Sciences, University of Arizona. In a letter to his employer Simonds in 1924, Alowese Penfield suggested that Deusner could provide more details about the inception of the arboretum, but unfortunately no such record remains. Although Simonds is not mentioned in the history, circumstantial evidence points to the Thompson Arboretum as the project that gave him the expertise to write the chapter on arid landscapes in *Landscape-Gardening*.

Colonel Raymond Robins (1873-1954) of the American Red Cross, famously the only American officer to meet personally with Lenin, was a close enough friend of Thompson's that, upon Robins's return from Russia, they enjoyed driving through the west together in 1917.[56] Gifford Pinchot (1865-1946), former director of the U.S. Forest Service, was a close friend and correspondent of both men, and perhaps unofficial advisor on both of Thompson's plant conservation projects in the 1920s.* The further development of both the arboretum and the institute provide an engaging account of Thompson's fascination with botany and his financial ability to leave a lasting legacy.[57]

---

* Pinchot also corresponded with Robins in January 1919 about Governor Frank O. Lowden and J.T. Williams of the Woodlawn Farm Company, "Breeders of Purebred Livestock, Sterling Illinois." Robins's sister Frieda Maynard lived at Ravinia, the Highland Park, Illinois neighborhood where Jens Jensen had his home and studio.

PERSONAL GLIMPSES

The European tour the Simondses and Garfields took the summer of 1922 was a vastly different experience from Robins's revolutionary travels in Russia. In letters back to Roy West, not only can we glimpse what caught O.C.'s attention, but also get a sense of the pleasure he took in observing the scene, whatever it was, and describing it in detail.

He took the time while in London on July 31 to write a letter relating travels through France and Switzerland. The elegance of the interior of the train carriages, the graciousness of the conductor—the group found it all better than traveling at home in a Pullman! Looking out the window, Simonds enjoyed every changing nuance of color in the sky. In England, he had to reconsider his typical method of planting for railways. He told Roy, "You know we generally think that we must plant out a railroad. The English hedges shutting out at times in a most aggravating way the views we were anxious to get made me think that we should consider people riding in a train as well as those who own the adjoining land." He concluded by reflecting on "our great enjoyment of the grand display in the heavens and the fact that people we met in London had not seen it made me think also of the good fortune of those people who live on a hill in the country like Ernest Warner [Simonds's cousin in Madison for whom he designed subdivisions] and who can observe with deliberation and no interruption the unexcelled beauty of clouds and sky and all the wonderful changes that are continually taking place out of men's reach." He signed it, as he did many letters to Roy in the 20s, "Tra la la, O.C.S."[58]

CHAPTER NINE ENDNOTES

[1] Thomas Wakefield Goodspeed, "LaVerne Noyes," *The University of Chicago Biographic Sketches*, Vol. 1 (Chicago: The University of Chicago Press, 1922), 257-77.

[2] Copy personally addressed to Simonds, SFC.

[3] Goodspeed, 274.

[4] Trustees, Board of, *Minutes*, Vol. 10, 1917-18, 403, University of Chicago Archives.

[5] Ibid., Vol. 11, 1919-20, 17.

[6] Goodspeed, 96-99.

[7] "The Campus," *Report of Iowa State Board of Education*, 1916, 266. Special Collections, The Parks Library, Iowa State University.

[8] Robert William Werle, *A Historical Review and Analysis of the Iowa State University Landscape from 1858 to 1966*. Unpublished master's thesis: Iowa State University at Ames, 1966.

[9] L.H. Pammel to President R.A. Pearson of Iowa State College, March 21, 1916, PP-1, 25/5, Grounds Committee, University Archives, Iowa State University.

[10] Goodspeed.

[11] "Dean of Cemetery Field."

[12] Martha Simonds's diary.

[13] Bruegmann, "Glen View Club—Boy Scout Fountain," Vol. 2, 138.

[14] Simonds, "Landscape Gardening in its Relation to Roadside Planting," *Journal of the International Garden Club*, Vol. II, No. 2 (June 1918), 187-201 & 300-301; "Care of Woods and Ravines," Ibid., No. 3, September 1918, 421-24.

[15] Ibid., 421.

[16] Martha Simonds's diary; plans at MA.

[17] Simonds, *Landscape-Gardening* (New York: Macmillan Company, 1920), 1.

[18] Quoted in Kenneth Clark, *Landscape into Art* (London: J. Murray, 1949), 74.

[19] Ibid., 6-7.

[20] Ibid., 17-18.

[21] Ibid., 24-25.

[22] Simonds's 1931 desk diary.

[23] "Book Reviews," *Landscape Architecture*, XI, No. 3 (April 1921) 155-57.

[24] Martha Simonds's diary.

[25] Ida Hay, *Science in the Pleasure Ground: A History of the Arnold Arboretum* (Boston:

Eastern University Press, 1995), WHT.

[26] Cynthia Zaitzevsky, *Frederick Law Olmsted and the Boston Parks System* (Cambridge, MA: Belknap Press, 1982).

[27] Sterling Morton to the Director of the Arnold Arboretum, December 22, 1920, Sterling Morton *Correspondence*, Archives of Sterling Morton Library, Morton Arboretum, Lisle, IL. All subsequent correspondence is from the Morton Arboretum's archives.

[28] "A Brief History of the Morton Arboretum" brochure (Lisle, Illinois: The Morton Arboretum, 1996).

[29] Morton to Sargent, June 1921. This appears to be the earliest reference to Simonds's poor health.

[30] Simonds to Morton, July 13, 1921.

[31] Ibid.

[32] Ibid.

[33] Morton to Simonds, July 11, 1921.

[34] Simonds to Morton, July 13, 1921.

[35] Ibid.

[36] Simonds to Morton, January 18, 1922.

[37] Morton to Simonds, September 6, 1921; "Morkrum Mfg. Co." at 1410 Wrightwood, Chicago, owned by Howard Krum and Sterling Morton, with labels and markers made by Ryerson & Sons; letterhead, MA.

[38] Morton to Sargent, October 12, 1921.

[39] Sargent to Morton, November 26, 1921.

[40] Simonds's bills for the month on behalf of Morton, December 1, 1921.

[41] "New Parks and Improvements," *Park and Cemetery* (December 1921): 266.

[42] Sargent to Morton, December 27, 1921.

[43] Godshalk and his wife Margaret were guests of the Simondses at Pier Cove the next summer, signing the Cove Book on September 6, 1923.

[44] Godshalk to Simonds, February 8, 1928, Morton Arboretum, Sterling Morton Library archives; Simonds, 1921-1923.

[45] Bruegmann, entry #925.

[46] Morton Arboretum, *Bulletin of Popular Information*, May and July 1925.

[47] Simonds to Morton, January 18, 1922; plans for the Morton Arboretum. MA.

[48] Morton to Sargent, May 1, 1922.

[49] Simonds to Morton, July 8, 1922.

[50] Simonds to Morton, August 1, 1922.

[51] Scott Mehaffey, "Laying the Foundation: Landscape at the Morton Arboretum, O.C. Simonds and Clarence Godshalk, 1922-1953," *The Morton Arboretum Quarterly*, Vol. 31, No. 3 (Autumn 1995), 36.

[52] Bruegmann, #925.

[53] Clarence Godshalk to Genevieve Gillette, May 12, 1943; Bentley Historical Library, University of Michigan, School of Natural Resources Collection, Box No. 55, Department of Landscape Architecture.

[54] http://www.bti.cornell.edu

[55] Alowese Penfield to O.C. Simonds, 1924, SFC.

[56] *Raymond Robins Papers*, 1878-1951, State Historical Society of Wisconsin.

[57] http://ag.arizona.edu/BTA/history.html; *The Magnate*, Herman Hagedorn's 1935 biography is available through this site as well.

[58] Simonds to West, July 31, 1922, Garland's Hotel, Suffolk Street, Pall Mall.

chapter 10

"A BETTER HERITAGE
FOR LATER DAYS
CAN NO MAN LEAVE"

1922-1960

Turkey Tail Mushroom amid White Oak leaves

THE "CHURCH BEECHES" at Simonds's Michigan property in Pier Cove. AUTHOR PHOTO

YORK HARBOR

On their return from visiting European gardens in September 1922, O.C. and Mattie stopped to visit their son Robert in York Harbor, Maine. Twenty years earlier, Simonds had designed grounds for Bryan and Helen Aldis Lathrop's summer home here, created by Holabird and Roche. Concerned with the town's appearance, Lathrop had campaigned for planting more street trees, and engaged his friend Simonds to come and work on the project.[1] By 1910, Lathrop began to purchase property for a subdivision (400 acres). Simonds prepared the plat for him and also became an investor in the undertaking.[2]

They named their development York Harbor Hills, and their group the Seabury Land Company. As with College Hills and the Highlands in Madison, which were platted around the same time, the lots did not sell quickly and few houses were built. Simonds kept pursuing its development, however, and Robert—now a graduate of the Landscape Design Department at the University of Michigan—was sent to oversee the work. By 1926, when Robert married Gladys (Jerry) McConnel (also a landscape architect from the University of Michigan program), the York Harbor Hills promotional brochure listed Herbert R. Simonds (the oldest son) as a company director, Robert as Superintendent of Improvements, and Simonds and West of Chicago as Landscape Designers. It boasted that

The plotting has not been done on paper in the conventional manner; rather the land was studied and the house sites selected to afford the best ocean view without disturbing the outlook from other houses . . . Only after the house sites had been carefully located were the plot boundaries fixed. Roads follow the natural curves and grades so as to preserve the park-like beauty of the rolling hills. The result is a plan which gives to small acreage the freedom and seclusion usually associated with large estates.[3]

Efforts to develop a successful subdivision dragged on, though, throughout the

MONTROSE CEMETERY, with American elms, Chicago, Illinois.   AUTHOR PHOTO

depression of the early 1930s, until the Simonds family finally relinquished its interests.[4]

In 1922, Simonds commissioned his old friends Holabird and Roche to design a storefront building for part of his property fronting on Montrose Avenue, although he never did build it.[5] That spring and fall he went back to Dixon to work on residential projects. He also redesigned Montrose Cemetery in Chicago that year, one of many such projects. Situated on the city's northwest side, it had been in operation for several years before Simonds created a comprehensive plan.[6] Simonds gave his "Nature as the Great Teacher" lecture for students at the University of Illinois that year too. The talk expressed his conviction that by studying the natural elements of a site, the configuration of woodland borders, and the groupings of plants as they occur in the wild, a designer could learn some of the most important lessons for creating beautiful and satisfying landscapes. While the designer's task was to make the site look as though Mother Nature had gone to art school and learned the elements of composition, he or she would learn just about everything else directly from nature.

ABOVE: O.C. and Martha Simonds
at their 50th wedding anniversary
celebration, Grand Rapids, MI.
RIGHT: O.C. Simonds, late 1920s.
SIMONDS FAMILY COLLECTION

FLORIDA

By 1924, Simonds had become interested in tung oil, a quick-drying varnish ingredient and wood preservative extracted from *Aleurites fordii*, discovered in China twenty years earlier. The tung oil tree, as it is commonly known, was under investigation at the Agricultural Experiment Station in Florida. Charlie Garfield, Simonds's cousin, owned property in DeLand, in central Florida and Simonds's initial purchase was five acres near DeLeon springs. He owned about twenty-five adjacent acres by the mid-1920s. Simonds enjoyed Florida's mild winters, which were easier for him to handle when his health began to deteriorate in the early 1920s. The couple that cared for his Michigan property, Sven and Louisa, came down to DeLand with him. The second season Sven helped to clear thickets in which he then planted tree seedlings to see what would grow and "shaped the ground to inclose pools of water." A fire killed off most of the seedlings, though, and hogs running loose rooted up the rest. Florida was not the Midwest!

By his third season in DeLand, Simonds bought seventy-five additional acres and a lake with more property. He decided to name his place Spring Hammock and he called a piece of water Alligator Pond because Sven was sure he had see one there. Always interested in new plants and projects, Garfield and his cousin became fascinated with the prospect of raising tung trees to make money and of the opportunity to appreciate plants that could flourish in the south.[7] Unfortunately, their enterprise did not take off because they were about ten years too early—the industry grew rapidly in the mid-1930s.

By January 1929 Simonds had accumulated 160 acres and decided it was time to divide and sell his land, perhaps remembering his father's theory that land makes more money by selling it than by working it. He hoped to make the development a nature sanctuary with residences. When the *DeLand Daily News* interviewed him and asked what motivated him to buy here in the first place, Simonds responded with stories of his youth seventy years earlier on a farm in Michigan. He vividly described how as a boy he had grown to love the woods and streams and all the natural scenery, and he saw the same kinds of untouched nature here. He came also, he said, because his most intimate friend did—referring of course to his cousin Charlie. His thoughtful approach to developing the property, though, could not attract buyers, given the glut of Florida property on the market at the time, left over in large part from Charles Ponzi's real estate schemes a few years earlier.[8]

Because he had developed an intimate knowledge of his land, its topography, its animals, and its peculiarities, when he decided to subdivide, he wrote a far more detailed and accurate description of the properties than the typical Florida real estate brochure offered.[9] In recollecting the whole adventure in the winter of 1931, Simonds said he had bought the land "primarily as a place to play in. That is, a place to make paths, pools and pictures."

Simonds also sold his house and lot on Montrose in Chicago in 1927, investing some of the profits in a thirty-six-unit apartment building on Greenleaf Street in Rogers Park.[10] The local paper expressed what the neighbors

MONTROSE AVENUE ca. 1890 (top, looking west) and in 2011 (bottom, looking east).

were all thinking—the neighborhood "beauty spot" that they had enjoyed for forty-five years would be destroyed to make room for a large building. The *Chicago Tribune* reported on July 31, 1927, that "Noted Mansion to be Replaced by Skyscraper; North Side Garden Spot to Fade," as Simonds sold his three and a half-acre estate to a developer for a ten-story apartment hotel. The reporter, Philip Hampson, took a few column-inches to reminisce about the neighborhood circa 1880, when Simonds bought the property for $1,000. Lake View Township grew from a few lonely farms to the bustling business district of the 1920s. He let readers know that the property sale contract stipulated that Simonds could remove any and all plants to relocate to his home in Michigan.

As it turned out, the market crash occurred after Simonds's property had been razed and bulldozed, but before the apartment and retail structure was begun, and so the property sat vacant and was used as a parking lot for many years. O.C. and Mattie moved in with their daughter Gertrude and her husband William Walker, who lived around the corner on Junior Terrace, just a few blocks from their old home. While the Simondses were in their seventies now and still had properties in Florida and Michigan, one can only imagine their sadness at seeing their home and gardens of forty-five years destroyed.

ASLA WORKS OF MEMBERS AND A GOLD MEDAL

P. H. Elwood, the same professor of landscape architecture at Iowa State who remodeled the campus after Simonds and Noyes left, published the first photographic collection of works of ASLA members in 1924. For Simonds's section of the book, he printed a few pictures of Graceland and two of unidentified private estates. The frontispiece of the book was a small, also unidentified, photograph of a tree with tulips around its base, beside a gently curving road. It, too, was a scene in Graceland. Yet, in his introduction to the collection, Elwood was unequivocal in his insistence that to conform to current professional standards a designer had to be equally proficient in both formal and naturalistic styles. Although he chose Simonds's rustic design for the front of the book, his emphasis on the *two* design methods was a harbinger that the end was near for the landscape-gardener. The 1920 *Landscape Architecture* review of Simonds's book foretold the same.[11]

Despite landscape-gardening's decline within the landscape design profession, the Architectural League in New York award Simonds its gold medal for landscape design in 1925. This was especially prestigious because the League only gave an award the years it could find a worthy recipient. Simonds served on a special ASLA committee planning a memorial for Frederick Law Olmsted and as concerned as ever with proper professional standards, he was also a member of the ASLA's newly formed Ethics Committee beginning in 1926.[12] The Society held its annual meeting at the Hotel Sherman that year, and guest speakers included architect Dwight Heald Perkins and landscape designer Jens Jensen, who, naturally, talked about the native landscape.

OTHER OBJECTIONS TO LANDSCAPE-GARDENING METHODS

The American Mercury, a sophisticated, up-to-the-minute publication edited by the formidable H.L. Mencken, published landscape architect Elbert Peets's denunciation of "The Landscape Priesthood" in 1927. Aiming specifically at "the true Olympians, the fifty Fellows of the American Society of Landscape Architects," Peets claimed that "the introduction of the English landscape style of gardening was a calamity of the first magnitude." It had stifled any real creativity in American design, was antithetical to vernacular gardening styles, and the society's rhetoric about the unique requirements of a landscape was so much "foliage of logical distinction [under which] will be found the fungi of economic interest," according to him.[*]

By name, he mentioned the three Olmsteds, the two Eliots, and Henry Vincent Hubbard and Theodora Kimball of Harvard.[13] Formal design was not off the hook, either, though; he expressed disdain for the American Academy in Rome and the landscape architecture department in general at Harvard. Peets never mentioned Simonds, but his invective against the natural style of

---

[*] Peets's invective was a response to one of his Harvard landscape architecture professors who had found fault with the style of his work. Mencken's attitude encouraged such outbursts. During his days as *Baltimore Herald* drama critic, he reportedly said, "The first job of the reviewer is to write a good story . . . It doesn't make much difference whether what he says is fundamentally sound or not . . . Don't hesitate to use the actors roughly; they are mainly idiots." (as quoted in *Indian Hill: The first 75 years, 1914-1989*, privately printed by the club), 7.

design included the precepts Simonds employed.

> Cemeteries, as everybody knows, are always landscaped . . .It is truly
> pitiful to see normally straight-edge minded engineers trying to equal
> the trick streets and yawpy intersections of the initiates.

As for "Rural Beautification," Peets briefly touched on the edition of
Landscape Architecture that dealt with landscape extension work, singling out
a "photograph of a previously gaunt farm home beautified with a curved walk
and flocculent shrubbery," perhaps the very same two photos found on page
54 of *Landscape-Gardening*. Other than suggesting that students have their
minds opened with "pedagogical dynamite," however, Peets did not propose
any remedies to what he saw as a dire situation. He went on to a respectable,
explosive-free career, designing such historical revival sites as the copy of
Colonial Williamsburg for the town center at Greendale, Wisconsin.[+]

UNIVERSITY OF MARYLAND

The University of Maryland at College Park sought campus-planning
assistance from Simonds in early 1927. The next two years' correspondence in
the University archives related to this project provides a rare look into the issues
with a large project and client reactions to Simonds's work. It also makes clear
that even prominent, highly-regarded designers can become overly confident
in their big vision, overlooking crucial details.

As with other larger scale projects, Simonds was excited about the
forestation possibilities here. He also was curious to know about soil
experiments being conducted at the school to hasten the decomposition of
straw, leaves, and "other refuse for fertilizer." Simonds had read an article about
research at the Rothamsted station in England using sulphate of ammonia and
chalk as reagents, and wondered if this had been tried at Maryland, and if so,
with what results. He hoped that he might be able to use such a mixture for the
grass cuttings and leaves in Graceland's compost to speed up the process.

By May 2, 1927 Simonds had finished a preliminary sketch of the campus

---

+ Williamsburg was much in vogue at the time. The Rockefeller-funded restoration was guided by
landscape architect Arthur Shurcliff, who was imaginative and imaginative in his approach, if not a stickler
for historic authenticity.

and had sent it to the client. He considered the placement of roadways, grading that would be necessary on the hilly site, vistas that could be incorporated, and of course the plantings that could create a pleasant and welcoming ambiance. Simonds corresponded with both President R.A. Pearson and Professor of Floriculture A.S. Thurston (the university had some time before put the supervision of planning and maintenance for the grounds under the supervision of the horticulture department). He also heard back from A.G. McCall, the man in charge of the soil investigations, that he had not found the reagent to stimulate quicker composting (apparently everyone here used only his initials, not his first name).

Simonds would visit the campus when he was in the east on other business, either en route to his property in Florida, or to work with the Grosvenors on Wild Acres, just a few miles away in Bethesda. He, Pearson, and Thurston kept up a frequent correspondence to keep the planning moving forward. By June they were considering the issue of car parking and where and how to site locations for this new necessity. Pearson also explained that most of the design would need to be phased in as funds became available. Simonds was, as always, the most discreet of landscape designers in answering Thurston's query at the end of June as to whether he might be able to visit the campus in the middle of July. He would not know until he had an answer from "a friend in Nova Scotia," he wrote, rather than dropping the names of his clients, the family of Alexander Graham Bell.[14]

Simonds's very naturalistic design was, as at the University of Chicago, not to everyone's liking at this campus, and in October 1927 the school asked Frederick Law Olmsted (junior) to give his advice on locating buildings, roads, and the overall treatment. Simonds wrote to Pearson that he would "be glad" for him to get Olmsted's opinion. He and Olmsted worked with architects Smith and May in Baltimore, as well as a University of Michigan landscape graduate named Mark Shoemaker, now employed here in the extension service. After Olmsted's visit, Simonds wrote a short report for President Pearson to assure him that the two landscape designers were in agreement regarding the placement of the new library (the biggest concern of the moment). He went on to discuss the things that he most cared about when he planned a site. The library was to be in a "location [that] commands the whole region" and he took his cue from that. He asked Pearson to "Please remember that I look upon landscaping as one of the

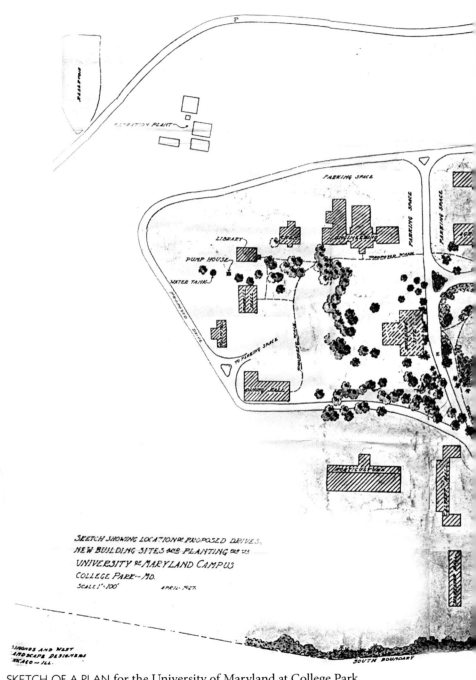

SKETCH OF A PLAN for the University of Maryland at College Park.

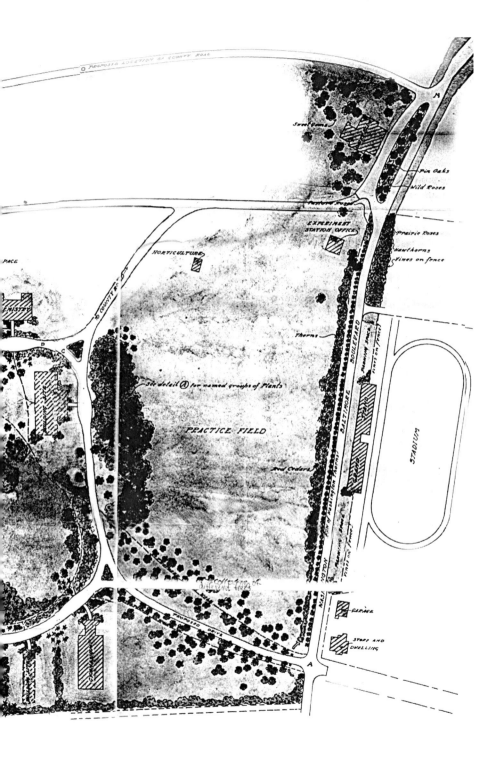

fine arts comparable to painting, architecture, sculpture, music and poetry." He saw what he was creating as the equivalent of "a great painting" for the school to own. Simonds and Pearson seem to have been well-acquainted on a personal level as well; one letter from Simonds thanked Pearson for the payment of an invoice as his company's bank account was low; in another, Pearson expressed the wish that "some of us" could meet him in Locust Valley (where Hill House, the estate of Simonds's long-time friend and client Anton Hodenpyl was located); and in January 1928 Simonds began a letter "Last night I lay awake for an hour or two thinking about some of your problems. Let me give you my thoughts."[15] Simonds was not an overly casual soul, so his correspondence here suggests a personal as well as a working relationship.

By that January, Charles Eliot II was working with Simonds on the campus,[16] and by early February they had together submitted two possible plans. "Scheme B" was accepted by the Board of Regents. Harrison's Nurseries of Berlin, Maryland offered to quote special pricing on the plants specified. Harrison's owner was Senator Orlando Harrison (1867-1928), who was a highly regarded nurseryman and orchardist. With his four sons and 200 to 500 seasonal employees, he grew 10,000,000 trees and seedlings a year, and boasted one of the largest peach orchards in the world. Harrison had also been instrumental in transforming the small state college into the University of Maryland, and had supported the bill for the county extension service.[17] The firm's interest in the campus plan was further supported by Harrison, who, as mayor before 1910, had been instrumental in Berlin's first street-lighting and city water systems, and was the Chairman of the Committee on Roads and Highways when he served as state senator.

Pearson wrote to G. Hale Harrison, one of the four sons running the nursery, and who had graduated from Cornell, in the middle of February 1928 to emphasize the importance of the selection of plants, that "we do not want to spend money on any planting material that does not offer reasonable promise of growing successfully." He had given the Simonds list to Professor Thurston to discuss with university horticulturists, and asked for Harrison's input too. "I have the highest opinion of the ability and judgment of Mr. Simonds, but I have the reservation that persons who are most familiar with this particular locality are competent to criticize and offer suggestions in connection with his recommendations as to planting."[18]

Simonds, typically willing to take account of his clients' views and with nearly fifty years of landscape design experience to his credit, seems to have over-reached on some elements of this project, the selection and placement of plants being just one. He had ordered the removal of several evergreens that were alongside the campus greenhouse. H.J. Patterson, the Director and Dean of the Agricultural Experiment Station, wrote to President Pearson on April 10, 1928, to defend the evergreens, saying that they served as a windbreak northwest of the greenhouse, which would otherwise be exposed. On June 25, Pearson wrote to Simonds to ask (in a very kind and straightforward tone) about an "expense item . . . that they had received no advance notice" about and to try in the future to avoid incurring costs not in the budget.

Things went along well enough until September, when the grounds superintendent, H.L. Crisp, started to complain about elements in Simonds's design. Crisp had been in this position previously, but, due to some issues with his work, the management transferred the responsibility to the horticulture department under the aegis of Dr. Auchter, then to Professor Thurston, and then reinstated Crisp in the position. He did not take kindly to Simonds. Pearson sent him a letter on September 12 instructing him to follow Mr. Simonds's directions for a new sidewalk near the gymnasium. Crisp replied two days later, saying "I have your letter of September 12th. It contains much in which I do not concur. However, I will follow in detail Mr. Simonds' instructions. You, of course, will then hold Mr. Simonds responsible for results."

Even at this early stage Crisp did not to want to cooperate with any of "Scheme B." Thurston wrote to him on September 26 to explain that, instead of buying the 2,150 English ivy plants specified by Simonds, he had had them propagated by student workers in the greenhouse. The plants, he wrote, were still in the greenhouse, not in the ground. He concluded the note by asking Crisp, "May I hear from you shortly as to just when you will be ready to take care of these plants." Administratively things were moving along; Pearson wrote a cordial letter to Simonds on October 27 with the good news that the Board of Regents had agreed to the siting of the library building. Out on the grounds, though, things were more difficult. Thurston wrote to G. Hale Harrison in January 1928 regarding the plantings of the previous season. Harrison had complained the new plantings looked like they had not received proper care. Thurston defended his crew's maintenance, saying that the soil was clayey and baked hard when dry, that some plants had been heeled-in for a while,

> but this should not be detrimental to them provided they were properly
> heeled-in by your men . . . The delay in planting was due to your men
> not being able to open holes fast enough to keep other men busy
> planting. In order to assist your men and hasten the planting, I finally
> had several of our men go to digging holes, and in the time so spent the
> first week they helped in this way, 965 holes were dug by them.

Plantings did not thrive this first year. Thurston continued,

> In regard to the rhododendrons in front of the Agricultural Building,
> I will say upon receiving Mr. Symons' [sic] plans, I questioned the
> feasibility of planting them in that location, and suggested that a
> change be made. While on the Campus he looked at this location and
> said, "I don't think we need to make any change. We'll plant them
> there." The question of replacement and replanting, I will take up with
> . . . and let you know about this later.

However these various situations resolved, Simonds was still on board the following year. The *Minutes of Meeting of Committee on Campus Maintenance and Improvement for February 2nd, 1929* included discussion by Mr. Crisp and Mr. Thurston regarding evergreens at the entry gate that obscured the road, a potentially dangerous situation. Crisp questioned Simonds's suggestions for a parking area next to the gym and his grading proposals. Thurston explained the use of a six percent grade was for a walkway with an easy incline. But on May 7, 1929, Crisp wrote to Thurston reporting completion of the walk on the south of the old Chemistry Building, and that "quick action" needed to be taken to keep the soil from now washing into the sewer. He saw other flooding problems continuing if "due consideration" was not given to the area that was already not draining properly. In the meantime, Pearson wrote to Simonds to ask his assistance with campus light placement.

On May 11 Thurston responded by letter to a telephone conversation that morning with Crisp, who had informed him that he would be sodding a small triangle north of the gym, although Simonds's plan called for shrubs. He

O.C. SIMONDS at work in his office,
ca. 1929.
SIMONDS FAMILY COLLECTION

reminded Crisp that he had asked that nothing be done until Simonds arrived that coming Monday. Thurston also commented on the new walk being installed at the chemistry building, and asked that work be stopped until its placement and shape could be resolved. After Simonds's visit, Thurston then wrote to H.C. Byrd, also involved in the campus planning, to explain his views on this walk. Simonds wanted it to be in the shape of a Y; Thurston was convinced that was overkill for the little use this area had. He discussed this with Simonds while the latter was on campus, but again Simonds told Thurston it was fine and saw no reason to change it.

Crisp then wrote to Pearson on May 22 with a list of problems, all of which he blamed directly on Simonds's work. This included basement flooding in buildings that had "received 'professional' landscaping'"; sewers filling with silt; drainage problems; and several other similar issues. Thurston replied to Pearson on the 27th, after "giving careful consideration to the enclosed letter of Mr. Crisp . . . " He answered the "criticisms of Mr. Simonds's recommendations" as best he could and suggested they be forwarded to Simonds for response. Several of Crisp's complaints seemed to be regarding actions he had taken on his own recognizance, and others due to Crisp's lack of attention to maintenance of plantings (the reasons he had been removed from the position before). Thurston then consulted Dr. Auchter, who, one suspects, had been through these kinds of difficulties when he was in Thurston's position. Auchter concluded that Crisp would not have these problems if he would "follow standard landscape practice."

The last letter from Simonds was to Thurston, dated February 9, 1930, in which he said he hoped to get back to the campus the end of March. This seems to be the last of Simonds consulting with the University of Maryland. Whether Olmsted or Eliot continued to consult, it would seem that Simonds did not bring anyone else from his firm to this project. The university continued to expand its campus and over time Simonds's work was altered or swallowed up in the changes.

WORKING WITH THE BELL FAMILY

Despite the new trends in landscape, Simonds still believed whole-heartedly in his design philosophy, and so did many others. In 1928, he went to Bethesda, Maryland to consult with Gilbert Grosvenor, Alexander Graham Bell's son-in-law and founder of the National Geographic Society, about his estate, Wild Acres. Simonds was further engaged by the family to plan a fitting last resting place for Bell on their property in Nova Scotia, and to engineer the relocation of a sixteen-ton boulder as his grave marker.[19] (Chapter 12 on the Lathrops and Bryans includes more information about the Bells and Grosvenors.)

"A STAUNCH DEFENDER
OF THE NATURAL CHARM
OF AMERICAN LANDSCAPES"

By the mid-1920s, Simonds was commuting to Madison to lecture on landscape-gardening at the University of Wisconsin. He was also occupied with enlarging his tree nursery at Pier Cove.[20] Walter Studley, a young neighbor, acted as nursery manager in Simonds's absence. They tested new plants and experimented with pushing climate zones a few numbers in the relatively temperate climate of his Michigan ravine. Studley bought a new Ford truck for the business, which he and Simonds hoped to develop into a commercial venture. Simonds's alma mater the University of Michigan awarded him an honorary Master of Arts degree in 1929. The school spokesman called him "a staunch defender of the natural charm of American landscapes . . . A better heritage for later days can no man leave,"[21] the kind of compliment that would have pleased Simonds greatly.

Simonds continued to work, but he was not well. He went to a clinic called the "Health School" in Chicago that year and received some stringent dietary suggestions, but the diet did not relieve his difficulties. That winter, O.C. and Mattie went to Florida to escape the Midwest's bitter weather, and sent fruit back to his partner Roy West and to a few neighbors.[22] Their son Marshall, who had been superintendent of the Green Bay, Wisconsin Parks Department, moved to Chicago to join his father's firm and take on some of the responsibilities. *The American Cemetery* published a charming and informative interview with O.C., calling Simonds "The Dean of the Cemetery Field." The article included his own recounting of his early days at Graceland with Jenney, experiences transplanting trees, and his impressions of Adolph Strauch at Spring Grove.

And he continued to write. In its March 1931 issue, *Monument and Cemetery Review* published a three-page article on "Landscaping Cemeteries," just eight months before Simonds's own death. In it, he discussed his major precepts, now honed to very simple and explicit concepts. First, beauty mattered, the kind of subtle aesthetic one would appreciate in a painting by Jean-Baptiste Camille Corot or Jules Dupres. Second, seclusion mattered. Although not a religious man, Simonds certainly believed in a kind of natural sacredness to death and the natural environment. Third, convenience—a cemetery needed to be accessible, and the graves within it needed to be easily reached. The roads ought to be curved because this was more beautiful and economical than straight drives (not for Peets, of course). Cemeteries, he felt, were more appealing than a park because they were quiet and lacked crowds, and "how restful to the eye is a surface covered with the green leaves of a vine." As always, he encouraged using local plants, writing "I would especially advocate the use of native shrubs . . . Do not discard a bush because it is common or abundant." He addressed scale, something not often written about then in landscape design, making the common sense suggestion that plants on smaller lots should be on the same scale as the lot. Good advice for any type of site, he said the cemetery should be designed as a whole (advice followed more for parks probably than cemeteries, which are often expanded in an ad hoc fashion).

The work that the Lathrops and Bryans had begun with elm trees in the 1850s continued to flourish. The Pfund Bell Nurseries Company and Elmhurst Nurseries took out an ad in the September 1930 issue of *The American Cemetery* for their elm trees; the text read "The 'Elmhurst' Elm, Grown by us from seed gathered from the famous old elms of Cottage Hill Avenue admired everywhere for their cathedral arch over this Avenue." The Elmhurst Elms were indeed outstanding until Dutch elm disease reached Chicago in 1954.[23]

SIMONDS'S LAST YEAR

In Florida again, with his property still on the market, Simonds ordered more tung oil trees in January 1931. Wilson Pettibone in Hannibal, Missouri, who had hired him several times to create and guide his Riverview Park, contacted him to work on a new park along the Mississippi and, on January 6 Simonds sent him a preliminary plan for Nipper Park.[24] In July he spoke at a meeting of the Association of American Cemetery Superintendents at Oakland Cemetery in Freeport, Illinois, one of his former projects.[25] Next he went to visit Anton Hodenpyl, his old friend from Grand Rapids, at his estate Hill House in Locust Valley, Long Island. Simonds combined a personal visit with a landscape consultation. While there, Simonds became increasingly ill; his health did not improve when he returned to Chicago and in November he entered Lake View Hospital. He continued to enjoy what he could in his hospital bed, singing songs that his mother had taught him when he was a boy. On Saturday, November 21 Simonds died of complications from a gastric ulcer.

A funeral service was held for him at Graceland's chapel at 2 p.m. the following Monday. Later that day, the cemetery's plant propagator named two of his new chrysanthemum varieties for Marshall's two daughters, Margaret and Barbara, in Simonds's memory. In accordance with his own wishes (and despite his fifty-three year affiliation with the place known as his masterpiece), Simonds's remains were cremated in Graceland's oil-burning facility that he had helped to engineer in 1892. His ashes were spread under his favorite trees, the "church beeches," in the ravine at Pier Cove. *American Cemetery* ran his obituary in its December issue and described his approach to landscape as "greater simplicity, greater naturalness, and greater beauty." It further credited him, saying "His knowledge of the ultimate development of trees and shrubs under proper care enabled him to create effects in landscape gardening seldom equaled and *never* surpassed."[26] When Mattie died seven years later, she, too, had her remains cremated and her ashes spread under the church beeches in Pier Cove.

LASTING INFLUENCE

O.C. Simonds had an influence on the style and standards of landscape design in the Midwest for decades (as did his mentor Bryan Lathrop). While most of his plantings have either deteriorated or overgrown beyond recognition, or have been planted over, the general scheme of many of these sites still follows his original plan. Some of our favorite streets and gardens continue to reflect his belief that design was the most comprehensive art. (See Appendix A for a catalog of his work.) Throughout the more than five decades he practiced his art he became a true master of his painterly approach to design. He knew the characteristics and growth habits of native plants so well he could design with them in combination without hesitation, and still create a site that was comfortable and serviceable. He was, as a biographer has said of Hamerton, "if not an originator of trends, a conduit of taste."[27] He was pleased to be such, to develop landscape gardening as taught by Bryan Lathrop and Adolph Strauch, to create the kinds of scenes that Hamerton described, and to make places in a manner similar to Olmsted's. It meant a great deal to him to speak for our natural environment, for the cause of reforestation, and for the appreciation of our landscape. As *American Cemetery* recounted in his obituary, "to come upon a lady's slipper or gentian in an artistic natural setting meant more to him than a bed of a thousand dahlias or peonies."

After Simonds's death, his firm continued to provide a range of landscape work until the late 1950s (see Chapter 11). However, his own naturalistic approach was superseded by a variety of other styles, and only became popular again with the resurgence of ecology and an awareness of natural systems in the early 1970s. The post-modernists practicing landscape design in 2011 have again moved on from the motive of "landscape painting."

CHAPTER TEN ENDNOTES

[1] York Harbor booklet, SFC.

[2] Map, O.C. Simonds & Co., 1910, showing roads, rivers, and vegetation, SFC.

[3] Seabury Land Company, "York Harbor Hills, Maine," brochure, n/d (date established by the company name of "Simonds and West," to which "O.C. Simonds and Co." was changed in 1925, according to announcement cards.

[4] Miscellaneous records and correspondence between Simonds and his sons Robert and Herbert, SFC; author's conversation with Roberta Simonds, 1997.

[5] Bruegmann, Vol. 2, 240.

[6] Thank you to cemetery historian Diane Lanigan for alerting me to this project.

[7] *Preliminary Report on Experiments with the Tung Oil Tree in Florida*, U.S. Department of Commerce and University of Florida Agricultural Experiment Station, Bulletin 171 (May 1924); and miscellaneous other brochures about tung oil, SFC. Simonds purchased $12.50 worth of tung oil trees in January of 1931, according to his desk diary.

[8] *DeLand Daily News*, January 23, 1929, 1; John Kenneth Galbraith, *A Short History of Financial Euphoria*. (Whittle Books, 1990), 73.

[9] "Spring Hammock: Reflections at the End of the Season," January, February, & March 1931; Simonds typescript; Bentley Historical Library, University of Michigan, Ann Arbor.

[10] *Real Estate News*, 1970, MA.

[11] P.H. Elwood, Jr., ASLA. *American Landscape Architecture*. (New York: The Architectural Book Publishing Co., 1924).

[12] *Transactions*. 85-86.

[13] Elbert Peets, "The Landscape Priesthood," *The American Mercury*, Vol. X, No. 37 (January 1927), 94-forward.

[14] Simonds to Thurston, June 29, 1927; Mark Shoemaker papers, Archives and Manuscripts Department, University of Maryland Libraries.

[15] June and August 1927; January 1928; President's Papers, Ibid.

[16] Pearson to Simonds and Eliot, February 7, 1928; letter is addressed to Charles Eliot 3rd, but that is not likely to be accurate.

[17] http://www.taylorhousemuseum.org/pages/harrison.html

[18] Pearson to Harrison, February 15, 1928, President's Papers, Ibid.

[19] Author's conversation with Robert C. Simonds (son of Robert O. and grandson of O.C.), July 1997; photographs of the planting and boulder-moving in his collection.

[20] Simonds to Walter Studley, April 10, 1928; several plant inventories and nursery order forms dated throughout the 1920s (for as many if not more non-native trees as indigenous), SFC.

[21] Louis E. Ayres, "Ossian Cole Simonds," *University of Michigan Alumnus*, December 12, 1931, SFC.

[22] J. Roy West to Simonds, January 6, 1930, SFC.

[23] Nature Bulletin No. 411-A, March 20, 1971; Forest Preserve District of Cook County.

[24] Memo on Simonds's desk calendar.

[25] *Park and Cemetery*, December 1931, 301-302.

[26] *American Cemetery*, December 1931, 15. There was also an obituary for Helene Van Oven, who with her brother developed Naperville Nurseries, just a few miles from the Morton Arboretum, and one of the vendors used by Simonds and West for clients in that vicinity.

[27] Czach, referring to Hamerton, 477.

chapter 11

SIMONDS & COMPANY
WITHOUT SIMONDS

1931-1956

Red Pine

TRILLIUM ON THE FOREST floor of Simonds's ravine at Pier Cove, with invasive
barberry from his nursery in the 1920s.   AUTHOR PHOTO

O.C. SIMONDS & COMPANY

In 1925 the company became known as Simonds and West, with West relieving Simonds of many administrative responsibilities. During the last few years of his life, Simonds wintered with Mattie in Florida, while West ran the office in his absence, writing frequently on the status of projects. Simonds sent him fresh oranges when he was in Florida (a rarer treat in 1930 than today) and apples from Michigan, and West reminisced about his early years in the firm. His gentle sense of humor and his warm relationship with his boss—whom he still addressed as Mr. Simonds in 1931—come through in his correspondence. Writing to Simonds in Florida on February 6, 1930, West mentioned attending a lecture by landscape architect Fletcher Steele the day before at the Fortnightly Club, which, he wrote, "is a house you must have visited hundreds of times in bygone years." It had, of course, been Bryan and Helen Lathrop's Georgian mansion at 120 East Bellevue Place, designed for them by McKim, Mead, and White during the construction of the World's Fair. West continued, "I recall when I was eighteen years old that you sent me down to hoe in Mr. Lathrop's back yard. I used to carry a hoe back and forth on the street-car and wear a nice suit of blue overalls . . . there are very few of our young men who would be seen carrying a hoe on the street."

West and the younger designers had been taking the firm in the new directions that the clients of the 1920s demanded; the sites were smaller, the designs more formal and modern. So West appreciated Steele's remarks on modern gardens, and noted that "people are using the outside of their houses so much more now" that they nearly always included a terrace or small outdoor room adjacent to the house in their plans. A real change for him; West continued, saying "a few years ago I thought that the wild portions of a house lot should extend up to the walls of the house."[1] No doubt he learned that early on from Simonds, and while Simonds never did change his approach, West did.

Not only did tastes in garden design change in the '20s, but new types of projects began to develop as well. Simonds and West were closely involved in the planning and development of Skokie Road (formerly called Highway 57).

Throughout the winter of 1930 West and Erle O. Blair met with industrialist William V. Kelley (for whom Jens Jensen designed the grounds of "Stonebridge," his Lake Forest estate), Charles G. Sauers, the superintendent of the Cook County Forest Preserve District, and Robert Kingery. Kingery (1890-1951) had worked for O.C. Simonds and Company for six years, leaving to work as an engineer at the recently founded Portland Cement Association for the next six years. In 1924 he had the honor of being asked to start the new Chicago Regional Planning Association's office, function as its secretary, and hire its staff. Not surprisingly, then, West, Blair, and another staff designer named Arnold Roehl attended the Chicago Regional Planning Association annual dinner in 1930. In 1933, Henry Horner, the governor of Illinois, asked Kingery to serve in Springfield as the Director of the Department of Public Works and Buildings; he continued to return to Chicago on his own time to work with the CRPA. He volunteered as well with a number of local planning agencies and park boards. Perhaps his best-known legacy is the regional planning work that culminated in Daniel Burnham, Jr.'s 1956 *Planning the Region of Chicago*, an updated version of his father's 1909 Chicago Plan. Although Kingery had died five years before its publication, the CRPA's general manager divided his prefatory remarks equally between Burnham and Kingery's contributions. The Kingery Expressway on Chicago's south-east side was named for him in 1953.

Marshall Simonds resigned his position with the Green Bay (Wisconsin) Park Board in January 1930 to join his father's firm. Along with West and Blair, he helped keep the firm going for throughout the early years of the Depression. The name of the firm was altered again around 1931 to Simonds, West, and Blair, reflecting further changes. By the mid-1930s Marshall left to work for the Civilian Conservation Corps (CCC), as did his younger brother Robert, who moved with his wife Jerry and their young son Robert O. to Channahon, Illinois, where he managed CCC crews.[2] Marshall left the firm to return to Green Bay by 1938. The firm now billed itself as "Land Designers." Promotions did not come quickly with Simonds, apparently. West was not promoted from "draftsman" to "landscape-gardener" until 1913 (having started there in 1896); Blair had been working for Simonds since at least 1914, if not earlier, but only moved up from "draftsman" to "gardener" in 1916.[3]

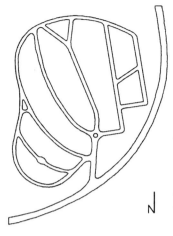

ACACIA PARK cemetery near Buffalo, NY. The original southern portion (show here) exhibits a split character with curvilinear paths amid older trees to the west and orthogonal pathways with more recent plantings to the east. The project was handled by J. Roy West.

J. ROY WEST (1880-1941)

West was born and raised in the Hubbard Woods section of Winnetka, the same small neighborhood as Marion Mahony Griffin (1871-1961) and her cousin Dwight Heald Perkins (1867-1941), two of the shining stars of the Chicago architectural scene in the early 1900s. Winnetka was also Kingery's residence in the Chicago area. A life-long bachelor, West gave generously of his time and energy to his community and to nature organizations. He served as a Winnetka Park Board commissioner for many years, and was a charter member of Jen Jensen's Friends of Our Native Landscape, a group that was instrumental in saving such endangered landscapes as the Indiana dunes. West was a charter member of the Chicago Society of Landscape Architects, which he helped organize to educate and encourage young designers, serving as the chairman of the board in 1935; Sauers of the Cook County Forest Preserve District was the group's president. West also continued to work with Graceland Cemetery; the Simonds, West, & Blair office continued in the 1101 Buena station building at the east side of the cemetery until the building was slated for demolition in 1951. In 1928, Simonds and West were hired to design a Masonic cemetery called Acacia Park, near Buffalo, New York; West would be the partner to handle the project.[*]

---

[*] Information from conversation between John Bry, Acacia historian, and Diane Lanigan of Graceland Cemetery, March 2008.

For Graceland, West offered advice to the cemetery superintendent Herman Reich in 1937 on restoring plantings at the Martin Ryerson plot, and on the difficulty of using the number of evergreens that had been planted previously because of "the increasing amount of smoke in the atmosphere" that caused problems for these species. He recommended spreading hawthorns instead. West also continued to uphold the standards that Simonds and Lathrop had begun setting for the cemetery grounds in the late 1870s. The cemetery staff was discussing the idea of making a denser group of plantings for the front of the Ryerson mausoleum (Louis Sullivan), but West advised that it would "mar the beauty" to do so, and that the plots on the other three points of the intersection—the Schoenhofen mausoleum (Richard Schmidt), the Pullman neoclassical column and exedra (Solon Beman), the Goodman berm (Howard Van Doren Shaw), the Potter Palmer monument, and the Kimball family colonnade (both by McKim, Mead, and White)—required a cohesive landscape. He thought maintaining the wide lawn to harmonize with these other lots was the most appropriate approach "and restful in appearance." He finished by saying that "I would also restate your old ruling of the Cemetery that Graceland should not allow outside nurseries to do work in the cemetery as it would lead to a great deal of trouble . . . This rule has been repeatedly proven to me to be a good one as I travel around the country and visit cemeteries where people are allowed to enter and plant their cemetery lots in their own way and with the type of material they chose." West had himself been involved with the cemetery's landscape for forty years when he wrote to Reich, and knew it as intimately as Simonds had before him.

West lived his entire life in the same home in which he was born, and after her husband's death, his sister kept house for him in his later years. Naturally, he practiced his design ideas on his own home grounds, turning part of them into a wild garden densely planted with early scilla and spring blooming dogwood. When he died in November of 1941 at the age of sixty-one, West was cremated at Graceland, and his ashes returned to his family.[*] George C. Cone, who had worked for Simonds from around 1910—the beginnings of the landscape department at University of Michigan—died the following March.

---

[*] West's nieces and nephews lived in the area. For more details about West's career, see my short biographical essay in *Shaping the American Landscape*, ed. Charles Birnbaum and Stephanie Foell, University of Virginia Press, 2009, 368-71.

AFTER WEST

After West's death, Blair continued to keep the firm of Simonds, West and Blair in business. The office was still in its original location at 1101 Buena Avenue, in the Holabird and Roche-designed former station on the east side of Graceland, as late as January 1951. Lake Hazelmere, the second of the two lakes created by Jenney and Simonds early on, had long since been filled in and turned into additional burial ground. By April 1951 the rebuilding of the main office on Clark Street was complete and the old Buena Avenue building had been vacated; demolition was soon to follow.[4] As of 1956, the company's offices were located at 7530 Sheridan Road, Chicago.

Unfortunately, the firm's trail peters out in the 1950s, with just occasional references to its projects. In 1951 Arch Van Deusen of the Indian Hill Realty Company in Winnetka recommended Blair, along with four other prominent practitioners including S. Herbert Hare and A.D. Taylor, to Horace Holley, administrator of the Baha'i Faith in the United States, as a candidate for designing the grounds around the newly completed House of Worship in Wilmette. As "Van" wrote, "Every one I have talked to about landscaping the temple grounds agree that only a very fine job will do, or the whole effect of the wonderful building may be spoiled." He went on to say that they needed to have a "first class architect" create the plans, and then he might "even let the job go to some spade and shovel boys."[5] Whether or not Holley contacted any of these landscape architects, the job eventually went to Hilbert E. Dahl, a staunch Baha'i himself and a landscape architect who had been trying for twenty-five years to shepherd the development of the grounds.[6]

The winter of 1952 found Simonds, West, & Blair planning the landscape for the new Alexander Hamilton monument in Lincoln Park. John Angel of New York sculpted the statue, which he completed in 1941 but was subsequently stored in Chicago for a decade. Finally in 1952 the monument was set atop a twenty-six and a half ton granite base, reportedly the biggest in the Midwest.[7]

Until the end, the firm continued to design cemeteries. Two Chicago area projects included Mount Emblem Cemetery in Elmhurst, the near-west suburb that the Bryans and Lathrops had called home as early as 1860, and Rand Hill in northwest Arlington Heights. The Mount Emblem history states that circa 1936 "It took eleven years for the architects of Simonds, West, & Blair to transform 75 acres of flat farmland into a picturesque, tranquil scene with tens of thousands of new trees and shrubs as well as the creation of Lake Emblem."[8] Best known for its iconic 1867 wooden Dutch windmill, the cemetery is a favorite haunt of local painters—something that would surely have delighted Simonds.

In 1955, the company designed a new Jewish cemetery as part of the larger non-sectarian Rand Hill Cemetery. Blair also designed a new entrance for this section along Wilke Road.[9] They continued with the landscaping until at least 1956; any trace of Simonds's company disappears after this project, and nothing more is known of Erle O. Blair.[*]

FRANK M. BUTTON (1860-1938) AND FLORIDA

Button and Simonds first worked together on the Fort Sheridan project from 1889-1893, and continued to associate on and off well into the 1920s. Button lived at 2365 Magnolia in Chicago while in Simonds's office in 1909, just about two miles directly south of their office at Graceland. He came to Florida with Simonds around 1910 to assist with Charles Deering's first Florida estate, Buena Vista. Just north of downtown Miami, Deering created test gardens on 200 acres, giving an additional twenty-five acres to the United States Department of Agriculture. As the estate developed, Deering asked Simonds to lay out gardens and drives, and it was Button who continued to oversee it for several more years. Charles's brother James began his extravagant Italian Renaissance estate Vizcaya in 1910 south of Miami in Coconut Grove, but given the ornate and formal style developed by architect F. Burrall Hoffman and landscape designer Diego Suarez, this project would have been out of Simonds's province. He and/or Button, however, may have created some of the more naturalistic areas away from the building compound. Charles later bought the old Cutler estate southwest of Miami and developed an extensive nature preserve, now called the Deering Estate at Cutler and owned by the Miami-Dade Park District, but Simonds and Button do not seem to have been involved here either.

A few years after his wife's death in 1916, Button moved to Florida. He had

---

[*] The Cove guest book lists two visitors who may be related: Alowese Traer Penfield, mentioned in an earlier chapter, and Dorothy Penfield Blair, who would seem to have been Alowese's sister, and could have been married to Blair.

already established a good career for himself, and had served as vice-president of the Mid-West chapter of the ASLA in 1919 before he moved to the then-new town of Coral Gables in 1920 to work with its founder George Merrick on its development. Button also took on a number of private projects over the next eighteen years.[10] His involvement with Buena Vista allowed him to develop design skill with tropical plants, something that would be most useful in Coral Gables. Landscape architect Laurie Olin credits Button's plantings here as "spectacular flora that anticipates the work of Roberto Burle Marx," the noted Brazilian landscape designer.[11] His reputation for successful landscapes in the unique Florida climate brought him the Coral Gables commission in 1924. Developer Merrick hired a stellar group of designers including an artist named Denman Fink, architects George Fink and Phineas Paist, and, of course, landscape designer Button. Coral Gables was a completely planned community in the Mediterranean Revival style then sweeping the country. The town was zoned for residential, business, and industrial areas, as well as recreational and country club sections—at a time when major metropolises like Chicago were just enacting their first zoning regulations.

That same year a developer named D.P. Davis on the other side of the peninsula hired Button to design landscapes for his two man-made islands off Tampa's coast, a project taking full advantage of the real estate boom at the time.[12] As ambitious a plan as that of Coral Gables, Davis Islands would not attain the same success. Interestingly, Simonds made his initial purchase of about twenty-five acres in DeLand to grow tung oil trees at the time Button worked on these two towns.

Button was one of only a handful of landscape architects in this part of the country at the time he moved there in 1920. Arthur Shurtleff* wrote to him a few years later asking about starting an ASLA chapter in Florida, but Button wrote back to say that there just were not enough practitioners there yet to keep it going. The ALSA *Illustrated Works of Members – 1931* contains two photos of Button at the Ponce de Leon and Alhambra Plazas, with architect Denman Fink; the buildings are in the old Florida-Spanish style, and the landscapes very informal and naturalistic. Button continued to manage a busy practice and was still taking on projects when, at the age of seventy-one, he was struck

---

* Shurtleff would shortly thereafter change his name to Shurcliff and would be the principle landscape architect for John D. Rockefeller's restoration of Colonial Willamsburg.

and killed by a passing truck while he was supervising a garden installation in Coral Gables. His remains were brought back to Chicago and buried in the Simonds family plot at Graceland Cemetery. His first wife Florence is interred there with him.

THE SIMONDS FAMILY

The Simondses' real estate investments were hard-hit by the financial crash of 1929. Even though their Montrose Avenue property would have sold for several hundred thousand dollars in 1927, the building on Greenleaf and the land in Florida had no buyers. After O.C.'s death, Mattie was forced to auction off their furniture in Michigan (much of it had come from their Chicago home) for a few dollars. If her daughter and son-in-law had not bought their Pier Cove property, she would have lost that as well.[13]

Daughter Gertrude and her husband William Walker were founding members of the Prairie Club. Dedicated to learning about the natural ecology of the southern Lake Michigan region, with instruction from dunes experts Henry Cowles and Jens Jensen, the group frequently traveled to Simonds's ravine at Pier Cove on its excursions. After her father's death, Gertrude kept the Michigan property as close to his intentions as she could, and when the state proposed building a highway through the ravine in 1960, she saved the property a second time by fighting to have the road moved farther east, leaving his beloved ravine unscathed.[14] The property that O.C. and his friend J. B. Johnson purchased in 1891 is still held by their respective families, and the ravine, while much overgrown from Simonds's original plan, still contains the church beeches, wild roses, and many other plants from the old nursery.[15] When Gertrude's mother-in-law died in 1933, she was buried in Chicago at Graceland.

Julia Simonds Fletcher, Simonds's sister, lived in Grand Rapids throughout her life. Holabird and Roche designed a house for her, built on property adjacent to the old family farm, which their cousins the Garfields had purchased. Her brother and their cousin Charlie created a small subdivision in the area immediately south of their land. Together, Julia Fletcher and Charlie Garfield donated remaining acreage from the farm to the city of Grand Rapids for a public park, and Garfield and his wife are buried there, with a large boulder for their gravestone. Originally called Garfield-Fletcher Park, now known simply as Garfield Park, it was renovated with funding from the National Park Service in 1997.

Hodenpyl Woods, a few miles northeast of Garfield Park, is another enduring Grand Rapids heritage created by Simonds. Developed and financed by his childhood friend Anton Hodenpyl, the two men created this woodland park and drive to preserve a small piece of the area's forests as they were before the early settlers arrived.

CURRENT CONDITIONS

Lacking Simonds's artistic guidance, the landscape pictures he created for properties of family and friends are gone, but because they shared his concerns, the landscapes themselves still endure "for generations to come" (as he had expressed it to Morton) as open, green spaces in otherwise urban settings. The landscape-gardening profession lost one of its greatest practitioners when Simonds died, but his heritage of respecting and preserving "nature as the great teacher" still enriches our lives in these spaces.

CHAPTER ELEVEN ENDNOTES

[1] JRW to OCS, February 6, 1930.

[2] Author's conversation with Robert C. Simonds, 1997.

[3] Lakeside Directories for the years 1910-1925.

[4] Graceland Cemetery *Minutes of Managers/Shareholder meetings, 1938-1973*; April 10, 1951, 62.

[5] Van Deusen to Holley, n/d; Baha'i National Center Archives.

[6] For a short biography of Dahl, see my entry in *Shaping the American Landscape*, University of Virginia Press, 2009. Per her obituary in *Winnetka Talk*, Susan D. West, J. Roy West's sister-in-law, was the first resident of the Baha'i Home for the Aged in 1958, although she was not a Baha'i.

[7] "Granite Block for Hamilton Monument Set," *Chicago Tribune*, February 7, 1952, A10.

[8] www.mountemblem.com

⁹ "Jews Plan 60 acre tract in N.W. cemetery," *Chicago Tribune*, September 29, 1955, W4.

¹⁰ "The City of Coral Gables: Still an Oasis," *Florida History and the Arts*, Summer 2004; undated typescript written by Debbie Lang of Coral Gables.

¹¹ *Vizcaya: An American Villa and Its Makers*, Witold Rybczynski and Laurie Olin. University of Pennsylvania press: 2006.

¹² http://www.tampapix.com/dpdavis.htm

¹³ Author's conversation with Roberta L. Simonds, 1996; inventory of Simonds's household furnishings, SFC.

¹⁴ "Battle is Won; Road Won't Go Through Simonds' Sanctuary," [unidentified Grand Rapids newspaper] May 31, 1960, SFC; author's conversation with Roberta Simonds, June 1997.

¹⁵ Site observations, July 1997 (and subsequent years up to spring 2010); Simonds's original plan redrawn by Roberta Simonds, SFC.

chapter 12

THE BRYAN AND LATHROP FAMILIES

Silky Wild Rye,
Woodland Brome,
and Bottlebrush Grass

JOHN CONSTABLE'S *Study of the Trunk of an Elm Tree* (1821).

THE BRYAN AND LATHROP FAMILIES

Bryan Lathrop and his family, through their connections, influence, and interest in landscape-gardening, are at the heart of the story of O.C. Simonds's life and career. While William LeBaron Jenney invited Simonds to Chicago to work for him on the Graceland project and introduced him to the profession, it was Lathrop who mentored Simonds in the subject of landscape-gardening, introduced him to important future clients, and hired him to work for the Lincoln Park Board of Commissioners. Chances are he also advised Simonds on real estate purchases and investments. His gratitude to Lathrop, as mentioned earlier, lasted until the end of his own life. The Lathrop family is relatively unknown today, but it had a powerful and significant influence on the development of Chicago from the 1850s through Bryan Lathrop's death in 1916.

LAYING THE GROUNDWORK

The Bryans and Barbours were old Virginia families and the first member of the family to emigrate from Virginia to Chicago was Thomas Barbour Bryan (1828-1906), the founder of Graceland Cemetery discussed in Chapter 2. Bryan was born in Alexandria, Virginia, the son of Daniel Bryan, a postmaster and state senator, and Mary Barbour, daughter of James Barbour, a governor and senator. Bryan studied at Harvard, graduating from law school there in 1848. He married Jane Byrd Page in 1850. Her father, Charles H. Page, was chaplain at the Newport barracks, and her mother a daughter of the influential Byrd family.

The couple moved to Chicago in 1853, and by 1856, had purchased 1,000 acres in Cottage Hill, Illinois. Bryan sold some of his acreage to painter George Peter Alexander (G.P.A.) Healy (1813-1894) the following year. Healy painted the Bryans' portraits in 1857 and went on to great acclaim as the presidential portrait painter who captured the likenesses (mostly from other sketches, paintings, and photographs) of eleven United States presidents, including Abraham Lincoln. Bryan practiced law in Chicago and developed much of downtown's real estate in early, pre-fire Chicago. His best-known building was Bryan Hall, an auditorium and theater on Clark Street that was the city's entertainment mecca until it burned in 1871.

While living primarily in Chicago, the Bryans also built a summer and weekend house on their Cottage Hill property in 1859. It was a twenty-one room showplace named "Byrd's Nest" for Jane's mother's family, with a billiard room, a bowling alley in the basement, greenhouses, and a room just to house a solar telescope from the London World's Fair. But most relevant to the story of Graceland and Simonds was Bryan's proclivity for transplanting trees. *The Prairie Farmer*, which covered all sorts of news its editors saw fit to print, reported that the Bryan residence not only had an "artificial lake" on its grounds but the property was "surrounded by thousands of newly transplanted trees," including several elms with trunks up to eighteen inches in diameter, collected from the banks of the nearby Des Plaines River.

Bryan began buying property in Lake View Township, five miles north of Chicago's central business district, and chartered Graceland Cemetery in 1860. The body of his infant son Daniel Page Bryan was moved from the now-defunct city cemetery and was the first burial. With the start of the Civil War, Bryan, a staunch Union supporter, outfitted his own company called "Bryan's Blues." To benefit the U.S. Sanitary Commission after the war (headed by Frederick Law Olmsted for the first few years), Bryan sponsored the Sanitary Fair in his Hall. Later he sold facsimiles of the Emancipation Proclamation to raise funds for the Chicago Soldier's Home. A personal friend of Lincoln, Bryan served as his pallbearer at both his Chicago and Springfield funerals; he transformed the bowling alley at Byrd's Nest into a chapel so that he could hold a memorial service there for Lincoln in April 1863.[1]

In 1889 Bryan began working "zealously for the Columbian Exposition to be held in Chicago," along with his namesake nephew who was director of the Chicago Real Estate Board.[2] His official Exposition letterhead read "Office of Special Commissioner at Large," and he served as vice-president of the World's Congress Auxiliary in 1892. He died in 1906, the year Burnham began to develop the Plan of Chicago; Bryan surely would have been a subscriber had he lived a few more years.

THE FAMILY BRANCHES

Thomas and Jane Bryans' son Charles Page Bryan (1855-1918) was several years younger than his Lathrop cousins, traveled in Europe after the war from 1865-67 (his cousins were sent abroad earlier by their father during the war to keep them out of the war) and attended the University of Virginia and Columbia Law School. He was admitted to the Washington bar in 1878. When his father and his cousin Bryan Lathrop served as directors of the World's Columbian Exposition, Charles assisted by procuring foreign exhibits in 1891-92. Charles then served in the Illinois General Assembly from 1892-97 before answering his real calling of international diplomacy. Over the years he was stationed in Switzerland, Brazil, Portugal, Belgium, and Japan, but, after an accident, he returned to Elmhurst, where he became involved in municipal water and electric company investment.

The Bryans and Lathrops had close connections with a number of important Chicago families at Graceland including that of Edward Swift Isham, who, with Robert Todd Lincoln, formed the legal firm Isham and Lincoln in 1872. Lincoln also assumed the directorship of the Pullman Company upon George Pullman's death. Lincoln's daughter married Charles Isham in 1891 and they named their son Lincoln Isham.

Thomas Barbour Bryan's sister Mariana (1820-1893) met and married New Englander Jedediah H. Lathrop (1806-1889) while he was in Virginia on business. When the family visited her brother in Cottage Hill in 1864, they decided to stay and bought twenty-six acres from Bryan at the corner of St. Charles Road and York Street, on which they built a villa they named "Huntington" after Jedediah's mother's family. Jedediah's career had flourished when he joined the East Boston Timber Company in 1837, to supervise logging in upstate New York and oversee the lumber mill. He learned much about trees and forests from this experience, which may have given Lathrop the inspiration to transplant trees twenty-five years later on his estate in the Midwest. Once settled here, Lathrop became a real estate developer like his brother-in-law, but he focused more on suburban residential development than downtown office blocks. He saw opportunity in a near-west community that would be called River Forest, and created a sub-division there in 1868; Lathrop Avenue is still a reminder of his activities there. The elm trees left from that project were brought back home to Cottage Hill and planted in rows along the main street, becoming so majestic and so beloved by the community that eventually the town's name was changed to Elmhurst.

The Lathrops had four children: Bryan, born in 1844; Barbour, born in 1846; Minna Byrd, who was born in 1857 and died at the age of twenty; and Florence, born 1858. Jedediah sent his two sons to study in Europe for the duration of the Civil War, to keep them out of the army and especially to keep Barbour from joining the Confederates for a second time.

FLORENCE

Florence Lathrop (1858-1921) was sent to school in Paris and, after returning to Cottage Grove, at the age of twenty-one married Henry Field in 1879 in Byrd's Nest Chapel at her uncle Thomas's estate. Henry was the European buyer for his brother Marshall's business and so the couple returned to Paris shortly after the wedding. They had two daughters, Florence and Minna. Henry died in 1890 and Florence and her girls returned to Chicago, living at Huntington in the summer and at the Field mansion on Ontario Street in the winter. (Henry's body was brought back to Chicago and interred at Graceland Cemetery, in a plot between the Marshall Field family and the Lathrop family.) After seeing the work of renowned animal sculptor Edward Kemys at the World's Columbian Exposition, Florence commissioned two bronze lions as a memorial to her husband. The statues were placed on either side of the main entrance steps at the Art Institute of Chicago, where they still stand today, having become the museum's icons. In keeping with the Lathrops' preference for anonymity, there is no plaque honoring the donor, and Art Institute publicity does not mention the Field or Lathrop names in connection with the lions. Mrs. Field also donated their collection of Barbizon school paintings, including the important *Song of the Lark* by Jules Breton; as with her brother Bryan, this subtle and nature-focused style appealed to her sense of good taste and propriety.

Florence Field met her second husband, Thomas Nelson Page (1853-1922), the year before the Fair opened, and they were married in early June 1893 at Byrd's Nest Chapel—after what the papers referred to as a very proper courtship up and down the east coast. He was a cousin of her aunt-by-marriage,

Jane Page Byrd Bryan, and apparently the quintessential southern gentleman, although without financial resources. Page was a writer known for his "local color stories," such as *Meh Lady: A Story of the War*, in which he described what he saw as the mystery and delicacy of southern women.[3] Florence's father had died four years earlier, so what he would have thought of this union with an ardent Southern supporter did not become an issue. Their primary residences were an elegant McKim, Mead, and White-designed townhouse in Washington, D.C. and Rockledge, a large shingle-style summer home in York Harbor, Maine, designed for Florence by Holabird and Roche. With his wife's wealth and devoted support, Page went on to a distinguished career as an ambassador to several countries, most famously to Italy during the years of World War I. Mrs. Page's cousin Charles Page Bryan had a somewhat parallel career in a number of places. When Mrs. Page died in early June 1921, she left behind a fortune estimated by the *New York Times* at about $2,000,000, thanks to her brother Bryan's assiduous management of her resources. For decades he had increased her wealth through astute and various financial transactions. He had hired Simonds in 1900 to create a plat of subdivision for property she owned in LaGrange, a suburb near Elmhurst on the west edge of Chicago, and then aggressively sold individual lots for development. He managed her stocks and bonds as well, and, although Florence deferred to his judgment, she asked that he inform her of any transactions.

She saw to it that her husband was well provided for in her will, but left most of her money to her two daughters. Minna had impetuously married a Yale football player named Prescott Gibson when she was just seventeen and they had one child, Henry Field Gibson. It was not a happy marriage and they divorced several years later bringing both relief and distress to Minna's very traditional mother. Minna's son Henry felt closest to his mother's family and in his twenties dropped the name Gibson, calling himself Henry Field after his mother's father. Minna wed a second time in 1908, marrying into the English aristocracy by becoming Mrs. Algernon Burnaby of Baggrave Hall, Leicestershire. As can be imagined, Henry's growing up years were difficult for him, belonging neither to his native United States nor to his step-father's England. Mother and grandmother worried greatly about his future until his great-uncle Barbour Lathrop appeared on the scene and introduced him to Dr. Henry Wellcome of the pharmaceutical firm Burroughs, Wellcome &

Co. [*sic*], and an ardent archaeologist. Archaeology was also Henry's favorite interest (he greatly appreciated the Field Museum in Chicago, founded by his great-grandfather), and Wellcome encouraged him to study with Henry Balfour at Oxford. This was a turning point in his life; he went on to become a renowned anthropologist, "discovering the earliest known wheel," and serving as an advisor to presidents Franklin Roosevelt and Harry Truman.[4] While the Lathrop, Field, and Aldis families owned large plots at Graceland Cemetery and many family members have been buried there over the decades, Henry eventually moved to Coconut Grove, Florida, and in 1959, signed a quit-claim deed to his rights to a Graceland burial over to his aunt Florence Field Lindsay. His move to Coconut Grove resulted from his appreciation and perhaps affection for Uncle Barbour (his grandmother's brother), who spent winters here in later years with his dear friends, David and Marian Bell Fairchild. Field contributed to Fairchild's botanical garden and funded publications. Florence's younger daughter, also named Florence, led a less colorful life than her sister, marrying a teacher named Thomas Lindsay, who went on to a successful career as a Boston lawyer.

BRYAN LATHROP

Bryan Lathrop (1844-1916) was Simonds's mentor and a life-long influence. But he had an even broader impact upon Chicago's cultural institutions, its commercial real estate market, and its transformation from a grimy, money-grubbing town into a world-class metropolis. Like his uncle and his sister, Lathrop endowed many institutions in Chicago and was well known to fellow citizens in his day, yet he preferred to keep his name off buildings and out of the papers, and so has quietly disappeared from Chicago history. If for no other reason, Lathrop deserves to be remembered for his business acumen and his professional integrity, which seems to have been beyond reproach.

Lathrop was born in Virginia on August 6, 1844. When the Civil War began, his father Jedediah sent him oversees to study and to remove him from the possibility of being drafted into the army. Young Bryan thrived amidst the opportunities his father had arranged for him, traveling the continent and British Isles, learning music and developing an appreciation for art (especially his taste for the works of the Barbizon painters). He became interested in

English landscape-gardening, which would have far-reaching influence on the landscapes of the American Midwest. The family had moved north from Virginia to Cottage Hill in 1864, and after returning from his European sojourn, Bryan went to work managing Graceland Cemetery for his uncle Thomas. His uncle had already set the style for the cemetery by employing such top designers as William Saunders and H.W.S. Cleveland to develop the grounds. Lathrop saw an opportunity to create an exceptionally beautiful cemetery; when Simonds came along as Jenney's apprentice in 1878, he found the long-term collaborator he needed to develop his vision. Lathrop served as the Graceland trustees' treasurer for many years, and eventually replaced his uncle as president. In 1875 he married Helen Lynde Aldis (1849-1935) of Washington, D.C. and York Harbor, Maine. Her father was Washington judge Asa O. Aldis; her brothers were Owen and Arthur, who would play significant roles in the development of downtown Chicago over the next three decades.

Like his uncle and his father, Bryan became extremely successful in the real estate business. He was also a brilliant manager of estates and trusts for the wealthy in Chicago and New England, seeming to have an innate sense of what and when to buy and sell when it came to property. He did equally well with the investments he oversaw for his sister Florence and brother Barbour, and with the passing years their wealth continued to increase. Lathrop and his uncle T.B. Bryan (and Lathrop's brother-in-law Owen Aldis) were among the forty-five Chicago businessmen on the World's Columbian Exposition management board. Charles Follen McKim of the New York firm of McKim, Mead, and White came to Chicago to meet with Burnham to assess the site of the fairgrounds (he was pretty well aghast at the swampy, unbuildable conditions, as were all the out of town architects), and to begin planning the fair's Agriculture Building. Lathrop asked McKim to design a new townhome for him at what is now 120 East Bellevue Place, on the lot just west of William Borden's French Renaissance house at the corner of Lake Shore Drive (designed by Richard Morris Hunt in 1884). Part of Potter Palmer's subdivision, Palmer only leased the land to Lathrop until 1922, when Helen Lathrop sold the house to the Fortnightly Club and the Palmer estate sold it the property. *The Chicago Economist* reported in August 1891 that the house on the drawing boards was "in the Colonial style of architecture with a decidedly Beacon Street twinge to it"; Alfred Hoyt Granger called the finished product, "the most perfect piece of Georgian architecture in Chicago".[5] It was an interesting choice of descriptors; one of the half dozen streets in the Sheridan Park development north of Graceland was called Beacon Street too.[1*]

The Bellevue house was a perfect symbol of Helen and Bryan Lathrops' approach to life. In a highly desirable, newly popular part of town, the house was elegant and conservative, yet socially on par with the more ostentatious dwellings in the neighborhood (the Palmer castle being the most conspicuous; LaVerne and Ida Noyes would settle a few blocks away in another stone pile many years later). With some homes costing nearly $1,000,000, the Lathrops spent just $67,400 on theirs. But it was hardly a little pied-a-terre; the Lathrops employed a full-time, live-in staff of ten, whose rooms were on the third floor of the house. McKim did the original design and William Holabird and Martin Roche created construction documents and interior drawings and supervised the actual building of the structure.[6] Holabird and Roche also remodeled the Lathrops' summer home in York Harbor, Maine. Since Simonds's early days at Graceland, Lathrop used this firm almost exclusively for his building projects, whether personal or commercial.

THE ALDIS IN-LAWS

In 1889, Holabird and Roche designed the Caxton Building for Lathrop at 328-334 South Dearborn (502 South Dearborn in the current numbering system), south of Congress Street. A twelve-story, steel-framed office building of brown pressed brick, the Caxton was a pioneer in that part of town, rising just two years after Charles Heisen's Temple Court and Como Block buildings, put up by 1887. Other developers at the time shied away from the southwest corner of the central business district with good reason. The area from Van Buren Street south along Clark Street was known as "Little Cheyenne," reputedly the toughest and raunchiest area of the city.[+] Owen Aldis (1853-1925), who began his career in Chicago in 1879 managing the Portland Block for Peter and Shepherd Brooks of Boston (and in which the fledgling firm of

---

[*] Sam Brown, the Sheridan Park developer, discussed in an earlier chapter, hired Holabird and Roche to design his own home in the subdivision, at 4608 North Beacon Street (originally 3203 in the old numbering system) for $5,000 in 1890, as noted in Bruegmann's *catalog raisonne* of H&R's work.

[+] The infamous Levee district was a few blocks farther south along Clark and Dearborn between Harrison and Polk, and filled the gap when Little Cheyenne became an early victim of gentrification. In the meantime, Cheyenne, Wyoming called its vice district "Little Chicago" in response.

Holabird, Simonds, and Roche rented space), saw the potential of putting up office blocks in this underdeveloped neighborhood. Aldis began to build here, investing the money of the Brooks brothers for whom he was now acting as agent. He also believed the future would be in office towers when many still refused to build more than a few stories high. His persistence on both counts paid off handsomely as the buildings quickly leased fully. Aldis began planning the Monadnock building in 1888, to be erected on the southwest corner of Dearborn and Jackson, still an unacceptable part of town. Aldis worked with John Root of Burnham and Root on this project, as he had on the Montauk (where Lathrop had offices for a time). Edward Renwick (1860-1941), Simonds's old family friend from Grand Rapids who would work for Holabird and Roche/Root for his entire career, later reported that, "Everyone thought that Mr. Aldis was insane to build way out there on the ragged edge of the city. Later, when he carried the building through to Van Buren Street, they were sure he was."[7] From the success of his buildings it was immediately obvious that Aldis was far from "insane." His younger brother Arthur moved to Chicago in 1889 and became a partner in their new property management firm, Aldis and Company, and they continued to build major office buildings.

When Root died suddenly in January 1891 (during the beginning stages of planning for the World's Fair), Aldis switched his architectural commissions to Holabird and Roche, who then designed the south half of the Monadnock for him immediately after the fair. Although Aldis served prominently on the board of directors of the fair with Lathrop and T. B. Bryan, he apparently found Burnham a little too unrefined for his tastes (no comment on record from the other two). As head of the Buildings and Grounds Committee, Aldis (along with most of the fair's directors) thought the downtown lakefront (future home of Grant Park) to be the best location for the fair. But the Illinois Central Railroad's tracks cut across the entire frontage from Twelfth Street to Randolph, and despite Aldis's high-level negotiations with the railroad's president, no agreement could be reached. Aldis then decided on the South Park location (now Jackson Park), had his committee present Root's famous sketch plan of the exposition site with buildings and features in place, and the decision was made.*

---

* Most accounts of the site choice credit Frederick Law Olmsted with selecting the South Park location; perhaps it was more of a collective decision amongst Aldis, Olmsted, and Burnham.

Aldis was as successful in siting his office buildings and his brother-in-law Bryan Lathrop followed his lead in building major office towers in this questionable area of the southwest Loop, putting up the Caxton and then the Old Colony—another Holabird and Roche design that is still standing—at Dearborn and Van Buren in 1894 on behalf of another Boston investor, Francis Bartlett. According to Miles Berger in *They Built Chicago*, "By 1902, almost one-fifth of Chicago office space was Aldis-produced and -managed."

Aldis and his brother-in-law apparently got along quite well, having similar tastes and proclivities. Both Aldis and Jedediah Lathrop were on the board of managers of Graceland, along with Bryan and, of course, uncle Thomas. Owen had married Leila Houghteling in 1878. She was the daughter of lumber executive William De Zeng Houghteling and presumably sister of Simonds's Winnetka client James Houghteling. She died just seven years later and Aldis eventually moved into the Lathrops' Bellevue Place home, where he lived for many years.

One of Burnham's specific goals in creating a beautiful city was to encourage wealthy Chicagoans to stay here and spend their money at home instead of the capitols of Europe. Aldis, Lathrop, and James Houghteling were all subscribers to the Burnham plan when it was published in 1909. But in May 1912—less than a month before Burnham died in Germany while himself traveling and spending money abroad—fifty-nine year old widower Aldis was driving through Germany with his brother Arthur and his wife Mary Reynolds when he met a twenty-two year old French woman from an aristocratic but impoverished family and by the end of the year they were married. Aldis lived out his life in France, where he died in 1925. His brother Arthur continued to manage the firm in Chicago, living in an unusual Holabird & Roche-designed residence modeled after a Venetian palace, at 1258 North Lake Shore Drive (two blocks north of Lathrop's home and also still standing); he retired to France in 1918 and his son Graham assumed company leadership.

LATHROP'S CULTURAL CONTRIBUTIONS

Thus Bryan Lathrop and his relatives, with their preferred architects, developed an appreciable part of downtown Chicago, set precedent for how Chicago real estate firms operated, and made large fortunes. Throughout all these decades, the city's cultural institutions also benefited from his financial and real estate expertise. He joined the Newberry Library board in 1896 and was actively involved until his death twenty years later. His Newberry appointment came not a moment too soon. The Library owned large amounts of property in the city, these holdings being a part of its endowment. In 1896 it was in the midst of difficulties with the Lincoln Park Commissioners over the Library's holdings in Blocks 43 and 44 of Kinzie's Addition, along Pine Street (now Michigan Avenue) between Chicago Avenue (just south of the water tower) and Ohio Street. The property owners and the Commissioners had agreed that if the City gave authority over this stretch of Pine Street to the Commissioners, they would develop it into a boulevard privately funded and maintained by the owners. Already in June that year the Lincoln Park Commissioners had won a judgment against these "shore owners" (their properties were bounded on the east by Lake Michigan) to pay $100 per linear foot of their lake shore frontage for another shared concern. Although the lawyer's letter did not specify what the money was for, later correspondence explained it was to pay royalties to Major William L. Marshall for the patented Marshall Combined Breakwater and Beach that had already been installed. The Library's lawyer recommended the trustees pay, assuring them that to do so would not "hurt their position."[8]

The Commissioners, though, seemed to waffle on just what their management of the lake shore and the boulevard actually meant. In February 1898 their attorney contacted the owners again, informing them that Marshall was willing to settle for $3.50 per linear foot, waiving interest. The letter further explained that, "This breakwater was built, as you are aware, by the shore owners under their contracts with the LPC. Consequently the Commissioners do not feel that it is their duty to litigate the claim of Maj. Marshall. The litigation of his claim will be at your expense if the litigation is continued."

There were other issues with this property as well (just half a mile directly south of Lathrop's house on Bellevue Place, the area was well-known to him). The infamous Captain (as he called himself) George Wellington Streeter and others were once again suing owners, claiming rights to these properties. The Land Department in Washington, D.C., was the final authority in such matters (this involved riparian rights along the lake shore) and had "finally decided adversely to the claimants" (Streeter, et al.). Then a new claim to 160 acres of unsold land had been presented by a man named Benner, so the Library and fellow property owners Marianna Ogden and N.K. Fairbank had again hired lawyers Needham and Cotton to defend their interests. Benner's claim was denied in 1898; Streeter continued to defend his squatter's rights until 1916.* Lathrop's real estate expertise benefited the Newberry on several occasions, although sometimes even he could not solve issues satisfactorily. In January 1897 the same group of owners came to an agreement with the Lincoln Park Commissioners, and quite an agreement it was. The ordinance passed on January 4 transferred Pine Street from the City of Chicago to the Commissioners; the property owners along Pine signed the document, taking full responsibility for improving and maintaining the new boulevard. Not only was it a covenant but also a lien, and not just against the property but against the owners to the effect that they and their heirs and representatives "shall be personally responsible and bound and obligated by the same even after we have sold and conveyed . . . said parcels of land . . . until we . . . file with the said Commissioners, a personal agreement in like form . . ." to the next owners of the property. There were enough owners' signatures to fill four pages, and Eliphalet W. Blatchford, as president of the Library, signed for its 109 feet. Lathrop became a Lincoln Park Commissioner himself in 1903 and wrote about the corruption of the previous board; it would seem that these ongoing wrangles must have influenced his decision to join.

Then in 1901 Captain Streeter was back in court again, to "enjoin [these same owners] not to erect any buildings, fences or other obstructions upon the premises owned by said complainant . . . or doing upon the said premises or in any way or manner depriving your orator of the unlimited use and occupancy of the same until the further order of this Court." The expertise of real estate men like Lathrop, the power of this well-to-do group of civic leaders, and the Chicago police force could not settle the squatter issue of Streeter.

By 1904 Lathrop was a vice-president of a new organization, the North Central Improvement Association, whose goal it was to keep certain north side streets clean and in good order, at private expense. His co-directors included

---

* Years before Streeter's boat had run aground on a sandbar in Lake Michigan and he made no effort to dislodge it. Overtime more sand accumulated around it and Streeter claimed ownership of the newly formed land, declaring it to be the "District of Lake Michigan." Amazingly, he held out here for two decades, until the police were able to arrest him and his group on charges of selling alcohol on Sunday, tearing down his shack, the "Oasis," in November 1916. (Who is to say Burnham, Lathrop, et al, did not get their ideas for landfill from watching Streeter?)

an impressive roster, including: J. Lewis Cochran, Franklin MacVeagh, Edward Ryerson, Rockwell King (another Simonds client in his own neighborhood), La Verne W. Noyes, Charles Wacker, Mrs. Charles Henrotin, Mrs. A.C McClurg, Mrs. E.B. McCagg, Mrs. Cyrus McCormick, Mrs. Harold McCormick, Mrs. Potter Palmer, and Mrs. Theodore Thomas (wife of the Chicago Orchestral Association's director). Other subscribers included James Deering (Simonds's client Charles Deering's brother and the builder of Villa Vizcaya near Miami), Harry Gordon Selfridge, and Octave Chanute. Simultaneously Lathrop was involved in the beautification of York Harbor, Maine, his summer retreat. The enthusiasm such groups as the American Park and Outdoor Art Association engendered had far-reaching influence around the country in the early years of the twentieth-century, and Lathrop practiced what the organization preached.

LINCOLN PARK COMMISSIONERS

Lathrop joined the commissioners in 1903 with another new member, Francis T. Simmons, who owned a successful glove company in Chicago. The two served for ten years, making changes in how the Commission conducted business (honestly) and in the configuration of the park itself. Lincoln Park had its start in the 1860s with a generic "Lake Park" appellation, on the land around North Avenue and Clark Street that had formerly been the last city cemetery. The park was renamed for the assassinated president from Illinois and over years additional tracts were added to make this a large landscape-style park. Shortly after joining the Commission, Lathrop delivered a paper at a meeting of the APOAA in Boston. He began by saying that, "My first experience as a park commissioner was a surprise and a shock. For about eight years Lincoln Park had been given over to the politicians, with the usual result—extravagance, mismanagement, neglect and decay." He was especially dismayed at their approach to hiring a new superintendent (Chicago had several independent park districts before their consolidation in 1934, of which Lincoln Park was one). The top runner, for whom they were "deluged with letters" of recommendation, "had every qualification for the office except one; he knew nothing of the making and care of parks; nothing of soils and fertilizers; of artistic grading; of planting and pruning; of the maintenance of lawns; of the nature and habits of trees and shrubs, or the effect of time on their for and color in masses; in short, he had no knowledge of even the rudimentary principles of landscape gardening."[9]

Why have parks? Lathrop's belief was that the purpose was to provide "a refuge to the dwellers in cities," to give them someplace "where the eye may feast on the beauties of nature, and where the body and mind may relax and find repose." Who should design and manage parks? Lathrop said they should be landscape-gardeners,* and that brought him to a "vital question": "Is landscape gardening one of the fine arts, or is it only a by-product of the arts, unworthy of the life-long devotion of a serious mind? One is almost forced to believe that its professors are ashamed of it. Few of them even call themselves landscape gardeners any more." He said further that it was the only art form to have progressed in the nineteenth-century—"all of the others have distinctly retrograded . . . architecture as a creative act has ceased to exist." Strong views indeed on the subject, and Lathrop's opinions had a direct and enduring influence on Simonds.

Lathrop hired Simonds to work as consulting landscape-gardener at Lincoln Park, the position that had been vacant since Annette McCrea's hasty departure three years before. He held the post until 1913 when Lathrop left the commission, then again from 1917 until 1921, when Francis Simmons, his other supporter, died. As a team, they promoted lake fill from Fullerton to Diversey, with plans to create an addition five miles of fill up to Devon Avenue (see Chapter 6). They removed Victorian tchotchkes and fountains, removed many little winding paths, and took down outdated structures. They hired architect Dwight Perkins to fashion new buildings and fixtures, and Simonds developed meadows and naturalistic massings of native trees and shrubs. A high-profile, significant project, the restoration of Lincoln Park's landscape and of its commission's integrity perhaps gave the West Parks Commissioners and Jens Jensen inspiration and motivation for their 1906 housecleaning.

As well as working to beautify and expand Lincoln Park, Lathrop kept an eye on the lakefront. A proposal to build a break water along the shore from the Chicago River north two miles struck him as inadvisable and in December 1911 he wrote to Charles H. Wacker to object to the idea because he believed that, "The greatest natural beauty we have in Chicago is Lake Michigan," and asked that the matter be taken up by the Chicago Plan Commission (of which Wacker was a prominent member).

THE PRAIRIE SPIRIT

Well-known in landscape-gardening circles, Lathrop also received the questionnaires that Wilhelm Miller distributed in 1915 to Simonds and Jensen. Not one to pull his punches or back-pedal like Simonds, he wrote to Miller that, "Mr. O.C. Simonds is the one gardener whose work as far as I know has any distinction, and there is not one thing new in his principles. His main inspiration came from Adolph Strauch who was a man of genius." (Being Simonds's teacher and mentor, Lathrop ought to know; Simonds himself never claimed to have created the style.) He explained further, "Mr. Simonds works as easily and as naturally by the sea or among the mountains as on the prairies . . . it should be so since the basic principles of the fine arts are immutable." He summed up his perspective on the matter writing that, "I do not believe that there is any prairie style of landscape gardening and I hope that there never will be one, any more than that we shall have another American language in place of the English language." Lathrop spent seven pages exploring the topic, describing what to him was appropriate landscape design for the Midwest, and leaving it at that.[10]

Lathrop continued to manage trusts and real estate and he began to put money into industrial properties as well. In 1912 he started investing in factory sites at the Indiana Harbor in East Chicago through the Philadelphia Land Company. Burnham's 1909 Plan of Chicago had very directly suggested moving freight transfers, warehousing, and industry to outlying areas as a way to expedite traffic and clean up the city. Suddenly investors were exploring sites with excellent transportation potential around the edge of the city, and East Chicago was very well situated. Not only did it have a harbor on Lake Michigan, the Calumet River flowing through the town, and several freight lines traversing its borders, but it was also adjacent to steel plants and locomotive works. Whether or not Lathrop realized any profit from these ventures is hard to say, as there were still subscription installments due a year after his death in 1916.

On May 10, 1916, Lathrop wrote what *The Chicago Daily Tribune* called "His Last Act." He had been elected president of the "recently organized Illinois Society for the Prevention of Blindness," and his letter to the editor was a means of promoting its work. The letter began, "I am appalled to learn that there are in the state of Illinois between two and three thousand blind persons who might be seeing today had their eyes been given proper care when their sight was endangered." The society was promoting the use of silver nitrate drops in the eyes of newborns as a simple preventative, and Lathrop finished his letter with that recommendation. He died at home on Bellevue Place three days later. *The Chicago Tribune* reported that "Bryan Lathrop, Civic Leader, Dies Suddenly; Succumbs to Heart Disease as He Recovers from Effects of an Operation." Lathrop had just drawn up what would be his final will on April 29, 1916, so perhaps his death was not all that unexpected. He was as generous in his will as he had been during his lifetime.

A trustee of the Art Institute of Chicago, Lathrop left to it, "all of my etchings and lithographs by James McNeil Whistler (a total of 379 and valued by the estate appraisers at $75,000), whether in frames or portfolios. It is my desire that these etchings and lithographs shall be kept together..." To the Chicago Orchestral Association, the organization that was closest to his heart, he left a legacy of about $700,000 as an endowment with which to start a public school of music. He stipulated that his "name shall not be given to it," Lathrop's penchant for privacy being stronger than any desire for public acclaim. That July, though, Illinois poet Edgar Lee Masters wrote *A Poem in Memory of Bryan Lathrop, Who bequeathed to Chicago a School of Music.*

Lathrop left monies to the Children's Memorial Hospital and United Charities. His will enumerated disposition of his possessions including other works of art, clothing, fishing equipment, and miscellaneous items to friends and family. He left all 2,000 volumes in his library to the Newberry, excepting books that would duplicate what was already in its collection. Nieces Minna Field Burnaby and Florence Field Lindsay each received $25,000, "as a mark of [his] affection" because, he wrote, he knew they were "already well provided for." Each of his servants was included, with the proviso that they were still in his employ at the time of his death. "To Joseph Egert, my gardener at York Harbor, Maine, if he shall be in my employ at the date of my death, I bequeath any and all his notes which I may hold at the time of my death, and also such a sum of money to equal $1500" (about two years' salary) was a typical bequest.[11]

Lathrop's funeral was held in the chapel at Graceland Cemetery. William Holabird was listed among the pallbearers, but not Simonds who, perhaps, as a landscape-gardener, was not of the social standing required for that honor. Or perhaps there were other reasons. One can only imagine the grief he felt upon the death of the man he held in highest esteem, who had set him on his professional path, had taken him to Europe to visit gardens, had introduced him to a blue-chip network of clients, and with whom he shared a steadfast devotion to the calling of landscape-gardening.

Lathrop was laid to rest in a simple grave on a low grassy hill north of the Field family plots. His sister Minna and their parents Jedediah and Mariana were already buried here. Bryan arranged to have the stately elm, mentioned earlier, moved many miles from Wilmette to his father's grave site at Graceland in the early 1890s. His wife Helen Aldis, her brother Owen, and his first wife would all be laid here as well over the next twenty years. Brother Barbour, who died in Philadelphia, was buried in the east and sister Florence, who died at her home in Maine, was interred in Rock Creek Cemetery in Washington, D.C.

Helen Aldis Lathrop continued to live at 120 East Bellevue Place until she sold it to the Fortnightly Club in 1922 (she had been a member of the club for forty years). Bryan's grand-nephew Henry Field (Minna Field Gibson Burnaby's son) reminisced fifty years later about visiting "Auntie Helen" at York Harbor and at a beautiful villa in Fiesole, near her namesake city of Florence. (Some of his personal correspondence is in the collections of the Chicago History Museum.) She was always interested in and encouraging toward his interests in archaeology. Uncle Bryan he recalled as "a very genial friendly person who was always kind to me and gave me my first fishing rod to use in Scotland." Helen and Bryan stayed with them often at Baggrave Hall, Leiscestershire, which must have been a delight for Henry. He also remembered a lovely anecdote about Bryan's courtesy when they were traveling through Europe. Apparently Auntie Helen did not like some aspects of train travel, and when this could not be avoided on a particular trip, his uncle arranged "for a charming and talkative young man" to ride in their compartment to distract his wife as they rode backwards through a tunnel. Also pleasing to Henry was that the Field family home in York Harbor was right next door to Helen and Bryan's.

When Helen died in 1935, her body was returned to Graceland and buried along side her husband's. Chicago society must have had to make some adjustments when Bryan Lathrop died and six years later Helen sold the town house. They had no children. The musical events and parties held there regularly, including their traditional Thanksgiving gala with music by Chicago Symphony members, were over. Their Elmhurst estate had already been sold to Dr. Henry Lindlahr by 1914 and turned into a vegetarian sanitarium (the Battlecreek Sanitarium was widely copied). Bryan's sister Florence lived primarily in Washington, D.C. and at her home Rock Ledge in York Harbor. Brother Bryan called the Bohemian Club in San Francisco home and wintered in Miami. Helen's brother Owen Aldis had retired to France and Arthur, the other brother, would soon do the same. The anonymous lions guarding the steps of the Art Institute were the only visible remnant of this remarkable clan.

AND THEN THERE WAS BARBOUR

To call Thomas Barbour Lathrop (1846-1927) the family black sheep would be like calling a Maserati a car—technically true, but mostly missing the point. Barbour's career, oddly enough, leads the Lathrop story right back to Simonds. Two years younger than his brother Bryan, Barbour had a radically different personality. A rebel to the core, at the age of fifteen he ran off to join the Confederacy as a drummer boy; his abolitionist father brought him back home and then took him to boarding school in New York. Barbour was the only southerner amongst his Yankee classmates and although they hated his "imperious manners" and southern sympathies, he believed he was superior and was mostly unfazed by their ridicule and ostracism. He was not there long for before another dispute with his father prompted Jedediah to send him, at the age of sixteen, to the University of Bonn "with plenty of money." Barbour took to the situation like a proverbial duck to water. He learned German quickly and instantly adapted to the European class system which reinforced his belief in his own superiority, his right to come first, and to always have the best of everything. With his ample resources, he took frequent trips to Paris–the Paris of the Second Empire. Extremely bright, with "an undefeated self-assurance," Barbour soon became a sparkling conversationalist and splendid storyteller, with a sophisticated and charming personality (or an insolent one depending on one's point of view).[12]

The Civil War ended in 1865 but Barbour stayed in Europe for two more years, finally sailing for home in 1867, having been abroad for four years. Upon his return, his father insisted he study law at Harvard (after all their arguments and after Barbour's four years of independence one wonders what Jedediah thought would happen). Barbour submitted and graduated with his law degree in 1869 at the age of just twenty-two. Back in Chicago with the family, he was put to work in Wirt Dexter's law office and did so well that Dexter soon offered him a partnership. Barbour turned it down, saying later, "A lawyer cannot tell the truth, he cannot express what he thinks about a case. I wouldn't be a lawyer for all the wealth in the world." This was the final straw for Jedediah who cut off Barbour's money as result and the two did not speak for many years. Barbour, however, was unfazed by his father's action and went to New York to find a job. He wrote for the *Ironmonger's Gazette* briefly–an unlikely match of interests. Then he crossed the country to San Francisco seeking a job reporting for the *San Francisco Morning Call*, a well-regarded newspaper. By then the young man was broke and in order to eat was reduced to stealing milk and bread from door stoops—he later repaid his debt to those he stole from many, many times over. Lathrop finally got the job and became a top reporter, energetic, and somehow always dressed elegantly and expensively, despite the small wages he earned at the paper. As can be imagined, none of this endeared him to his fellow employees and in what Marjory Stoneman Douglas referred to as a "non-fight with the newspaper ringleader," an echo of his boarding school experience ten years before, he soon left that position. It was during this time that he became one of the early members of the Bohemian Club in San Francisco, founded in 1872 by journalists wanting a place to gather. Lathrop would be a lifelong member and considered the club to be his permanent residence. The club's notorious midsummer "High Jinks" out under the redwoods was his favorite club activity, but talking came in a close second. His fellow members nicknamed him "The Man with the Iron Jaw" and thought that the only person who could outtalk Barbour was Rudyard Kipling, with whom he became good friends.

During these years of estrangement from his father Barbour did visit his mother several times. Father and son reconciled enough before Jedediah died in 1889 (incorrectly dated as 1887 in Douglas's book) that Barbour had been fully reinstated in his father's will. This was the beginning of the great wealth he would soon accumulate so that "with his brother's expert care and advice, and his own natural and acquired shrewdness, he became, very early, a millionaire." He quit his job, and knew that he wanted to travel and that he did not want to marry. Described as eccentric, tough, and kind, Lathrop smoked fat Egyptian cigarettes continuously, dressed impeccably, and lived the life of an upper-class Bohemian, traveling constantly and circling the world thirty-eight times in his life. He always had the best stateroom on a steamer, but that did not keep him from active and interested involvement in what went on around him. On one of his trips to Japan, Barbour gave up his room to a family with a sick child. When the ship arrived in Singapore he learned that the girl had died, perhaps of cholera, as everyone else immediately deserted the ship—a typical response when this dread disease struck. Lathrop, however, returned with a boat to bring the parents ashore with the body, found a coffin, and made sure the child had a proper burial. He was known for helping families of students, and for giving any lady he knew $500 for her first trip to Paris, to spend on anything she liked. During his travels in the early 1890s, Barbour also collected artifacts for the World's Columbian Exposition for his brother Bryan, one of the managers of the fair.

Barbour would be remembered especially for his support of plant exploration and importation. He became interested in plants on his first trip to Peru. The locals were building a railroad for his host, Henry Meigs, high in the Andes, but despite the altitude and the heavy loads they were hauling, the workers seemed not to tire. He discovered that this was the result of chewing a plant called "coca" (*Erythroxylon coca*). Lathrop collected some of the leaves and sent them to the California Academy of Science to analyze. Lathrop's protégé David Fairchild remembered years later that, "Much to Mr. Lathrop's disgust, nothing was ever done in the matter. He was particularly annoyed later when a German chemist isolated the useful drug cocaine from coca leaves, a drug which soon became the best known alleviative of human suffering. It was a bitter disappointment to Mr. Lathrop that he had not had the satisfaction of bringing cocaine to public notice."

Lathrop was off on another voyage in November 1893, the month after the World's Fair closed. He sailed on the *Fulda*, one of the largest steamers of the day, bound for Naples. This was to be a turning point in his life for it was on this trip that he met David Fairchild. Fairchild was a twenty-four year old horticulturist who had just left his job with the United States Department of Agriculture, after working in its pavilion at the fair for six months. He was sailing to Naples on the *Fulda* to pursue his dream of studying in Europe. Lathrop was a forty-three year old millionaire man of the world. Forty-five years later Fairchild still vividly recalled his first sight of the man who would become his mentor and friend. One morning as he was walking around the deck, he noticed a tall, handsome man, dressed in pajamas, standing in the sun in the doorway of the Second Officer's cabin. Fairchild had never seen pajamas before—everyone he knew wore a nightshirt. His sophisticated sleepwear and his occupancy of such a prestigious cabin made it clear that this was an important passenger. Fairchild assumed their paths would never cross, or, as he put it, "still less did I dream that we would become intimate companions and friends for life."

Meet they did, introduced at dinner shortly thereafter. Lathrop regaled him with stories about his time in Java, and Fairchild told him about giving up his dream of traveling there because it cost too much. After that, Fairchild turned his thoughts to the Biological Station in Naples, where he would be working. Much to his surprise, Barbour Lathrop called at his pensione. In the course of conversation Lathrop offered to give him $1,000 to make the trip to Java, saying it was "an investment in science, nothing personal." Fairchild felt his knowledge was not up to the offer and spent the next two years studying to prepare himself for the trip. By 1895 he accepted the money and sailed for Java. Lathrop, curious about a plant hunting expedition, joined him, bringing Bryan and Helen Lathrop and one of the McCormick daughters from Chicago. Thanks to Barbour's support, David Fairchild became an expert in the discovery of plants with economic value, and returned to the USDA by the end of the century to become the chief of its new Department of Foreign Seed and Plant Introductions.

Over the next decade he made a number of voyages; the list of Fairchild's contributions to American horticulture from expeditions made on his own or with Lathrop eventually included plants ranging from Japanese flowering cherries to avocados to tung oil trees (the plant that two decades later Simonds and Garfield would plant on their property in DeLand, Florida). David's zeal for plant exploring gave Barbour a useful and fascinating reason for continuing his world travels. Barbour's intelligent participation, knowledge of far-flung places, and financial support gave David a solid base for his work. He was also able to introduce the younger man to helpful connections around the world. Lathrop's cousin Charles Page Bryan (Thomas Barbour Bryan's son) was minister to Brazil when they visited Rio de Janeiro and he provided hospitality. He was transferred to Portugal about 1903 and Fairchild and Lathrop stopped there on another of their many trips. Fairchild had come to believe that Lathrop "had phenomenal luck" regarding weather and that whenever their ship came into port the sun shone. However, this time, upon their arrival in Lisbon, the rain was pouring down so hard the two men did not know how they could get their luggage to shore without it being drenched. While they were considering their options, a launch came alongside, and in it was "Cousin Charlie," Charles Page Bryan in his black Prince Albert coat and top-hat. Sopping wet, "but with the same unruffled dignity" he always maintained, Bryan took control of the situation.

By this time Lathrop and Fairchild had virtually become members of one another's families. Upon returning from a voyage to Tunis in late summer 1901, Fairchild received a telegram from Lathrop inviting him to York Harbor, which he found to be popular with literary people. He especially enjoyed the gatherings at Mrs. Thomas Nelson Page's (Florence Lathrop) "cottage", where he met William Dean Howells and Bryan Lathrop. Fairchild was also a guest at Mrs. Page's home in Washington and he thought she had the "most brilliant salon" in the city. A few years later Fairchild stopped in Chicago on his way west and "spent a memorable day with Mr. Bryan Lathrop [who] had excellent taste and was convinced that America should develop its own types of landscape gardening along naturalistic as opposed to formal lines." Lathrop introduced him to Simonds who "had accomplished some of the first successful moving of large trees." Writing in 1938, Fairchild recalled that Simonds told him that "in landscape gardening, the plants native to a region should compose the major part of any landscape, and this idea sank deeply into my mind and affected everything that I have done in the way of landscape planting." Lathrop then took him to Highland Park just south of Fort Sheridan to see a friend's property. It was small but Fairchild found it planned so well that it seemed to be many times larger than its actual size. After going over the grounds thoroughly, Fairchild found that this "oasis" had changed his mind about the formal gardening popular at the time. Compared to this naturalistically designed landscape, the typical American garden featured "garish shrubs [and] trees" that had no relationship to one another. Lathrop explained to him his dislike for variegated plants also, saying that the white on the leaves looked "as bad as a stray piece of paper" on the lawn; Fairchild recalled that Sargent had said the same thing at the Arnold Arboretum. He would remember these comments and experiences when he began to design his own properties near Washington, D.C. and in Florida.

It would not be too long after this visit that Simonds and Button were working on Charles Deering's estate "Buena Vista", using these same principles right in Fairchild's Miami neighborhood.

After Fairchild's marriage to Marian Bell (Alexander Graham Bell's daughter) in 1905, "Uncle Barbour" visited frequently at their home in Washington, D.C. and later at "The Kampong," Fairchild's experimental garden in Miami. Marian and "Fairy," as Barbour called him, named their son Alexander Graham Bell Fairchild; their first daughter they named Barbara Lathrop Fairchild in honor of her father's mentor. (Their third and last child was Nancy Bell.) Lathrop's interest in botany and horticulture had flowered over the years of traveling with Fairchild so much that when he unexpectedly came across a grove of *Phyllostachys bambusoides*, the most widely cultivated timber bamboo in Japan, growing twelve and a half miles south of Savannah, Georgia on the Ogeechee River, he bought it and gave it to Fairchild's Plant Introduction office. They named it the Barbour Lathrop Plant Introduction Garden. Lathrop became a part of the Bell family circle too, and shared Mrs. Bell's interest in Japanese udo plants (*Aralia cordata*), which she was growing in her garden at their home in Baddeck, Nova Scotia.

Lathrop had adopted modern technology and owned a long black Cadillac, driven by his chauffeur. The other side of a brilliant mind and personality often seems to be a short and hot temper, and Barbour was no exception. Fairchild made few comments in his memoirs about this side of his mentor, but those he wrote provide a glimpse at the more difficult parts of his personality. On one trip he "[left] Mr. Lathrop to vent his wrath on the luckless staff," and back in the States in the early twenties, "his long-suffering black servant Tom" tended to his needs. There was no mention of bequests to servants in Barbour's will.

When Barbour died in Philadelphia on May 17, 1927, he left an estate valued at $1,750,000, mostly in personal property. Although his primary residence was the Bohemian Club in San Francisco, he was considered a legal resident of Chicago and his will filed here. He left money to his two nieces (his sister Florence's daughters), and to other relatives and friends. There was a bequest to Children's Memorial Hospital, and $50,000 to the Orchestral Association of Chicago "in memory of my brother Bryan Lathrop." Jesse

Lathrop Moss of Lake Forest received $10,000 and functioned as an executor. He had become the Newberry Library's financial agent shortly after Bryan joined its board and was presumably a cousin. Barbour left "curios" from his travels to the Golden Gate Museum and "To John McLaren, Superintendent of the Golden Gate Park, San Francisco, $1,200 to purchase something in memory of his old friend and admirer." The list of personal effects read like the inventory of a fine haberdasher and included a Vacheron and Constantin 18 karat gold watch with chain, a medal from Verdun, gold stick pins, and a sterling silver whisk broom. For the man who was in some ways the son he never had, Barbour left, "To my friend and long-time traveling companion, David Fairchild, now Chief of the Section of Plant Introduction, Department of Agriculture, District of Columbia, the sum of $15,000, in remembrance of the pleasant years we passed together, said sum, in case of his death before my death, to be paid to his wife, etc." Lathrop also left a small sum to each of Fairchild's three children. The bamboo grove was not forgotten either. He left $10,000 to Fairchild and a law firm in Savannah "to be spent on the Bamboo Grove Government Experiment Station, leased from me by the Government and situated on the Ogeechee Road." Fairchild called him "The Patron Saint of Plant Introduction," and Lathrop deserved the title.

Barbour Lathrop outlived his responsible, dutiful brother by eleven years and his gracious, proper sister (who was twelve years younger than he) by five years. Although Florence did not mentor someone directly as her brothers had done, she provided the wherewithal for her second husband Thomas Nelson Page to pursue a distinguished diplomatic career and was the picture-perfect diplomat's wife. And she gave the Art Institute its lions which have become a widely-recognized symbol of Chicago. Barbour, like his brother, found a protégé worthy of mentoring, generously sharing knowledge, connections, and resources. It was through Barbour that Bryan's protégé Simonds met such important clients as the Bells and the Grosvenors and had the chance to converse with Fairchild. While there was always a certain formality between Bryan and O.C. Simonds, Barbour and David Fairchild developed a level of friendship between equals that seems to have been full of shared humor. In both instances, though, the Lathrop brothers enabled two brilliant careers and, perhaps inadvertently, contributed significantly to the nascent professions of American landscape architecture and horticulture.

DAVID FAIRCHILD, THE BELLS, AND THE GROSVENORS

Born in Lansing, Michigan, David Grandison Fairchild (1869-1954) was the son of an English professor at Michigan State Agricultural College— Charles Garfield and Liberty Hyde Bailey's alma mater. When David was a child his father George accepted the presidency of the state agricultural college in Kansas and the family moved west. David graduated from this school as a botanist, and between family connections and his own profession, he got to know the legendary Michigan horticulturists. Professor Beal he described as a "gentle Quaker" burying seeds in bottles to test germination. Regarding Bailey he said that it was "hard to overestimate the influence of his publications . . . his stimulating and forceful personality has been outstanding in the horticultural world." He knew Eugene Davenport, too, whom he found to be "quite as great in his way" for helping to create the school of agriculture at the University of Illinois. It is surprising that he had not met O.C. Simonds before Bryan Lathrop introduced them, given the colleagues they had in common.

After graduating from Kansas State, Fairchild went to work for the United States Department of Agriculture in Washington, D.C. as a plant pathologist in 1889. The department had been started during Lincoln's presidency in 1862, discontinued during the war, and reestablished later. The same William Saunders who had recently designed parts of the original section of Graceland Cemetery was named head of the Plant Propagation section.[*] Fairchild worked in the agriculture exhibits at the World's Columbian Exposition in 1893, in the Agriculture Building designed by McKim, Mead, and White. Of course, even if Fairchild had met the Bryans or the Lathrops during the fair, being just a junior USDA employee, he would not have been formally introduced. Yet he met Barbour by serendipity on the *Fulda* the month after the Exposition closed. After four years with the USDA, Fairchild felt the wider world calling him, and having been encouraged by his Aunt Sue when he was a boy to travel and learn all he could, he took the plunge and left his job. After the Foreign

---

[*] This William Saunders was born in Scotland, came to American about 1845, worked as a landscape-gardener and horticulturist, and was an important contributor to the development of the USDA. He died in September 1900. The Dominion Experimental Farms in Canada was headed up by another William Saunders (1836-1914) from England, who was succeeded by his son Charles.

Seed and Plant Introduction section was started in 1896, Fairchild came back to manage it. In the intervening years he met Barbour, traveled to Europe and Java, and found his calling as a plant explorer.

Over the course of his career, Fairchild introduced a number of plants to America that have become staple crops: avocados, seedless grapes, Siberian alfalfa, Lapland barleys and turnips, bamboos, filberts, Japanese flowering cherry—and tung oil. Fairchild discovered this new varnish on a trip to Canton in late 1901. A junk caught his attention because it was not painted, but instead was oiled or varnished. He made inquiries and found that it was coated with tung oil (also called China wood oil), made from the fruit of the *Aleurites fordii*, known as the tung oil tree.

It was an intriguing product that formed a thick crust and shriveled when exposed to air, and it dried better in moist air than in dry so was an excellent product to use for boats. The more Fairchild learned, the more promising the plant became. Deciduous, fast growing, no bigger than an apple tree when mature, it bore fruit within four years, and was hardy to zero degrees. By 1907, 800 trees had been distributed along the south Atlantic and Gulf coasts of the southeastern United States and by 1938 there was a 2,000 acre plantation near Gainesville, Florida. In the mid-1920s Simonds and Garfield had tried their short-lived experiment in DeLand, in central Florida, but tried too soon. By this time Fairchild had been established in his "Kampong" at Coconut Grove for about fifteen years when he and the landscape-gardener met each other again, upon Simonds's visit to his client Charles Deering at his estate Buena Vista on Biscayne Bay. Perhaps Fairchild told Simonds about the amazing plant, and at this time, Simonds, who was enjoying his nursery in Michigan, would have found growing a newly-imported and highly useful tree to be an exciting challenge. While the Garfield-Simonds experiment was not a success, by the mid-1930s the tung oil market boomed.

In 1901 Fairchild happened to meet Gilbert Grosvenor (1875-1966) at the Cosmos Club in Washington. D.C. Grosvenor was publishing a small magazine for the National Geographic Society and asked to include some of Fairchild's exotic photos of "Tunisian women fattened for marriage". They met again in 1904 and Grosvenor asked Fairchild to give a talk on his travels to Baghdad to the Society. Alexander Graham Bell (1847-1922) was president of the Society and was in the audience that evening; his daughter Elsie (1878-1964) was married to Grosvenor. Bell invited Fairchild to come to one of his "Wednesday Evenings," a salon he and Mrs. Bell held in their home in Washington. That evening he met Melville Bell, A.G.'s father; his mother Eliza Grace Symonds had died in 1897. Although she was deaf, her strong spirit refused to let that restrict any of her many activities and this was the amazing female model with which young Bell grew up.* Bell's wife Mabel Hubbard was completely deaf like her mother-in-law, yet she had learned to speak, lip-read, and sign in several languages. Obviously Bell's strong interest in hearing and communication stemmed from a desire to help the deaf. At dinner that first night at the Bells Fairchild found himself seated next to the other Bell daughter Marian (1880-1962), who had been working for sculptor Gutzon Borglum in New York City. It would have taken an unusual woman to understand Fairchild's travels and plant collecting, and it would have taken an unusual man to be a good match for a woman who had grown up with the inventor of the telephone and a hundred other new things. David and Marian seemed to fill those roles for each other nicely, and they were married in April 1905.

The newly-weds bought forty acres near Kensington, Maryland, just ten miles from the Capitol on Rock Creek. Uncle Barbour dubbed their place "In the Woods." Fairchild finally had gardens of his own and, as he soon learned, "in gardening you may as well not know anything at all as to know it in a theoretical way." He filled their land with the flowering cherry trees he brought from Japan. When he and Marian decided to sell "In the Woods" in 1928 to make the Kampong in Coconut Grove their permanent home, the thought of leaving his cherry trees made it nearly impossible for him to give the property up. Frances Hodgson Burnett, author of the highly popular *The Secret Garden*, was a dinner guest one night, and wrote a haiku in Japanese characters on her place card for him:

Only in dreams of spring
Shall I see again
The flowering of my cherry trees.

Mrs. Bell had bought the eleven-acre property on Biscayne Bay in Coconut

---

* Interestingly, Fairchild used the spelling of her name whenever he referred to O.C. Simonds in his memoirs.

Grove, Florida for them in 1916.* Fairchild named it "The Kampong," a Javanese word designating a family compound, and Barbour, who spent his winters in Miami now, visited each day. Architect Edward Clarence Dean designed their Spanish revival home. Their nearby neighbor was none other than Charles Deering who, as Fairchild recalled, "sent for O.C. Symonds, the landscape gardener I had met in Chicago," to work with his property, called Buena Vista. As at his Evanston home, Deering was mostly interested in plants and birds, and wanted to create a tropical arboretum here in Florida. Fairchild was impressed with the native plants growing at Buena Vista, including "one of the finest mangroves on the coast, an old grove of beautiful coconuts, and a magnificent banyan (*Ficus nitida*), with a hundred-foot diameter canopy cover."[13] Also among Simonds's circle wintering in Coconut Grove was client and childhood friend Anton Hodenpyl. Hodenpyl's Long Island tudor-style mansion Hill House was the last property Simonds visited before his death in November 1931.

The Deering brothers Charles and James both built estates in the Miami area. In his memoirs Fairchild reflected on the very different styles of the two properties and the rather strange destinies of each. As he and Charles were discussing Fairchild's experimental garden, James was in the next room planning Vizcaya with his architect. As Fairchild recalled, he came in and said to his brother, "Charles, don't let the botanists get all your money. The architects are getting all mine."[14] Buena Vista, dedicated to natural flora and fauna, was a paradise. Fairchild appreciated it greatly and remembered that it had canals winding through the mangrove forest and the coconut palm grove, a collection of rare trees, aviaries with egrets and cranes, and an island with monkeys. During the short but crazy land boom in 1925-26, the property was sold to developers. As Fairchild so poignantly wrote, "Even the magnificent *Ficus nitida* tree, the wonder of the Miami region, was torn to pieces and dragged out by tractors as the entire place was turned into a ghastly waste of suburban lots which to this day [1938] have not been sold." Buena Vista met the same kind of misbegotten fate as Simonds's Chicago home, but James's fantastic

---

* Elsewhere in his memoirs Fairchild wrote that in 1916 "Deering had expressed surprise that the garden should be located on rented land, and had offered to give us a tract near his new Buena Vista estate. This land was by far the best site offered to us, and we finally accepted it. Mr. Deering deeded it to the government with the proviso that in case the government should ever cease to use it as a plant introduction garden, the property should revert to his estate."

estate Vizcaya, created to replicate an Italian Renaissance palazzo and gardens, still stands and is owned by the county, attracting thousands of tourists each year.

Fairchild would have seen Simonds again at his sister- and brother-in-law's farm, Wild Acres, in Bethesda, Maryland. The Grosvenors had bought 104 acres in Montgomery, Maryland in 1912[15] and called Simonds in to look over their new property in January 1913, before they began to build (it was always Simonds's dream to have clients wise enough to do this). Writing from the Hotel Royal Palm on Biscayne Bay in Miami, Simonds reiterated the placement of the buildings and the road they had discussed in person. Views, woods, and location of the well were the primary considerations. He also encouraged them to plant trees to frame more vistas and provide shade, telling them, "An old friend of mine said that nothing grows into money faster than trees." The Grosvenors converted their farm into an estate in 1928, building a large Tudor-style house on the property that year and using some of the stained glass and other special features from the A.G. Bell house in Washington D.C. They asked Simonds for assistance again, which worked out conveniently in conjunction with his University of Maryland project. He brought his now-landscape architect son Robert into his Grosvenor projects.

FULL CIRCLE: ROBERT SIMONDS, THE GROSVENORS, AND YORK HARBOR HILLS

Robert O. Simonds (1899-1957) was O.C. and Mattie's youngest child, and the one to most closely follow in his father's footsteps. He went through the landscape architecture program his father had helped start at the University of Michigan-Ann Arbor, where he met his wife Gladys McConnel (Jerry), another landscape student who went on to practice professionally. The young couple became the landscape architects for the Grosvenor project and for the Bell grave site, with the senior Simonds advising.

The extended Bell family spent happy summers at Beinn Bhreagh, "Beautiful Mountain," so named by Bell, in Baddeck, Nova Scotia. Bell himself slept during the mornings, and worked during the night, continuing to think and experiment here at his retreat until his death in 1922. He was buried on the mountain and the family asked Simonds to create a fitting setting. Simonds and his son engineered the moving of a large boulder up the "beautiful mountain" to be used for a marker. Robert superintended the project in October and November of 1927. They contracted with a man named Totten from nearby Sydney, and his man Carson came by on October 10 to move the boulder. Robert wrote to Grosvenor back in Washington that Carson had made a sled of birch logs and loaded the stone onto it. Moving the boulder up the mountain was not an easy task. Robert continued,

> Wednesday the stone began to creep up the hill inch by inch. That day it moved 225 ft. which brot it up to 125 ft. below the road. Thursday and Friday the stone moved right along–going 800 ft. Friday. Saturday it poured and none of the men came except Norman. There were just 175 ft. to go so in the afternoon John MacDermid, Mr. Carson, Norman, Scot (the horse) and I went up and moved the stone the last lap. I was pleased with Mr. Carson's work and very little moss was disturbed in the moving.

He also cleared brush for Mrs. Grosvenor's "Surprise View," which Robert said surprised *him* as he "didn't know how much could be seen from there." Robert and Jerry continued into November working on the plantings to go around the stone.[16]

That December O.C. wrote to Grosvenor regarding Wild Acres to say that he hoped they could "keep the woods intact." He wanted to add native species including rhododendrons, mountain laurel, holly, inkberry, ferns, galax, shoria, partridgeberry, and pyrolas. Simonds was also pleased with the site selected for the new mansion and that he "wanted to help all I can in the development of your country home." The following April, Simonds made suggestions for creating a pond on the property that he thought could be "made tight with the clay soil." He also had plans for creating an "Evergreen Mountain" that would be seen as one drove up the entry road.

In mid-June of 1928 the elder Simonds attended his fiftieth college reunion in Ann Arbor, and continued to correspond with Grosvenor while he was there. Grosvenor's architect Arthur B. Heaton had plans for a croquet and bowling lawn, and Simonds advised on those. By the end of that October, Grosvenor had also asked his landscape-gardener to create a planting scheme for the grave of Rear Admiral Robert Peary (1856-1920) at Arlington National Cemetery.

AT BEINN BHREAGH, Nova Scotia, Canada, Simonds designed the grave site of Alexander Graham Bell (top). The view from the hilltop site (middle) was accentuated by clearing the brush. The marker for the grave is a massive boulder which was moved by a birch log sled (bottom).

The National Geographic Society had funded Peary's trips to the North Pole, including his historic journey in 1909, for which he claimed to be the first (non-native) to reach the Pole. Simonds wanted to plant hemlocks to "set off the monument," and then to create a "typical Virginia hillside" to the south of it with a variety of native plants that would provide year-round beauty as well as food and habitat for birds. He advised caution, though, suggesting that the shrubs should only be planted if the cemetery administrators were behind the plan.

Simonds continued to consult on the remodeling of Wild Acres, and in November 1928 his firm submitted a list of plants to be ordered from the Forest Nursery Company in McMinnville, Tennessee (established 1887 and still in business in 2011). The order included 3,700 trees of about thirty-five species; about 2,000 "hardy deciduous flowering shrubs" of about forty species; and 135 evergreens. By the next spring, Grosvenor wrote to O.C. to tell him, "I want you to know the very high opinion we have formed of the ability of your son, Robert, who has had immediate charge of carrying out your plans at Wild Acres. I believe this young man has unusual talent. He has also much energy and tact in directing laborers, and I predict for him a successful and brilliant future." O.C. wrote back in the middle of June 1929 to thank him, "Nothing, I am sure, can give a father more satisfaction than to have his boys make good, unless it is to have his daughters make good, so you can imagine how delighted I was to receive your letter of recent date. I am especially glad that you and Mrs. Grosvenor take such pleasure in the landscape work that has been done for you." He went on to say that there were several places that gave him a lot of pleasure because the owners enjoyed them so much. He listed Hodenpyl's Hill House estate on Long Island and an unnamed place probably in Dixon, Illinois.

Things were coming along well at the Grosvenors and in December 1929 Gilbert wrote to Robert to tell him so. "Everything that you and Mrs. Simonds did around Wild Acres was one-hundred percent good." O.C. and Mattie wintered in Florida as usual, but in January he wrote to Grosvenor regarding crabapples for the property, citing those at Mr. Higinbotham's place in Joliet as examples of how they could be used to good effect. (Simonds had done planning there in the late 1890s.) Their work was nearly finished at Wild Acres. On November 13, 1931, Grosvenor wrote to Robert, closing his letter by saying, "Hoping you and Mrs. Simonds and the boy are well." (Robert C. was not yet a year old at the time.) Simonds *père* died a week later, and Grosvenor wrote again on the 28th to say that "We shall always be glad that we had at Wild Acres the benefit of [your honored and distinguished father's] unusual talents." In December he sent his condolences to J. Roy West, "Mrs. Grosvenor and I shall always be glad that we had the benefit of Mr. Simonds' rare genius at our home, Wild Acres, in Maryland." In writing again in January, Grosvenor referenced Simonds's completed work for the University of Maryland, and that landscaping at his home was finished as well. The Grosvenors lived at Wild Acres for years. It was finally sold to the Natural Renewable Resources Foundation in 1973. Then in 2007 there were rumors that the property was to be sold and subdivided. Neighbors in the Wildwood Manor Association went to work to preserve it. By June 2009 it had been listed as a Montgomery County historic landmark and was at the heart of its historic preservation master plan.

The young Simondses soon took over another of O.C.'s old projects. The Lathrops had asked him back in 1901 or 1902 to design the garden around their summer home, Aldis Cottage, on the cliffs overlooking the sea at Millbury Cove, in York Harbor, Maine. He also designed the grounds of Florence Lathrop Field Page's home (Mrs. Thomas Nelson Page), Rock Ledge. Writing to George E. Marshall in Yorke Village, Maine, from the Hotel Netherland in New York, Lathrop told him about working on the development of new roads for the town. "I was fortunate enough to have Mr. Simonds, the best landscape-gardener in Chicago, with me, and he was kind enough to make some suggestions about the planting for the grounds about the Church and the Town Hall. In fact, he staked out the roads as he advised making them."[17] Although it was Lathrop who had introduced Simonds to the fundamentals of his art, to Adolph Strauch and other significant practitioners, and to the core writings of landscape-gardeners like Repton, Lathrop always referred to Simonds as the best in the business, with no hint of irony or mention of Lathrop's own role in Simonds's abilities.

Several years later York Harbor resident E.L. Gifford decided to subdivide parts of his property in what was called Seabury at the time, and for which he named his company the Seabury Land Company. The new town he named York Harbor Hills. Gifford asked Simonds to plan the subdivision, and Simonds found the whole setting so beautiful and promising that he and his friend Anton Hodenpyl invested in the project. Simonds assumed a large part of Gifford's holdings when the latter died. Sometime after 1922 the Seabury Land Company gave "Forris W. Norris of Oyster Harbors on Cape Cod an 11-month option to purchase the entire holdings of the Company."[18] Alas, Bryan Lathrop had been gone eight years or so; had he been available to advise, he would certainly have persuaded them against this decision. His policy was to never give an option on a property (clearly written out in his dealings with the Newberry Library two decades before). So the Simonds family continued its involvement with this unsuccessful project into the 1930s. Eldest son Herbert was one of its three directors, Simonds and West the Landscape Designers, Gladys LaFetra the manager, and youngest son Robert the Superintendent of Improvements. He, Jerry, and their little son Bob lived here for several years as they worked to establish the town. In June 1929 Charles and Anne Lindberg, on their honeymoon, stopped at York Harbor in their boat, the "Mouette", a rare celebrity appearance in this staid, upper-class resort town.[19]

Under Robert's supervision a beautiful stone model home was erected, and homesites established. O.C. had directed the layout. As a brochure promoted:

> The plotting has not been done on paper in the conventional manner. Rather the land was studied and the house sites selected to afford the best ocean views without disturbing the outlook from other houses. Only after the house sites had been carefully located were the plot boundaries fixed.
>
> Roads following the natural curves and grades so as to preserve the park-like beauty of the rolling hills. The result is a plan which gives to small acreage the freedom and seclusion usually associated with large estates.

They were creating a dream town. The firm sought a special kind of buyer, one who understood and appreciated the understated elegance of the development and of the Simonds approach. The brochure concluded by stating that, "The residents will be carefully selected and only persons in sympathy with the plan of development will be invited to purchase land." Unfortunately this kind of individual, with enough wealth and interest in such a community, proved too rare. Added to the seeming general lack of interest was the stock market crash that diminished the value of O.C.'s Florida, Chicago, and Michigan properties, and now the York Harbor Hills investment. Had Lathrop lived another decade or so, perhaps with his input Simonds's investments would have turned out very differently. In a way, though, this brought the father's long career full cycle: it was Lathrop who introduced him to landscape-gardening and brought him to York Harbor, and now it was Simonds's youngest son who wrapped up the last of the Lathrop projects.

CHAPTER TWELVE ENDNOTES

[1] Much of the information about the Thomas Barbour Bryans and the Jedediah H. Lathrops came from materials in the Elmhurst Historical Museum archives and the Bryan records at the Chicago History Museum. Additional sources include special collections at the Newberry Library, the Library of Congress, and Clerk of the Circuit Court of Cook County records.

[2] Bessie Louise Pierce in *A History of Chicago,* Vol. III.

[3] From Philip J. Funigiello's *Florence Lathrop Page: A Biography,* 1994: University Press of Virginia. While Florence Lathrop Field Page does not have an archival collection *per se,* Funigiello found her information in her husband's records at three institutions in Virginia.

[4] Ibid.

[5] Muriel Beadle, *The Fortnightly of Chicago: The City and Its Women, 1873-1973,* photocopy of pages courtesy of Elmhurst Historical Museum.

[6] Bruegmann.

[7] Miles Berger, *They Built Chicago,* 1992: Bonus Books, p. 44. Berger states that Renwick worked for Burnham in the 1890s; it is possible that he took a job there for a short time.

[8] Newberry Library Special Collections, Trustees of Newberry Library records, box 2.

[9] Bryan Lathrop, "Parks and Landscape Gardening," no date; Bentley Historical Library, University of Michigan. Lathrop did not usually hyphenate the term "landscape gardening," whereas Simonds did.

[10] Lathrop to Miller, April 27, 1915; University of Illinois archives, Horticulture Landscape Extension records.

[11] Bryan Lathrop will; Clerk of the Court of Cook County probate records.

[12] Much of the material on Barbour Lathrop and David Fairchild is from David Fairchild, *The World Was My Garden*, 1938: Charles Scribner's Sons; and Marjory Stoneman Douglas, *Adventures in a Green World: The Story of David Fairchild and Barbour Lathrop*, 1973: Field Research Projects. Douglas lived from 1890 to 1998—yes, 108! She was a brilliant woman who was the first to understand the threat of destruction faced by the Everglades and devoted her life to writing about them and lobbying for them. Additional material from "Barbour Lathrop" (obit), *New York Times*, May 18, 1927, 25 and "Barbour Lathrop, Capitalist, Leaves $1,750,000 Estate." *Chicago Daily Tribune*, October 9, 1927, 4.

[13] *The World Was My Garden*, 401.

[14] Ibid., 418-19.

[15] Montgomery Country Master Plan for Historic Preservation, Amendment, Sept. 2008.

[16] Correspondence between Robert O. Simonds and Gilbert Grosvenor, and between O.C. Simonds and Gilbert Grosvenor, 1927-1929; Library of Congress, Grosvenor papers, I:74 Personal Papers; Simonds, O.C. and Robert file.

[17] Lathrop to Marshall, March 26, 1902; Sterling Morton Library, Morton Arboretum.

[18] "Seabury Land Company Gives Norris Option on 'York Harbor Hills'"; York Harbor paper, no name, no date, no page number; Morton Arboretum.

[19] Brochures and newspaper clippings in Simonds family collection; interview with Bob Simonds, July 2009.

KEY TO PROJECT LIST SOURCE ABBREVIATIONS:

AIC　　Art Institute of Chicago
ALA　　*American Landscape Architect*
B/A　　Bergmann/Anderson archives
CELF　　*Country Estates of Lake Forest*
CLA　　*Country Life in America*
CPD　　Chicago Park District
DB　　Diana Balmori, "Cranbrook"
EHM　　Evanston Historical Museum
ER　　Edward Renwick memoirs
EW　　Ernest Warner biography
FLO　　Olmsted Client Card File, FLO Historic Site, NPS
HLR　　*Historic Landscape Report,* 1997
IHC　　Indian Hill Club
ISU　　Iowa State University
JRW　　J. Roy West correspondence
JRW obit　　West obituaries (ASLA and local papers)
LOC　　Library of Congress
MA　　Sterling Morton Library, Morton Arboretum
MPPDA　　Madison Parks and Pleasure Drive Association records
NC　　*National Cyclopedia of Biography*
OCS　　O.C. Simonds
P & C　　*Park & Cemetery*
RB-CHS　　Robert Bruegmann/Chicago Historical Society
RCS　　Robert C. Simonds
RG　　Robert Grese
SFC　　Simonds Family collection
SHSW　　State Historical Society of Wisconsin
WHTC　　William H. Tishler collection

The sources refer both to an actual plan or contemporary mention of an O.C. Simonds & Company (or successor firm) design as well to secondary sources.

PROJECT LIST

O.C. SIMONDS & COMPANY PROJECTS

Simonds and other members of his firm designed several hundred more projects than have so far been discovered. The sources refer to actual documentation of a Simonds & Company design where one exists; otherwise the reference is to supporting documentation. Updated May 2011.

DATE	NAME OR TYPE	LOCATION	SOURCE
	ARBORETUMS		
1921-1925	Morton Arboretum	Lisle, Il	MA
1907	Nichols Arboretum	Ann Arbor, MI	Nichols
	CEMETERIES		
1928	Acacia Park (Masonic)	Buffalo, NY	John Bry
1920s	Bell, Alexander G. gravesite	Nova Scotia	RCS
1908	Brady Hill Cemetery (entrance)	Saginaw, MI	RG
	Elmwood Cemetery	Detroit, MI	RG
1909	Forest Lawn Cemetery (entrances, northern section)	Saginaw, MI	RG
1878-1931	Graceland Cemetery	Chicago, IL	Graceland
1901	Lake Forest Cemetery	Lake Forest, IL	LF Cemetery
n/d	Memorial Cemetery [sic]	Oyster Bay, NY	FLO
1922	Montrose Cemetery	Chicago, IL	Montrose
1930	Mount Auburn Cemetery with junior partner Albin	Stickney, IL	JRW
n/d	Oakland Cemetery	Freeport, IL	*P & C*

DATE	NAME OR TYPE	LOCATION	SOURCE
	Oak Hill Cemetery	Cedar Rapids, IA	D. Cooper
	Oak Woods Cemetery	Chicago, IL	Oak Woods
1899	Seeley Cemetery	LaCrew, IA	WHTC
n/d	Washington Cemetery	Indianapolis, IN	ISU
n/d	Woodland Cemetery	Hastings, MI	on-site
	(extension by Robert Simonds)		SFC
1895	Woodland Cemetery	Quincy, IL	Cairns

ESTATES AND HOME GROUNDS

DATE	NAME OR TYPE	LOCATION	SOURCE
1915	Albright, Dr.	Milwaukee, WI	National
	(next door to Plankinton estate, grounds		Archives
	designed by Olmsted Bros. at same time)		
1905	Armour, J. Ogden	Lake Forest, IL	MA
	(Mellody Farm)		
1910-1915	Bassford, Lowell C.	LaGrange, IL	ISU
	Biddles, Francis	unknown	RG
1909-1922+	Booth, George G.	Bloomfield Hills, MI	Cranbrook
	(Cranbrook; also listed under Schools)		
1914	Bridge, George S.	Evanston, IL	ISU
1906	Burns, George	Ann Arbor, MI	RG
1914	Carpenter, Hubbard	Lake Geneva, WI	ISU
1904	Colvin, The Misses	Lake Forest, IL	MA
n/d	Cooper, A.A.	Dubuque, IA	MA
	Cooper, L.B.	Winnetka, IL	AIC
	(with Howard Van Doren Shaw)		
1906	Copeland	Ann Arbor, MI	RG
1900-1901	Cruikshank, John	Hannibal, MO	on-site
	(Rockcliffe Mansion)		
1904	Cruttenden, John	Quincy, IL	MA
1903	Cummer estate	Jacksonville, FL	J. Tankard
	Davenport, Eugene	Woodland, MI	SFC
	(The Maples)		
1910-1912	Dawes, Charles Gates	Evanston, IL	EHM
after 1895	Deering, Charles	Evanston, IL	Northwestern
1910	Deering, Charles	Miami, FL	
1907-1927	Douglas family	Cedar Rapids, IA	Brucemore
	(Brucemore)		

DATE	NAME OR TYPE	LOCATION	SOURCE
1906	Douglas family	Charlevoix, MI	WHTC
1894-1995	Fletcher, N.A. (Simonds's brother-in-law)	Grand Rapids, MI	RB-CHS
n/d	Frost, A.C.	unknown	MA
1905	Gaylord, Mrs. E.L.	Midlothian, IL	MA
1904	Goddard, Prof. E.C.	Ann Arbor, MI	MA
1920s	Grosvenor, Gilbert (Wild Acres)	Bethesda, MD	RCS; LOC
1906	Hardy, E.K.	Akron, OH	MA
before 1912	Hibbard	Winnetka, IL	*CLA*
1898	Higginbotham, Harlow (Forest of Arden)	Joliet, IL	*American Botanist*
1920s	Hodenpyl, Anton (Hill House)	Long Island, NY	SFC
1915	Ives, O.H.	Dixon, IL	ISU
1906	Jones	Ann Arbor, MI	RG
1905	Kackley, Thomas R.	Indianapolis, IN	MA
1899	King, Rockwell	Chicago, IL	MA
1907	Larned, Julia	Hubbard Woods, IL	MA
1890s	Lathrop, Bryan & Helen	Chicago, IL	ER
1900s	Lathrop, Bryan & Helen	York Harbor, ME	SFC
ca. 1915	Lawson, Victor (Lone Tree Farm/Lawsonia)	Green Lake, WI	SHSW
ca.1902+	Lowden, Frank & Florence (Sinnissippi Farm), with J. Roy West	Oregon, IL	P. Miller
1905-1908	Lowe, Edward & Susan B.	E. Grand Rapids, MI	*Bldgs of Mich.*
1900	Lyman, Bement	Indianapolis, IN	MA
1901	Martin, Horace	Lake Forest, IL	B/A
1906	Markely	Ann Arbor, MI	RG
1900	McCormick, Miss	Huntsville, AL	MA
n/d	Mumford, L.	Hastings, MI	RG
1905	Murdock, R.P.	Wichita, KS	MA
1906	Newcomb, Frederick	Ann Arbor	RG
1903	Peterson, Dr. R.	Ann Arbor, MI	MA
1909	Severa property	Cedar Rapids, IA	*HLR*
1909-1911	Shaver house	Cedar Rapids, IA	*Bldgs of Iowa*
after 1895	Smith, Byron L. (Briar Hall)	Lake Forest, IL	*CELF*

DATE	NAME OR TYPE	LOCATION	SOURCE
1905	Stack, J.L.	Midlothian, IL	MA
1905	Stillwell, Homer A.	Chicago, IL	MA
n/d	Wright, FL house	near Madison, WI	MA

GOLF COURSES

1912	Belle Meade	Nashville, TN	Emily Evans
1910s	Blackhawk Hills Club	Shorewood Hills, WI	on site
1894	Chicago Golf Club	Wheaton, IL	on site
1897	Glen View Club	Golf, IL	on site
1914	Indian Hill Club	Winnetka, IL	on site
	(originally Winnetka Country Club)		

PARKS

1905-1910	Ann Arbor Parks	Ann Arbor, MI	RG
n/d	Baltimore	Baltimore, MD	FLO
1898	Beloit	Beloit, WI	Beloit info
	Decatur	Decatur, IL	D. Sheaffer
1916	Detroit Zoo	Detroit, MI	RG
1905-1920	Dixon Parks	Dixon, IL	D. Sheaffer
1902	Lowell Park	Dixon, IL	SFC
1896-1901	Forest Park	Lake Forest, IL	LF
n/d	Frick Park	Pittsburg, PA	*NC*
1912	Anton G. Hodenpyl Park	Grand Rapids, MI	SFC
n/d	Garfield/Fletcher Park	Grand Rapids, MI	SFC
1931	Nipper Park	Hannibal, MO	Hagood
1908-1910	Riverview Park	Hannibal, MO	Hagood
1906-1907	John Henes Park	Menominee, MI	*Bldgs of Mich.*
1922	Kankakee parks (JRW)	Kankakee, IL	*P & C*
1900	Library Park	Kenosha, WI	Phillips
1903-1913	Lincoln Park	Chicago, IL	CPD
1903	Long View Park	Rock Island, IL	Oestereich
1900-on	Madison Park and Pleasure Drive Association (MPPDA):		
	Tenney Park	Madison, WI	SHSW
	Vilas Park	Madison, WI	SHSW
	Brittingham Park	Madison, WI	SHSW
1917	Lilac Garden, Marquette Park	Chicago, IL	CPD
n/d	New York	New York, NY	FLO

DATE	NAME OR TYPE	LOCATION	SOURCE
n/d	Pilcher Park	Joliet, IL	B. Newberg
1895-on	Quincy, Illinois parks:	Quincy, Illinois	various
	South Park		
	Indian Mound		
	Gardener		
	Parker Heights		
	Riverview		
	Berrian park		
	Sunset Hill		
1904	"Small Park"	Springfield, IL	MA
1907	Washington Park	Springfield, IL	U of I

PERSONAL PROJECTS OF O.C. SIMONDS

1881-1927	Own residence	Chicago, IL	SFC
1920s	Winter residence	DeLand, FL	SFC
1891-1931	Summer residence	Fennville, MI	SFC
1910-1931	Subdivision development	York Harbor Hills, ME	SFC

SCHOOLS

1910-13	Academy of Our Lady	Longwood, IL	MA
1905	Beloit College	Beloit, WI	WHTC
1904	Central States Normal	Mt. Pleasant, MI	MA
1909-1922	Cranbrook	Bloomfield Hills, MI	Cranbrook
1907	Ill. Industrial School for Girls	Park Ridge, IL	RB-CHS
1915	Iowa State University	Ames, IA	ISU
1892-93	Lake Forest College	Lake Forest, IL	LF College
n/d	Michigan Agricultural College (Michigan State University)	East Lansing, MI	FLO
1901	University of Chicago	Chicago, IL	U of C
1912	University of Chicago - Ida Noyes Hall	Chicago, IL	U of C
1916	University of Chicago - Midway Plaisance (changes were not incorporated)	Chicago, IL	
1918	University of Chicago	Chicago, IL	
1920s	University of Maryland	Baltimore, MD	U of MD; FLO

DATE	NAME OR TYPE	LOCATION	SOURCE

SUBDIVISIONS

DATE	NAME OR TYPE	LOCATION	SOURCE
ca. 1915	Belle Meade Farm with West Bloomfield Village Townsite	Nashville, TN / Bloomfield Hills, MI	JRW / Cranbrook
ca. 1890	Chicago - Buena Park streets	Chicago, IL	
ca. 1890	Chicago - Courtland /Palmer Square	Chicago, IL	
ca. 1890	Chicago - Sheridan Park	Chicago, IL	MA
1915	Huntington Woods	Huntington Woods, MI	MA
1911	The Highlands	Madison, WI	WHTC
1914	Indian Hill	Winnetka, IL	IHC
1913	Kincaid "The Coalectric Town"	Kincaid, IL	various
ca. 1902	Florence Page	LaGrange, IL	Funigiello
1915	Nokoma	Madison, WI	WHTC
1915	Palmer Woods	Detroit, MI	*Mich. Bldgs.*
1911-1923	Shorewood Hills	Shorewood Hills, WI	Brock
1912	Spring Harbor	Madison, WI	EW
n/d	Tuomy Hills	Ann Arbor, MI	RG
1910-1931	York Harbor Hills	York Harbor, ME	SFC

MISCELLANEOUS

DATE	NAME OR TYPE	LOCATION	SOURCE
n/d	Chicago Municipal Tuberculosis Sanatorium	Chicago, IL	
1920	Frederick Law Olmsted Memorial		FLO
n/d	Landscape plan	Birmingham, MI	DB
1905	Christ Church Memorial Church	Winnetka, IL	MA
1888-93	Fort Sheridan	Highwood, IL	OCS
n/d	Michigan State Capitol	Lansing, MI	MA
	Nelson Parkway	Beloit, WI	Beloit

PROJECTS BY PARTNERS

Below are later projects handled primarily by J. Roy West and junior partners. Dates are approximate; many projects presumably had been started with Simonds's involvement and were then managed by West.

DATE	NAME OR TYPE	LOCATION	SOURCE

RESIDENCES

DATE	NAME OR TYPE	LOCATION	SOURCE
ca. 1930	H.H. Bliss with Erle O. Blair	Janesville, WI	JRW
ca. 1930	Col. Buckingham		JRW
1938-1939	James & Betsy Getz Erle Blair; not built	Lake Forest, IL	*CELF*
ca. 1930	Goddard/St. Mary's	Freeport, IL	JRW
ca. 1930	Hafner family	Lake Forest, IL	JRW
n/d	Arthur Marks	Akron, OH	JRW obit
n/d	Arthur Marks	Westchester, NY	JRW obit
ca. 1930	Mrs. Marvin Miner	Barrington, IL	JRW
ca. 1930	L.C. Rose with Arnold Roehl	LaPorte, IN	JRW
1929-1930	Peter Schaefer with Arnold Roehl	Eagle River, WI	JRW
1930	Simmons	Greenwich, CT	JRW obit
1929-30	Henry Stanton		JRW
ca. 1930	Strom family with Albin		JRW
1930	Van Dyke family, Fox Point	Milwaukee, WI	JRW

OTHER PROJECTS

DATE	NAME OR TYPE	LOCATION	SOURCE
n/d	McMillan Park	Ft. Wayne, IN	JRW obit
n/d	Maytag Park	Newton, IA	JRW obit
n/d	Lake Forest High School	Lake Forest, IL	JRW obit
	"Many country clubs"		JRW obit
ca. 1930-on	Skokie Road, with Robert Kingery	Chicago to Highland Park, IL	JRW
ca. 1930	Muskegon County Sanatorium	Muskegon, MI	JRW

ROCKCLIFFE MANSION, covered with "Japan Ivy" and matrimony vines. HAGOOD COLLECTION

PLANTING LIST FOR ROCKCLIFFE MANSION, CA. 1901

The plant selection for this project is an excellent representation of the plants that Simonds typically used in his Midwestern projects. Plant names and numeration are given **as Simonds wrote them**; botanical names in brackets have been added.

PLAN NO.   COMMON NAME [BOTANICAL NAME]

1 Elm or hackberry [*Ulmus americana; Celtis occidentalis*]

2 Locust seedlings

3 Colorado blue spruces [*Picea pungens*]

4 Hemlocks [*Tsuga canadensis*]

5 Norway spruces [*Picea abies*]

6 Cherries [*Prunus sp.*]

7 Golden willows [*Salix sp.*]

8 Red willows [*Salix sp.*]

9 Golden lindens [*Tilia sp.*]

10 Red-buds [*Cercis canadensis*]

11 Norway maple [*Acer platanoides*]

12 Japan maples [*Acer palmatam*]

13 Elm seedlings

14 Linden seedlings

15 Ornamental apples

16 Buckthorn [*Rhamnus cathartica*] Invasive: do not use today!

17 Japan quinces [*Chaenomeles japonica*]

18 Red dogwoods [*Cornus sericea* 'redosier']

19 *Syringas* [mock orange; genus name was later changed to *Philadelphus*]

20 Common lilacs [*Syringa vulgaris*, European]

21 Snowballs

PLANTING LIST FOR ROCKCLIFFE (CONTINUED)

PLAN NO.   COMMON NAME [BOTANICAL NAME]

22 Highbush cranberries [*Viburnum trilobum; V. opulus*, European variety]

23 *Vibunum rugosum*

24 Hydrangeas [*Saxifracacea arborescens*]

25 Nine-bark [*Physocarpus opulifolius*]

26 Flowering currants [*Ribes alpinum*]

27 Forsythia [*Forsythia* x intermedia]

28 Double flowering plums [*Prunus* spp.]

29 Barberries [*Berberis japonica*; *B. Vulgaris*; *B. Canadensis*]

30 Thunberg's barberries [*Berberis thunbergii*]

31 Spirea in variety [*Spriea* x bumalda 'forebelli'; *S.* x b 'Anthony Waterer']

32 *Spirea van houttei* (one of Simonds's very favorites)

33 Indian currants [*Symphoricarpos orbiculatus*; *S. albus* (snowberry); *S. occidentalis* (wolfberry)]

34 *Rosa wichuriana*

35 "Michigan roses"

36 Sweet briars (*Smilax* spp.)

37 *Rosa rugosa*

38 Honey locust [*Gleditsia triacanthos*]

39 Horse chestnut [*Aesculus hippocastanum*]

40 Ornamental peaches [*Prunus persica*]

41 Persian lilacs

42 Japan ivy [*Parthenocissus tricuspidata*; better known as Boston ivy]

43 Matrimony vines [*Lycium vulgare*], wild grapes [*Vitis labrusca*], Indian currants [*Symphoricarpos orbiculatus*] and fragrant sumach [*Rhus aromatica*]

44 Goldenrods and asters

BIBLIOGRAPHY

O.C. SIMONDS' PUBLISHED WRITINGS: PERIODICALS

American Landscape Architect
"Graceland at Chicago," January 1932, 12 & 16, (WHTC).
"Notes on Graceland," (tribute to Bryan Lathrop), May 1930, 8-9.

Country Life in America
"The Planning and Administration of a Landscape Cemetery," September 1903, 350.
"Open Your Eyes," January 1913, 55.

Garden and Forest
"The Landscape-gardener and his Work," X, July 1897, 282.

The House Beautiful
"Home Grounds," V, No. 4, March, 1899 169-172.
"Home Grounds," V, No. 5, April, 1899 214-218.
"Home Grounds," V, No. 6, May, 1899 275-279.
"Home Grounds," VI, No. 1, June, 1899 25-30.
"The Surroundings of a Country House," VI, No. 5, October 1899, 227-232.
"The Surroundings of a Country House," VI, No. 6, November 1899, 282-286.
"Lawns and How to Grow Them," VII, No. 1, June 1900.
"The Surroundings of a Country House," VII, No. 3, August 1900.
"Country Life Near Chicago," 11 (?), No. 5, April 1902, 377-341.

Journal of the International Garden Club
"Landscape Gardening in its Relation to Roadside Planting," II, No. 2, June 1918, 187-201.
"A Plea for Landscape Gardening," letter attached to essay by Bryan Lathrop, II, No. 2, June, 1918 300-301.
"Care of Woods and Ravines," II, No. 3, September, 1918, 421-424.

Journal of the Western Society of Engineers
  "Parks and Boulevards," written discussion, V, No. 3, June 1900, 170-171.
  "John Butler Johnson: A Memoir," written with C.W. Melcher, T.L.
    Condron, and J.W. Schaub, n/d.

Landscape Architecture
  "Nature as the Great Teacher in Landscape Gardening," XXII, No. 2,
    January 1932, 100-108.

The Michigan Horticulturist
  "A Plan for Rural Grounds," October 1885, 1, 2.
  "Planting a School Ground," December 1885, 1, 4.
  "Twelve Good Native Shrubs," February 1886, 1, 6.
  "Rural Cemeteries," April 1886, 1, 8.
  "Take Home Lessons from the Woods," May 1886, 1, 9

Park and Cemetery
  (Title unknown), 5, July 1898, 83.
  "Announcements," XXXII, 8, October 1922, 203.

O.C. SIMONDS' PUBLISHED WRITINGS: BOOKS

"Drainage," in L.H.Bailey, *Manual of Gardening: A Practical Guide.* New York:
  MacMillan Company, 1910, 69-72.

*The Lakefront Park: A Few Suggestions from the Landscape Gardening Point of
  View.* Chicago: n/d, booklet, (1890s?) (SFC).

Landscape-Gardening. New York: MacMillan Publishing Co., 1920.

"Trees for the Home Grounds," Chapter IV in *How to Make a Flower Garden:
  A Manual of Practical Information and Suggestions.* Wilhelm Miler, ed.
  New York: Doubleday, Page and Company, 1903, 83-92.

O.C. SIMONDS' PUBLISHED WRITINGS: MISCELLANEOUS

"Residence Streets." *Annual Report for 1898 of the MI Horticultural Society* (SFC).

"Synopsis of Talk on Western Notes," *Transactions of the American Society of
  Landscape Architects*, February 5, 1907, 90-91.

"The Aesthetic Value of Wooded Areas in Michigan," *Report of the Michigan
  Forestry Commission for the Years 1903-04.* Lansing, MI: State of Michigan,
  1905, 77-122 (SFC).

O.C. SIMONDS' UNPUBLISHED WRITINGS AND PERSONAL FILES

SIMONDS FAMILY COLLECTION

Association of American Cemetery Superintendents charter membership certificate, October 20, 1897.

Correspondence, 1879-1931.

List of books in Simonds's personal library.

Pier Cove books from Simonds's farm in Michigan.

Records for farm and nursery at Pier Cove.

Seed and plant orders, seed packets.

York Harbor, ME real estate development plans.

Survey of DeLand, FL property, 1929.

Family photographs, various documents and letters.

STERLING MORTON LIBRARY

Correspondence between OCS and Joy Morton, between January, 1921-1931.

Midwest Landscape History Collection: Simonds's papers; List of Simonds's plans, 1899-1906.

STATE HISTORICAL SOCIETY OF WISCONSIN ARCHIVES

Madison Park and Pleasure Drive Association, Records, 1893-1938.

John Nolen, Letters, 1908-1935.

John M. Olin, Papers, 1872-1924.

UNIVERSITY OF ILLINOIS ARCHIVES

Department of Horticulture Subject File, 1898-1939:

  Simonds, Chicago, to Wilhelm Miller, July 20, 1915.

  Miller, Urbana, to Simonds, Chicago, July 23, 1915.

  Miller to Simonds, July 28, 1915.

  Miller to C.F. Fadeley, Waterford, VA, August 13, 1915.

  Miller to Simonds, November 15, 1915.

  Mrs. Elmer E. Kendall to Miller, May 1, 1916.

  Miller to Jens Jensen, May 5, 1916.

MISCELLANEOUS WRITING

"How to Develop Beauty and Seclusion in Cemetery Design," 1931.

"Progress of Rural Cemeteries," 1923.

"Nature in the Cemetery," address at the Chicago AACS convention, 1925.

BIOGRAPHIES AND OBITUARIES

Ayres, Louis E. "Ossian Cole Simonds, '78e, A.M. (Hon.) '29: An Appreciation by Louis E. Ayres, '08e." *University of Michigan Alumnus*, December 12 1931, n.p.n. (SFC).

Blair, Erle O. "O.C. Simonds," *Landscape Architecture*, XXII, No. 3, April, 1932, 235.

"Bryan Lathrop, Civic Leader, Dies Suddenly," *Chicago Tribune*, May 16, 1913.

Chicago Sunday Tribune, November 22, 1931.

"Charles W. Garfield," *American Fruit Grower*. (October 1934): 7 (SFC).

"The Dean of the Cemetery Field," *The American Cemetery*, September 1930, 20 & 37.

DuPuy, George. "O.C. Simonds: A Tribute." *The Lighted Cross.* [Ravenswood Congregational Church newsletter] (December 1931).

Garfield, Charles W. "Death of Ossian Simonds; Greatest Exponent of Landscape Art in America." *Michigan Tradesman*, 94 [December 1931] (SFC).

Leland, Ernest Stevens. "Ossian Cole Simonds, Master of Landscape Architecture," *The Pioneers of Cemetery Administration in America: A Collection of Biographical Essays*. Privately printed, Association of American Cemetery Superintendents, 1941, (SFC).

Marquis, Albert Nelson. "Ossian Cole Simonds." *The Book of Chicagoans: a biographical dictionary of leading living men of the city of Chicago.* Chicago: A.N. Marquis, 1911.

"Mr. O.C. Simonds." *The Lighted Cross*. December 1931.

"O.C. Simonds has Story on Reasons for Buying Land," *DeLand Daily News*, January 23, 1929, 1.

"O.C. Simonds Passes On," *Park and Cemetery*, December 1931, 301-302.

"Park Designer Taken by Death." *Chicago Sunday Tribune*, November 22, 1931 (WHTC).

"Simonds, Ossian Cole." *The National Cyclopedia of American Biography*. XXII. New York: James T. White & Company, 1932, 91.

(See also Grese, Robert E. "Simonds, Ossian Cole. An Annotated Bibliography," in *Pioneers of American Landscape Design*. National Park Service, 113-17.)

LITERATURE CONTEMPORARY WITH SIMONDS

American Society of Landscape Architects. *Transactions, from its inception in 1899 to 1908.*

_____. *Transactions, 1909-1921.*

_____. *American Landscape Architecture*. P.H. Elwood, Jr., ASLA, ed. New York: The Architectural Publishing Co., 1924.

_____. *Illustrations of Work of Members*. New York: The House of J. Hayden Twiss, 1931.

Annals of Horticulture. L.H. Bailey, ed. "Association of American Cemetery Superintendents convention meeting, 1889." New York; Rural Publishing Co., 1890 (WHTC).

_____. "AACS meeting, 1890." Ibid., 1891.

Andreas, A.T. "Graceland Cemetery," in *History of Cook County*. Chicago: A.T. Andreas, 1884, 720-21.

Art Institute of Chicago, Burnham and Ryerson Libraries
Daniel H. Burnham collection
William Le Baron Jenney papers

Bacon, Thomas H. *Mirror of Hannibal*. 1905; reprinted by Hurley and Roberta Hagood, Hannibal, MO: 1990.

Chicago Historical Society

Architectural Drawings: Holabird and Roche collection

Archives: Thomas B. Bryan collection

Henry Field, Jr. collection

The Cincinnati Cemetery of Spring Grove: Report for 1857. Cincinnati: C.F. Bradley and Co., 1857.

Civil Engineers Club of the Northwest. *Proceedings, including list of members*. 1869, 1879.

Cleveland, Horace William Shaler. *Landscape Architecture as Applied to the Wants of the West*. Pittsburg: University of Pittsburg Press, 1965 (reprint of 1873 edition; introduction by Roy Lubove).

_____. *A Few Hints on Landscape Gardening in the West*, with *The Relation of Engineering to Landscape Gardening*, by W.M.R. French. Chicago: Hazlitt & Reed, Printers, 1871.

Downing, Andrew Jackson. *Rural Essays*. New York: 1857.

The Forest Waters the Farm. New York: Forest and Stream Publishing Co., 1886.

Hamerton, Philip Gilbert. *Landscape*. Boston: Roberts Brothers, 1885.

Hunt, Anthony. "Landscape Architecture in and about Chicago," *The Architectural Record*. Vol. 23 (July 1912): 54-64.

Hubbard, Theodora Kimball. "H.W.S. Cleveland: An American Pioneer in Landscape Architecture and City Planning," *Landscape Architecture*, 20, 2 (1930): 92-111.

Kemp, Edward. *Kemp's Landscape Gardening*. Edited, revised, adapted to North America by F.A. Waugh. New York: John Wiley and Sons, 1911.

Kern, G.M. *Practical Landscape Gardening, with Reference to the Improvement of Rural Residences.* Cincinnati: Moore, Wilstach, Keys and Co., 1855.

Loudon, John Claudius. *Landscape Gardening and Landscape Architecture of the late Humphry Repton, Esq.* 1840.

Manning, Warren H. "How to Make a Formal Garden at a Moderate Cost," *Country Life in America,* March, 1903, 186-187.

Miller, Wilhelm. "The Illinois Way of Beautifying the Farm," Urbana: University of Illinois Extension, Circular No. 170, 1914.

_____. "The Prairie Spirit in Landscape Gardening," Urbana: University of Illinois Extension, Circular No. 184, 1915.

_____. "The Sargent Home Near Boston," *Country Life in America,* March, 1903, 199-201.

_____. *What England Can Teach Us About Gardening.* New York: Doubleday, Page and Co., 1911.

Olmsted, Frederick Law. *Papers, 1822-1903,* Library of Congress, MS62-4663.

Park and Cemetery, "Mark Twain Memorial and its Setting," 22, December 10, 1912, 236-38.

_____. "New Parks and Improvements," announcement of inception of Morton Arboretum, December 1921, 266.

Park and Outdoor Art Association. *First Report.* Lexington, KY: 1897.

Parsons, Samuel Jr. *Landscape Gardening Studies.* New York: John Lane Company, 1910.

Ravenswood-Lake View Historical Association Archives.
   By-Laws, Rules, Officers and Members of the Ravenswood Club, 1902-1903.
   List of Ravenswood residents in early 1900s.
   Ravenswood Congregational Church documents.

Root, Ralph Rodney. *Design in Landscape Gardening.* New York: The Century Co., 1914.

_____. "Country Place Types of the Middle West," *The Architectural Record,* 55, January 1, 1924.

Ruskin, John. *Lectures on Landscape.* 1897.

Van Rensselaer, Mrs. Schuyler [Marianna Griswold]. *Art Out-of-Doors; hints on Good Taste in Gardening*. New York: Charles Scribner's Sons, 1903.

Waugh, F.A. *Landscape Gardening*. New York: Orange Judd Company, 1899.

_____. *The Landscape Beautiful*. New York: Orange Judd Company, 1910.

Wight, Peter B. "Country House Architecture in the Middle West," *The Architectural Record*, XL, No. IV, October 1916.

Wilcox, David F. *Quincy and Adams Counties: History and Representative Men*. New York: Lewis Publishing Co., 1919, 488-89.

SECONDARY SOURCES ABOUT O.C. SIMONDS AND HIS WORK

Balmori, Diana. "Cranbrook: The Invisible Landscape," *Journal of the Society of Architectural Historians*, 53, March 1994, 30-60.

Beadle, Muriel. *The Fortnightly of Chicago: The City and Its Women, 1873-1973*, 2 photocopied pages.

Bettendorf, Elizabeth. "Preservationists hope local park 'registers,'" *Springfield State Journal Register*, December 14, 1991, 8 (SFC).

Boehme, Natalie. "City park gets its historic ranking," Ibid., June 12, 1992 (SFC).

Brucemore Report, in press, courtesy of William H. Tishler.

Bruegmann, Robert. *Holabird and Roche, Holabird and Root: An Illustrated Catalog of Works*. New York: Garland Publishing, Inc. in cooperation with The Chicago Historical Society, 1991.

Cairns, Malcolm. *The Landscape Architecture Heritage of Illinois* (WHTC).

Canaday, Tricia. "The Story of Nokoma." Unpublished seminar paper, Aug. 1992, (WHTC).

Chicago Park District."Lincoln Park Report," n/d, 12-15 & 19-20 (SFC)

Crese, Walter L. *The Crowning of the American Landscape: Eight Great Spaces and Their Buildings*. Princeton, NJ: Princeton University Press, 1985.

Edwards, Alice. "Chippiannock Cemetery: Rock Island's Landscaped 'Village of the Dead,'" *Historic Illinois*, 17, 3 (October 1994): 3-7.

Eifler and Associates. *Graceland Cemetery, Historical Report*. Unpublished, privately printed report, 1992, courtesy of Jay Womack.

Elmhurst Historical Museum Archives.

Fortnightly Club History, Chicago Landmark designation research (Bryan Lathrop house).

Elwood, P.H. Jr., ASLA. *American Landscape Architecture*. New York: The Architectural Book Publishing Co., 1924.

Gelbloom, Mara. "Ossian Simonds: Prairie Spirit in Landscape Gardening," *Prairie School Review*, 12, 1 (2nd quarter 1975) 5-18 (WHTC).

_____. Same title, photocopy of original typescript (SFC).

"Glen View Club, 1897-1987," booklet, courtesy of Anne Peschke.

Grese, Robert E. *Jens Jensen: Maker of Natural Parks and Gardens*. Baltimore: Johns Hopkins University Press, 1994.

_____. "Historical Perspectives on Designing with Nature," *Restoration '89: The New Management Challenge*, Proceedings of the First Annual Meeting of the Society for Ecological Restoration, Oakland, CA, January 16-20, 1989, H. Glenn Hughes and Thomas M. Bonnicker, eds. Madison, WI: Society for Ecological Restoration, 1990, 39-48.

_____. "The Prairie Gardens of O.C. Simonds and Jens Jensen," *Regional Garden Design of the United States*. Therese O'Malley and Marc Treib, eds. Washington, D.C.: Dumbarton Oaks, 1995, 99-124.

Hagood, Hurley and Roberta. *Hannibal, Too*. Marxelline, MO: Walsworth Publishing, 1986.

_____. Personal collection including chronology of Riverview Park construction; early Hannibal photos; news clippings; Rockcliffe Mansion National Register of Historic Places nomination forms.

_____. *Hannibal Yesterdays*. Hannibal, MO: Hannibal Free Public Library, 1992.

Hannibal Arts Council. Miscellaneous uncataloged photos and documents.

Hibbard, Angus. "Golf and the Glen View Club," An excerpt from Chapter XXXI: *Associations of Choice*, n/d, (GVC).

Himelick, Kirk. *Washington Park: Meeting Contemporary Demands, Preserving Historic Integrity*. Unpublished master's thesis, University of Illinois, Urbana, 1976.

McKenna, Marcia Nickles. "The Birth of Shorewood Hills," *The Story of Shorewood Hills*. Shorewood Hills Village Board: 1958, 7 & 14, (Tom Brock).

Landscape Architecture, "History in the Heartland," 86, 01, 18 (WHTC).

Mattern, Carolyn J. "Madison Park and Pleasure Drive Association," brochure, Historic Madison, Inc., 1994, courtesy of Tom Brock.

Mehaffey, Scott. "Laying the Foundation: Landscape Architecture at the Morton Arboretum, O.C. Simonds and Clarence Godschalk, 1922-1953." *Morton Arboretum Quarterly*, 31, 3 (Autumn 1995).

Meldman, Suzanne Carter. *Fort Sheridan Historic Landscape: Ossian Cole Simonds*. Report submitted to the Department of the Army Corps of Engineers, Champaign, IL, February 1995 (MA).

Prairie in the City: Naturalism in Chicago's Parks, 1870-1940. Chicago Historical Society, 1991.

Rusnak, Cecilia, ASLA. *Historic Landscape Report: Brucemore, Cedar Rapids, IA*. State College, PA: 1997 (WHTC).

Risjord, Norman. *Madison's Highlands: A Community with a Land Ethic*. Madison, WI: Highlands Association, 1988 (WHTC).

Simonds, Herbert. *Reminiscences of Herbert Simonds*. Privately printed, 1935 (SFC).

Tenney Park, National Register of Historic Places Nomination forms (WHTC).

The University of Michigan: An Encyclopedic Survey. Ann Arbor: University of Michigan Press, 1953.

Werle, Robert William *A Historical Review and Analysis of the Iowa State University Landscape From 1858 to 1966*. Unpublished master's thesis, Iowa State University at Ames, 1966.

"Village Planned for 'Good Life.'" *Wisconsin State Journal*, January 18, 1970, Sec. 6, 4, (WHTC).

Wyatt, Barbara, ASLA. Olin House: A Laboratory for Landscape Design. University of Wisconsin-Madison Grounds Department publication (March 1993).

Zube, Ervin. "The Advance of Ecology," *Landscape Architecture*, March/April, 58-67, (March/April 1983): 58-67.

SECONDARY SOURCES ABOUT CONTEXTUAL AND RELATED TOPICS

American Society of Landscape Architects. "Second National Conference on Instruction in Landscape Architecture, June 1921," Harvard University, typescript.

"Arbor Lodge: The Morton Family Estate," *The Architectural Record*, XIX, January 1906, 37-43.

Balmori, Diana, Diane Kostial McGuire, and Eleanor M. McPeck. *Beatrix Farrand's American Landscapes: Her Gardens and Campuses*. Sagaponack, NY: Saga Press, 1985.

Brott, Jody, "Pact Reached to Develop Ex-Army Base," *New York Times*, March 17, 1996, 27 (Fort Sheridan).

Crandall, Gina. *Nature Pictorialized: "The View" in Landscape History*. Baltimore: John Hopkins University Press, 1993.

Cronon, William. *Nature's Metropolis*. New York: W.W. Norton, 1991.

Deuchler, Doug. "Grave Matters: Burial Customs of early Oak Park and River Forest," *Oak Park Wednesday Journal*, October 30, 1996, 31, 40-41.

Ebner, Michael H. *Creating Chicago's North Shore*. Chicago: The University of Chicago Press, 1988.

Elliott, Brent. *Victorian Gardens*. Portland, OR: Timber Press, 1984.

Evans, Hilary and Mary. *The Victorians at Home and at Work*. New York: Arco Publishing, 1973.

Genskow, Karen M. "The Country Estate in Illinois," *Historic Illinois*, 10, February 5, 1988, 1-3 & 12-15.

Haglund, Karl. "Rural Tastes, Rectangular Ideas, and the Skirmishes of H.W.S. Cleveland," *Landscape Architecture*, 1976, 6 (1), 67-70.

Handlin, David P. *The American Home: Architecture and Society, 1815-1915*. Boston: Little, Brown and Co., 1979.

Hunt, John Dixon. *Gardens and the Picturesque*. Cambridge, MA: MIT Press, 1992.

Klim-Doell, M. Christine. *Gardens of the Gilded Age: Nineteenth Century Gardens and Homegrounds of New York State*. Syracuse: Syracuse University Press, 1986.

"Lawsonia" brochure describing subdivision of estate at Green Lake, WI.

Mack, Edwin F. *Old Monroe Street: Notes on the Monroe Street of Early Chicago*. Chicago: Central Trust Company of Illinois, 1914.

Marx, Leo. *The Machine in the Garden: Technology and the Pastoral Ideal in America*. New York: Oxford University Press, 1964/1970.

Meldman, Suzanne Carter. *The City and the Garden: The Chicago Horticultural Society at Ninety*. Chicago Botanic Garden, 1981.

Miller, Donald L. *City of the Century: the epic of Chicago and the making of America*. New York: Simon & Schuster, 1996.

Neckar, Lance. *The Design and Marketing of the Prairie: Progressives and Suburbs in Madison, Wisconsin, 1890-1920*. Unpublished master's thesis: University of Wisconsin-Madison, Department of Landscape Architecture, 1981.

Ottewill, David. *Edwardian Gardens*, Yale University Press, 1989.

Pellett, Kent. *Pioneers in Iowa Horticulture*. Des Moines: Iowa State Horticultural Society, 1941.

Pressman, Lenore. "Graceland Cemetery: Memorial to Chicago Architects," *Chicago History*, 13-18.

Saunders, William. Bibliography of materials available at the United States Department of Agriculture - National Agricultural Library, Beltsville, March, 1997. [Oddly enough, the founder of the Canadian Department of Agriculture, at this same time, was also named William Saunders.]

Schlereth, Thomas J. *Victorian American: Transformations in Everyday Life 1876-1915*. New York: Harper Collins, 1991.

Schuyler, David. *The New Urban Landscape: The Redefinition of City Form in Nineteenth-Century America*. Baltimore: Johns Hopkins University Press, 1986.

Shapiro, Mel, ed. *Golf: A Turn-of-the-Century Treasury*. Seacaucus, NJ: Castle Books, 1986.

Stern, Robert A.M. "The Anglo-American Suburb," *Architectural Design*, 1981, 51 (October/November).

Stroud, Dorothy, introduction by Christopher Hussey. *Capability Brown*. London: Country Life, Ltd., 1956.

Turak, Theodore. *William LeBaron Jenney: Pioneer of Modern Architecture.* Ann Arbor: UMI Research Press, 1967/1986.

_____. "William LeBaron Jenney, Pioneer of Chicago's West Parks," *Inland Architect*, March, 1981, 38-45.

Turner, Roger. *Capability Brown and the Eighteenth-Century English Landscape.* New York: Rizzoli, 1985.

Veblen, Thorstein. *The Theory of the Leisure Class.* London/New York: Penguin Books, 1899/1994.

Vernon, Christopher. *The "Illinois Way": Wilhelm Miller and the Gospel of the Prairie School.* Unpublished master's thesis, Urbana: University of Illinois, 1988.

Von Holst, Hermann V. *Country and Suburban Homes of the Prairie School.* New York: Dover.

Wind, Herbert Warren. *The Story of American Golf.* New York: Simon and Schuster, 1956.

Wright, Gwendolyn. *Moralism and the Model Home: Domestic Architecture and Cultural Conflict in Chicago, 1873-1913.* Chicago: University of Chicago Press, 1980.

KEY TO ABBREVIATIONS:

AIC	Art Institute of Chicago/Burnham-Ryerson Libraries
CHS	Chicago Historical Society
CHS	Chicago Historical Society
GVC	Glen View Club
MA	Sterling Morton Library
SFC	Simonds Family collection
WHTC	William H. Tishler collection

INDEX

AUTHOR

Barbara Geiger is a landscape historian specializing in late nineteenth- and early twentieth-century Midwestern designed landscapes. She teaches in the College of Architecture at the Illinois Institute of Technology, the School of the Art Institute of Chicago, and the Chicago Botanic Garden. Trained in cultural landscape research and preservation in the graduate program at the University of Wisconsin, Ms. Geiger has served in a number of preservation organizations. The goal of her courses, writings, and popular tours and lectures is to help people find ways to connect with their environment.

See **www.barbarageiger.net** for more information.

FERME ORNÉE PRESS

Ferme Ornée takes its name from the eighteenth-century term for a "decorated farm." Thomas Jefferson, William Shenstone, and Phillip Southcote were among a select group of men who taught themselves horticulture, landscape design, and soil management. With this knowledge they sought to develop productive, sustainable farms that were also beautifully composed scenery. O.C. Simonds's approach to design, and to the gentleman's farms he planned, was similar to their philosophy, making *Low-Key Genius* the natural project for launching Ferme Ornée.

New electronic and paper publications for history and land lovers seeking new and enriching ways to connect with our environment, in this spirit of combining the useful with the beautiful, can be found at FermeOrnée.com.

See **www.fermeeornée.com** for more information and products.

URBPUBLISHER

Low-Key Genius is the premier offering from this new producer of the printed word. It is with pride that this first effort is a 'real' book, the paper and ink giving literal and figurative weight to the fine work of the author. Urbpublisher produced this book in its entirety including content editing, layout design, and the cultivation a visual language respectful to the careful, deliberate talents of O.C. Simonds.

See **www.urbpublisher.com** for more information and products.

CPSIA information can be obtained at www.ICGtesting.com
Printed in the USA
LVOW101335211211

260510LV00001B/216/P